The Last Earth

The Last Earth

A Palestinian Story

Ramzy Baroud

Foreword by Ilan Pappe

Edited by Daniela Loffreda

PLUTO PRESS

First published 2018 by Pluto Press
345 Archway Road, London N6 5AA

www.plutobooks.com

British Library Cataloguing in Publication Data
A catalogue record for this book is available from the British Library

ISBN 978 0 7453 3800 2 Hardback
ISBN 978 0 7453 3799 9 Paperback
ISBN 978 1 7868 0287 3 PDF eBook
ISBN 978 1 7868 0289 7 Kindle eBook
ISBN 978 1 7868 0288 0 EPUB eBook

This book is printed on paper suitable for recycling and made from fully managed and sustained forest sources. Logging, pulping and manufacturing processes are expected to conform to the environmental standards of the country of origin.

Typeset by Stanford DTP Services, Northampton, England

Simultaneously printed in the United Kingdom and United States of America

Contents

To Zarefah, Iman and Sammy.
Stay Strong.

Acknowledgments

This book is the labor and vision of many people; without them, *The Last Earth* would not have been published and these Palestinian stories would have remained untold, thus unknown to the world.

I am tremendously grateful for the support I received from the Middle East Monitor and its director, Dr. Daud Abdullah. His insight has stood me in good stead.

I am greatly honored and privileged to have been a student of Professor Ilan Pappe, who supervised my Ph.D. thesis in Palestinian Studies at the University of Exeter, UK. Professor Pappe has been both a teacher and a friend.

Thank you to my Ph.D. committee examiners, Professors Nur Masalha, Ruba Saleh, and Sophie Richter-Devroe.

To my agent and friend, Carina Brandt, thank you for your tireless efforts and support. Working with you on a project so close to my heart impacted my work greatly. Many thanks also to Elena Sarjols and the entire staff at Brandt New Agency.

Daniela Loffreda and Yousef Aljamal joined me from the very beginning of this writing journey. Despite being the primary editor of this book, Daniela's contribution extended into research and, at times, co-writing. Yousef was a leading researcher in this project. His constant and devoted efforts resulted in interviews being arranged and transcribed. He was also involved in the vetting process for hundreds of people, many of whom we interviewed jointly. I thank both Daniela and Yousef for their invaluable assistance and contributions.

Salwa Amor helped me arrange interviews with Palestinian refugees in Syria and Lebanon. Her guidance was a cornerstone of my research on Yarmouk and Palestinian refugees in Europe. Thank you, Salwa.

A special thank you to the Pluto Press team. David Shulman, I am indebted to everything you have done to make the publishing of this book a reality. I also thank Kieran O'Connor, Emily Orford, Robert Webb, Melanie Patrick and the rest of the Pluto colleagues for their outstanding professionalism.

I would also like to thank the following people, each of whom contributed in a unique and essential way: Dr. Deepak Tripathi, Dr. Salman Abu Sitta, Professor Noam Chomsky, Professor Richard Falk, Hawa Monier, Sylvia Fernandes-DeMelo, Dr. Vacy Vlazna, Ahmad Al-Haaj, Romana Rubeo, Dr. Blake Alcott, Suzanne Baroud, Dr. Roger van Zwanenberg, Claude Zurbach, Mohammed Mushtaha, John Harvey, Tamam al-Assar, Hana Shalabi, Sara Saba, Khaled Abdul Ghani, Ali Abu Mghasib, Joe Catron and Baroness Jenny Tonge.

Foreword

Ilan Pappe

Al-Nakba al-Mustamera, the on-going Nakba, is by now a common Palestinian reference to the age and time they have been living in during the last seventy years. This means that discrete chapters in the history of the Palestinians, such as the catastrophe of 1948, are not just events in the past, but rather are part of a contemporary historical chapter. We are still in this particular phase, and thus when we write the history of certain historical moments, such as the Nakba, we write on contemporary issues as much as on past events.

This state of affairs has recently been recognized by scholars who adapted and applied the settler colonial paradigm to the case study of Palestine. The late Patrick Wolfe, who resurrected the paradigm, with a particular interest in Palestine, stated that settler colonialism is not an event but a structure. And indeed, examining the history of the Zionist movement in Palestine, it transpires clearly that the settler colonial project that commenced in the late nineteenth century is not over yet; as is the struggle against it.

This concept of an on-going catastrophe and the struggle against is encapsulated in the trials and tribulations of the heroes and heroines of this book who are of different Palestinian generations and come from different locations.

It is through minute, almost forensic personal stories over a generational spread that one can fully understand the full impact that such multifaceted experience has on the individual as well as the collective psyche of Palestinians in general and on Palestinian refugees in particular. The narration the readers are about to enter conveys very strongly this sense of a wholesome, homogenous time zone in which Palestinians live and of the inconclusive and precarious existential realities.

With this present phase in the life of Palestine and the Palestinians, oppression and victimization took different forms according to circumstances of time and place. In 1948, the Palestinians faced ethnic cleansing and massacres. Those who lived afterwards in Israel as a minority were under military rule that violated their human rights in almost every aspect of life. The refugees in the meantime were denied return and were joined by another wave of uprooted Palestinians in the wake of the 1967 war.

The methods of dispossession became more complex, and in many ways more sinister and brutal in the West Bank and the Gaza Strip in the last fifty years, and still continue in this vein, as this book goes to print. Israel employed new methodology of oppression since the changing circumstances rendered policies of ethnic cleansing ineffective after 1948. The methods have changed, but the main vision propelling them is the same, and typical to all settler colonial movements in the past: to have the territory without the people.

Ethnic cleansing as the principal means for implementing this vision was replaced by a matrix of dispossession, imprisonment, and spatial strangulation. This system was first imposed on the Palestinians who remained in Israel and were put under a harsh military rule between 1948 and 1967. The principle was quite simple, if you cannot remove people from a space, you have to enclave them so that they cannot move freely or expand their areas of habitation. This was executed brutally in the Palestinian areas inside Israel until 1967 and was then transferred as a system to the occupied West Bank and Gaza Strip.

Whatever the Zionist method it was met by Palestinian resistance. The Palestinians are victims, but they are not passive victims. The tragedy was and still is that due to military imbalance (Israel became the strongest military force in the Middle East and the Palestinians the weakest), every Palestinian act of resistance (including nonviolent ones) was met with all the ferocity of Israeli power. The various chapters and verses of this punitive repertoire are told in this book through the narration of its heroes and heroines and will acquaint you with this Palestinian experience. Notable among them are the imprisonment of men, women, and children without trial, who are incarcerated not because they are criminals but only because they are Palestinian.

Paradoxically, the biggest Zionist success of fragmenting the Palestinians into discrete groups that helped Israel to divide and rule was mitigated by the uniformity of this Palestinian experience throughout the years. This uniformity is very clear in the narratives unfolding in this book and it turns the Palestinian memory, oral history, and recollection into not just a register of atrocities but also tools of cultural resistance.

Antonio Gramsci used to say that cultural resistance is either the rehearsal for political resistance or the means employed when political resistance is not possible. I think both possibilities apply to the Palestinian resistance. Resistance here unfolds as individual acts enhanced by a strong solidarity of the collective. The oppression is daily and time minuscule, and so is the resistance. Small gestures, daily heroism, and survival accumulate into a story of *Sumud*, steadfastness. The message of this book, like many Palestinian books before it, conveys very clearly that Zionism is not a settler colonial project that is going to end with the elimination of the natives. They are here to stay.

One of the most impressive ways in which the Palestinians remained steadfast and will continue to do so is their ability, as so succinctly put by the late Edward Said, to narrate notwithstanding the ongoing Nakba. Their claims have been misrepresented over the years, even by some Palestinian politicians themselves, let alone foreign media and academia, and through the personal stories that insisted on their version of events that these fabrications and myths were successfully challenged and debunked.

The unique technique employed here by Ramzy Baroud makes these narrations as powerful as ever. It also elucidates clearly that the narrations are a potent tool of resisting colonization and dispossession. They are part of the cultural resistance mentioned earlier, one which was far more unified and homogenous than the political resistance that suffered, and still does, from factionalism and disunity. Memory became the principal means by which Palestinians inside Israel identified with the demand of the Palestinian refugees for their right of return and which broadcast clearly to the world at large, and to Palestinians wherever they are, that they are victims of the same settler colonial system. Therefore, any political solution that would perpetuate fragmentation and separation would prolong dispossession and suffering.

This unifying memory is accentuated by present-day experiences, but is not always recognized by the fragmented elite, which paralyzes the struggle. The act of symmetrically fusing the collective memory into an effective tool of cultural resistance comes from below, and it is through what Baroud calls "a history from below" that we reconstruct a very different narrative of the past and map the ambitions of the present.

The reader can use this book as source for the history of Palestine and Palestinians in tandem with other excellent books produced in recent years. It complements the existing scholarly tradition by adding the authentic voice of the people as the principal narrators of the past and juxtaposing it with the scholarly narratives based on documents and more conventional historical material, or media reports for the more contemporary period.

It also differs from what you will find in scholarly works in its literary style. History is a story; that does not mean that is false, or fabricated, or even fictional. But telling the story of history cannot be divorced from emotive undertones, anger, a sense of injustice, and hope. Scholarly work does not often succeed in reconnecting to these ever-present and normal aspects of humanity even when they write about human beings. The style allows us to connect to these vulnerable and at the same time empowering sides of humanity, even if at times they come through a mediating narrator.

It is probably only through such an approach that we can fully understand the connection between the destruction of the urban space in Palestine in 1948 and that of Syria since 2011. Among the many victims of the most recent of the two atrocities, the Palestinians again stand out (such as the dwellers of the Yarmuk camp in Syria), escaping this time from the Middle East and not just away from Palestine.

The inhumanity that engulfed the Palestinians once more has also affected millions of others in the region. The barbarity raging in Syria, Iraq, Libya, and Yemen deserves our attention and condemnation. Nonetheless we should not forget that this kind of inhumanity prevailed in Palestine for more than a century and that global indifference towards, and indeed quite often support for, it is one of the major reasons that the West feels and remains helpless in the light of the present carnage. It is only through paying attention to the Western role in the dispossession of the Palestinians, which began one hundred years ago with the Balfour Declaration, that the West's responsibility for the mayhem in the Middle East can be fully appreciated. One can absolve Arab societies and politicians for the dire state in which the Middle East finds itself today; this is recognized and has never been denied. The fate of the indigenous people of Palestine, as that of so many other indigenous people around the world destroyed by the West, is closely associated with a better and hopeful future for the Middle East as a whole. To understand best how it began, and what is meant, one needs to hear the voices of the people who were at the receiving end of Western Imperialism and Zionist settler colonialism. This book is a good place to start this journey.

The author of numerous books, Ilan Pappe is professor of history and director of the European Centre for Palestine Studies at the University of Exeter.

Khaled Abdul Ghani al-Lubani, otherwise known as "Marco," was born into a refugee family in Yarmouk, Syria and sought escape through an arduous path across continents. As a child, he was taught to believe he would never leave Yarmouk, unless the final destination was his adjoining village in northern Palestine. Only then would his family's honor be redeemed, and true freedom attained.

In our earliest exchange, Marco's first words to me were a verse from a poem by Mahmoud Darwish. Marco spoke of Palestine as if she were a woman; a beloved mother that was lost somewhere on the dusty trail of an unending journey.

1
Shit River

Let me re-arrange the evening with what suits my failure and her absence.

Mahmoud Darwish

Yarmouk was ever-present in Khaled's soul, pulling him in and out of an abyss of persistent fears, urging him to never return. What was he without Yarmouk, his first haven, his last earth? How could any place in God's unwelcoming universe be a home for him as a Palestinian first and foremost, and nothing else? When questioned, he answered without hesitation: "I am from the village of so and so in Palestine." Yet for him Yarmouk was all that remained of Palestine because the Palestine he knew existed only in books, or as the tattered map in his family's living room, and in old fables conveyed by long-dead grandparents.

At least he had her by his side to share his grief, for without her he would not have embarked on his quest. Her name was Maysam Saeed and she was Syrian. Her allure came from her seductive Mediterranean beauty and from the playful confidence she exuded. The impression that she gave was not one of arrogance, but rather was part of an innate game she would play with anyone she encountered.

They met as eager volunteers in Yarmouk's Palestine hospital. Innocent banter soon turned to flirtation that skimmed the boundaries of what was acceptable in the refugee camp. Their growing attraction drew them closer to a love that would become impossible to contain. Nor could they have foreseen that they would soon embark on an odyssey in search of their last earth, crossing a sea whose tumultuous waters had drowned many lovers and many innocents who barely had a start in life. Their love kept them afloat amongst the misery of war, but they knew there would be no true convergence of their two lives on the other side of the boundlessly dark sea. Even if their tiny boat could succeed in eventually evading the Turkish and Greek coast guard, love alone would still not be enough.

They first made love on February 4, 2013. When he closes his eyes and thinks back to that sublime moment, Khaled gets goosebumps. Despite all the tragedies that befell him in war-ravaged Yarmouk, nothing would have stopped him from sneaking into Maysam's family home during "the hunger siege". Though starvation had left his face pale and gaunt, and his skin dry and creased, Khaled always managed to muster up the energy for a night of passion. His hunger for love eclipsed all else including the fact that she was a married woman. For Maysam, her suffering at the hands of a cruel husband was sufficient justification for the taboo affair. Her three children, who all had her same handsome face, glowing skin, dark silky hair and adoring eyes, were not an obstacle either. No one and nothing else mattered more than their love.

Maysam's parents were from Deraa in the south. They owned enough land to classify them as "landowners", but not enough to buy them special status in Syria's burgeoning aristocracy. Such status required more than wealth; it meant that one had to know how to use that wealth to win favor with the ruling class. They sold some of their land to build a relatively large house in the affluent Zahira neighborhood in Damascus, and the rest was saved for a "dark day". That day did come, when what began as a restrained uprising in Deraa morphed into the era's most devastating war, forcing millions to flee their homes to escape the relentless bloodshed.

Khaled and Maysam's first attempt at crossing the sea was doomed to fail. The one thousand American dollars that Khaled's father had given him was almost depleted, and the money promised to him by his wealthy aunt in the United Arab Emirates hadn't yet arrived. By then they had settled in Izmir, Turkey's closest city to Greece. Seeking a chance at a normal life, they knew this was only a temporary stopover. After a short stay in a cheap hotel, they found cheaper accommodation in a small flat that cost them 400 Turkish lira each month. With money running out, and Maysam's anxieties increasingly suffocating her every thought, she wondered if she'd made a rash and grave mistake in leaving her children behind. As Khaled waited and waited for his aunt's money, he felt the pressure mounting and knew he had to take action.

Not far away from their flat in the Ucyol neighborhood, a makeshift Syrian Club was founded to serve refugees, but only those who declared their hostility to the Syrian government and swore allegiance to its enemies in the Free Syrian Army. Khaled and Maysam had learned about survival in times of war, and took on whatever identity they had to in order to keep a low profile. Whether facing an armed man or a feeble victim, in a split second they could gauge the situation and determine the role that needed to be played. At times Khaled claimed to be Syrian, denying any connection to Palestine. This they learned from the mistakes of Palestinian refugee friends, who were thrown in Turkish jails for significantly longer durations than their Syrian counterparts. Once, he walked the streets of a Kurdish village at the Syrian–Turkish border wearing army boots he had found somewhere by chance. Unaware that these old boots were the same kind worn by Kurdish PKK fighters, he was surprised when this footwear brought him the admiration of the locals who saw the Palestinian refugee as a

Kurdish warrior ready to fight for the Kurdish cause. Maysam, on the other hand, was saved by the grace of her beauty, and by the sorrow that was a constant in her hypnotic eyes.

It had been a month since they escaped the inferno in Syria, and after more weeks achingly dragged by, the prospects of freedom seemed dim. So they used their remaining money to join other refugees—Palestinians, Syrians, Iraqis, and Afghans—united by the belief that a quick death at sea was better than the continued insecurity of life in the shadow of eternal wars.

* * *

Khaled does not know when or why the family name "al-Lubani" was dropped, shortening the name to "Abdul Ghani." It might have had something to do with his grandfather's profession. Khaled's grandfather, Mohammed Abdul Ghani al-Lubani, was a proud man whose graceful manner of speaking earned him immediate respect. He was a well-regarded government employee serving as an assistant engineer during the British Mandate in Palestine where he designed and paved many roads in the north of the country. He wanted no more than a humble and honorable existence. But in 1948, his village, Al-Mujaydil, was destroyed and cleansed of Palestinians to make room for an Israeli town that was given a variation of the original Arabic name. Mohammed sought refuge in Syria. He had never imagined that he might one day have to flee his homeland to escape soldiers brandishing metal blades capable of splitting a man open, nor did he imagine he would end up languishing in a perpetual purgatory for sins he did not commit. In his naive mind, returning to Al-Mujaydil was merely a matter of time, for the village had survived since before it was officially listed in Ottoman records in 1596. Patiently and hopefully he and his wife waited, and waited, in Jobar, a small village outside the municipal borders of Damascus. This became their destiny—queueing at a never-ending charity line, waiting for their right of return, preparing for a meal that would never be served.

It was an irony of fate that the al-Lubani family settled in Jobar, an ancient village that was mentioned in the Talmud as one of several places near Damascus where Jews once lived. The area around its synagogue was now populated by Palestinian fellahin who had been violently forced out of their homes. It was the Jewish Zionist militia of the Yishuv Golani Brigade that violently expelled the al-Lubani family from their land, forcing them to seek shelter in this distant and unknown place where Jews had once sought safety.

With no jobs available for refugees, Mohammed al-Lubani had no other option but to shovel cow dung and sell it to local bakeries to fuel their ovens. It was a challenge to his sense of dignity, for the rotting smell made him feel like a walking piece of shit. But feeling like shit was better than death, he figured, at least for the time being. To motivate himself, he would imagine crossing a river of shit and emerging on the other side with a refreshing waterfall awaiting him, purifying him of all his suffering, and allowing him a clean slate, a new start, a new life. In time, Mohammed found a stable and a more dignified job. But the family name was ineradicably sullied by the stench of dung. To put his past behind him, he garnered his remaining pride and, without discussion, the family name 'al-Lubani' was dropped from all records, and they started anew.

Mohammed's beloved first born entered their lives in Jobar on December 16, 1959. In sync with the political mindset of most refugees, the name Jamal was bestowed upon him. Mohammed believed that the charismatic Egyptian leader Jamal Abdel Nasser was ready to liberate their land and facilitate the most important thing in the world—their return to Palestine. Heartache befell Mohammed when Nasser died soon after a painful and humiliating defeat in 1967, and the rest of Palestine was conquered by the ever-expanding State of Israel. So Jamal Abdul Ghani, who was born in Jobar, remained in Jobar; that is until he met Hana.

She was a kindergarten teacher in the Summo School. They fell madly in love, but when Mohammed went to ask for her hand on behalf of his son, he discovered that even the degradation of exile did not fully dismantle the class boundaries that governed the relationships between Palestinian communities before they had all become refugees. He returned home to tell his son: "I am afraid that those people do not see us as their equals."

The naked truth was they were equal—now. Both families had moved to Yarmouk as desolate refugees soon after the camp was established in 1957 for thousands of dispossessed Palestinians. Before the Nakba happened, Hana's family, the al-Khadras, were city dwellers who amassed wealth and owned plentiful fertile land in Safad. They could afford shopping in the best retailers, dressing in handmade clothing from the best artisans, and eating the tastiest food available. The al-Lubani family owned little land and came from a small village where food was not chosen from a fancy menu, and clothes were not fashion but another means of survival. Even in their prime, they were still bordering on poverty. With time on their side, and Jamal and Hana tirelessly fighting for their love, the stubborn delusions of Hana's family evaporated and the al-Khadras accepted the reality that their former status counted for nothing in the refugee camp. When this finally hit home, Jamal and Hana married, and it was then that the al-Khadras realized the raw truth of their family tragedy.

After years of unemployment, Jamal found a job making bread at Mazza Automatic Bakery, while his father became a tax collector, a position that provided financial security and a certain amount of prestige. Mohammed's self-image mired in cow dung was put to rest when he dumped his workman's uniform and tall rubber boots for shiny brown shoes, a golden tie, and a chocolate brown suit that matched his perfect felt hat. His tastes were so refined that he was easily mistaken as a well-to-do man from the high streets of Damascus. Just as his bad luck was beginning to change, Mohammed was ambushed by thugs looking to make a quick buck. Throwing him to the ground, they stole papers worth 40,000 Syrian lira from his prized leather bag. The coveted honor that he had redeemed slipped through his fingertips like dry desert sand. It was too much for Mohammed Abdel Ghani al-Lubani to bear; he died a few days later from a massive stroke.

Khaled was then a one-year-old toddler, born on May 4, 1988, followed by Sa'id a year later, and Majid the following year. The family lived in a two-story house in Sa'sa' Street. It was all that the old man had left behind for his wife, son and grandchildren, aside from the depressing legacy of dispossession and indignity.

Jamal was a resourceful man who inherited his father's ability to create something out of nothing. The older women of the camp loved Jamal, and would pinch his cheeks and praise God for creating such talent. He eased their stress by intuitively fixing fridges that had not kept food fresh in years, and made laundry machines stop their clunking. He ran a small carpentry shop naming it after his eldest son: 'Warshat Khaled'—Khaled's Shop. Furthermore, driven by a love for literature and the spoken word, he taught himself all he needed to know and more, without earning an official piece of paper from formal education. Soon his noble reputation was its own credential, and he eventually became a respected teacher at an UNRWA (United Nations Relief and Works Agency for Palestine Refugees in the Near East) school in the camp. Khaled, in a natural passing of the torch, inherited his father's fascination with science and technology and he too could fix any broken thing. In the time they spent together and in the passions they shared, Khaled grew closer to his father, and further away from the mother who he could never satisfy or feel loved by. To him, Hana was in a relentless state of irritability, as if she were fighting demons of unwavering pain and infinite disappointments.

Despite some good times in Yarmouk, the family was haunted by fears of the camp itself; a fear looming in the background like dark music in a horror film. Rarely did Khaled venture beyond his neighborhood. When he did leave his neck of the woods, he only did so in the company of his father, or to walk to Kawkab Elementary School and back; and it was always in one straight line, never deviating or pausing. His mother and father did not allow him to talk to anyone outside their sanctioned circle of friends and relatives, nor could he play marbles in the street, or use "bad language" even if others told him to "fuck off" a thousand times. Trust was not something easily earned by anyone, neither by the government, nor by the factions that spoke on behalf of the refugees and supposedly protected them. Only once did the teenaged Khaled disobey family orders when he joined a political discussion organized by Fatah loyalists in Yarmouk. The topic was "liberating oneself as a prerequisite to liberating Palestine," but he was not dazzled by what seemed to be pretentious words with no connection to the daily treadmill and despair of his family, so he never returned to their meetings.

Angst afflicted all of Yarmouk and permeated every facet of refugee life. The isolation felt at home was mirrored in the fear of every representation of authority. Even Khaled's second grade teacher, Wafa Zaghmout, behaved like a dictator running a terrifying fiefdom of her own, punishing pupils for no reason and beating children at will. Khaled, who was punished severely for "sweating too much," hated Wafa. When many years later she was diagnosed with cancer, a feeling of relief overcame him because he knew her oppressive reign would finally be over, and other innocent children would be spared her cruelty. She had finally received retribution for her malice, he felt. Fortunately, Khaled had one angel of goodness who gave him sanctuary, and that was Iman Ahmad, the fully covered Syrian teacher, and mother of his best friend, Ayham. To him, she was the saint who restored his faith in school and in women. She treated all the children the way she treated her own son. She was a fine woman and mother who embodied all that Khaled had wished for in his own broken experience as a son.

It was at the Kawkab School that Khaled was introduced to the adventures of Marco Polo. In class, when they read about his adventures, nothing would distract him. China skies were laid with bright red silken carpets, Japanese cherry blossoms bloomed in endless green fields, and the aroma of Indian spices whisked by his senses in dreams of life as Marco. Enthralled and excited by the prospect of life beyond his neighborhood, he urged his friends to call him "Marco." This nickname became his own and made him feel special. It allowed him to escape his very small world and stray from that one straight line he walked every single day, back and forth. His father Jamal was not impressed. He had chosen to name his eldest son Khaled because it was the name of the eldest son of Jamal Abdul Nasser. So, in this way, both father and son carried the same heroic names. Still proud of Nasser's legacy and his bloodline, despite its imperfection, it was as if the family never learned from past defeats.

Being a good son and wanting to please his father, "Marco" tried to live up to Jamal's high expectations and obtained a degree in English literature from a Damascus university. His ambition was to teach like his father, at an UNRWA school. He studied hard, obtained high grades and, like his father, was esteemed by his professors and peers. After a long day of study, he would fix broken appliances and repair batteries until the late hours of the night. Working long and hard, he showed his father that he was committed to the same legacy of problem-solving. Putting a smile on Jamal's face required more than the average son's efforts, and the rare times he saw that smile made it worth all the trouble. But a true connection between Jamal and Khaled never truly developed until 2013, when they were both besieged in Yarmouk, trapped together in a fight to stay alive, as hundreds perished under a rain of bombs amid the threat of an undignified death by hunger.

* * *

Marco had a powerful imagination. His mind travelled on endless journeys whenever life felt intolerable. Daydreaming helped him cope with his mother's humiliating punishments as a child; his father's rage; and Wafa Zaghmout's class of petrified little children. It came in handy whenever he was stuck in arduously long lines at UN feeding centers for Palestinian refugee children where unruly kids pushed, shoved, and tossed around all sorts of profanity. An adventure crafted by his rich mind would transport him to the front of the line, where he'd receive a slice of dried bread, half of an apple that had already gone brown, and part of an egg. On special occasions, a thin slice of canned beef was added to the mix, news of which would travel quickly through the line of giddy schoolchildren.

When the day came that Marco would walk in his father's footsteps as a teacher, to his great disappointment, teaching was an interminable exercise in boredom and he hated it. Something he had worked so long for, and which his father had spoken so endlessly about, made his stomach twist into knots each time he walked into a classroom. He had imagined that by teaching he would use language to help pupils escape the misery of the camp; to travel with him to new worlds where Marco Polo had travelled, and other places that Marco Polo never knew existed. While the bright students uplifted him and gave him a sense of gratitude, the daft ones crippled his desire to explore the farther reaches of knowledge and discovery. When they looked at him in total confusion or lack of interest, he imagined smacking their faces. He kept telling himself it would get better, easier, and that eventually even the slower ones would crave his lessons, greet him with a smile and maybe even thank him. But when the little voice in Marco's head would sometimes make itself heard in sarcastic comments he would murmur under his breath, he hoped on one hand that the students would not hear him, and on the other, he didn't care at all. His passion for the English language fizzled as most of his elementary school students never managed to crack the code of the English alphabet. A few months after claiming his position as a teacher at the same school where his mother once taught, he had all but given up.

When the Syrian conflict started, Marco cared little for the politics of war. He had reached the conclusion long ago that nothing good came out of politics and that anyone wearing a government or militia uniform was not to be trusted. However, the war inched closer to Yarmouk, despite the pleas of the refugees to the Free Syrian Army to leave them out of their feud with the government; and despite their pleas to the government to spare the camp its barrel bombs and indiscriminate rockets. Neither party cared for what the Palestinians said or felt. And no one cared for their safety, even after the old mukhtars of the camp visited the defected generals of the Free Syrian Army in Al-Hajar Al-Aswad. The generals dismissed the reasoning that Yarmouk should remain neutral since it was a Palestinian refugee camp operated by UN agencies. "It is all Syrian land, and Syria will not be divided," lectured a short officer with a massive scar on his face, and a gut so large it seemed to leak from his tightly buttoned uniform. With hearts crushed, the mukhtars returned to Yarmouk warning of ill-fated days ahead.

Some days later, those same ex-generals made their moves and entered Yarmouk, killing Palestinian fighters, and forcing the rest to flee following their four-day siege of Al-Khalisiya military compound in the south-western part of the camp. When the few Palestinian fighters were routed after a fierce fight, the government moved in to block its enemy's progress towards the Damascus suburb of Zahira beyond the furthest corner of Yarmouk. As the two warring parties made their moves, Yarmouk became locked in a death-trap.

In the first government strike, twenty-eight Palestinian civilians were killed in the camp's main mosque, and when the bloodbath ended, young men sobbed as mangled body parts were gathered and then buried. The trauma and shock was too much to bear. Many questioned if God really exists, and fear herded thousands, carrying whatever cherished belongings they had, out of the camp, in multiple directions—anywhere to get out of death's way. History was cruelly repeating their making as refugees, some of them for the third or fourth time.

Others opted to stay and face the lesser of two evils, since the siege had not yet become absolute and nowhere was safe for a Palestinian refugee anyhow. The Abdul Ghani family remained in their home and prayed to God for a return to normalcy, especially for the young children of the camp. The father began devising alternative ways to reach the besieged neighborhoods in Yarmouk so that trapped students would not miss out on their schooling. He was now an administrator who oversaw science curriculums for the UNRWA-operated schools in the Damascus area, so he knew every road and building. Teaching for Marco became more exciting and meaningful, and he took risks to reach Summo School and convey knowledge to traumatized children, the clever and the daft alike. Looking at their saddened eyes, they were all his children, and he wanted to save each and every one of their vulnerable precious souls. But the death toll grew and no amount of knowledge was enough to feed the thousands of ravenous refugees nearing famine's door or to fix a bullet hole in a neighbor's chest. Desperate to mend whatever he could, Marco rushed to Palestine Hospital to offer his services as a handyman to keep generators operating a while longer, fixing whatever machine was broken or destroyed by neglect or shrapnel.

The day came when his intuition and street smarts raised him to a new level of learning. Now the machines he was fixing were not made of cold metal, but were made of flesh and pumping blood. It began when Marco's neighbor on Sa'sa Street, Abdul Qader, arrived at the hospital with eight pieces of shrapnel piercing his back, and one thrusting deep into the core of one of his lungs. By then most doctors had fled Yarmouk, or were unable to reach the hospital. Only a few brave and dedicated doctors and nurses were left doing the work of a whole wing. Medical supplies were very scarce, so mostly they were amputating arms and legs rather than healing wounds. But the young Abdel Qader, the always-ready-to-help neighbor, was not meant to die, and Marco, the failed teacher who loved to fiddle with broken machines, had metamorphosed into an emergency room nurse determined to save the life of a childhood friend who knew more about European football than Syrian politics.

Abdel Qader survived, and Marco tackled other medical jobs in Palestine Hospital. First the simple ones came naturally, like assisting in amputations, giving CPR, making room in the morgue for new arrivals, and digging graves when no more space could be found in the hospital backyard. But when the medical staff shrank even more, Marco's newfound medical expertise extended to administering injections and taking X-rays. Soon he needed no instructions from a doctor when searching for bullets and shrapnel in the wounded Palestinians and Syrians who poured daily into the hospital's crowded wards and blood-splattered hallways. It became second nature for him and it gave him a sense of purpose in the midst of a war that did not have one.

Then Maysam came along. When she was dispatched by the Syrian Red Crescent Society to offer a consoling hand at Palestine Hospital, Marco was instantly smitten. He cared little for the ring on her left hand and was more taken by the tight jeans and t-shirt that she wore under her white medical gown. The overpowering chemistry they instantly felt transcended the gore around them as they both stood defenseless in front of their unexpected emotions. To him, her beauty resembled whatever hope could still be found amid the piles of dead and mutilated corpses in the walled-in graveyard. She too was on a quest to find a savior to rescue her from her domestic persecution. Marco embodied a hero with his darkened skin, palpable physical stamina, and bloodstained gown. As he helped the wounded, fixed batteries and transported the dead, she consoled bereaved families, and sought urgent arrangements with government shelters to accommodate the growing number of orphans in the area. Her loveless marriage gave her a sense of widowhood and so she cried alongside many widows, a status stamped on many hapless women as they arrived at the hospital, hopeful yet frantically looking for their husbands, only to leave with the life sucked out of them, pulverized and bruised.

Maysam Saeed was born on November 10, 1984. Her friskiness blinded people to her gossiping which knew no bounds, and her jealous nature led her to view any woman as a potential nemesis and every man as a sex-driven fiend. There were no shades of grey for Maysam. Everyone at

Palestine Hospital knew of her cruel husband and the endless hell that her life had become. Her vulnerability enticed Marco in his uninterrupted quest for love, and he was drawn to this most beautiful and appealing of all the ladies among the staff. Maysam was not just another notch in his belt, but for him being with her was quite a proud achievement since she was married, and a mother of three children—Saeb, Ahlam, and Wala. But their encounter did not end after that sinful February 4, or after their repeated further bouts of aberrant intimacy. The war around them was a reminder of the inanity of life and the abruptness of death, so the pleasure of the flesh was proof that they were still breathing. Maysam, justified her repeated actions as a way of asserting herself, as if she were saying. "Here I am world—living, fighting and loving as I please." For Marco, being together was like being rescued from Yarmouk, from the siege, from the war, and from the hopelessness of refugee existence.

Neither Marco nor Maysam sought love for emotional fulfillment, or a sexual affair to satisfy some unrestrained desire. They both sought an escape from the tragedy they were living in, a respite from the horrors forced upon them. Little did they know that one day they would create their own tragedy, and that these short-lived moments of bliss would become a distant memory. They made love in the evenings when the darkness could hide them. On the really tough days when unfathomable numbers of dead and wounded arrived, they made love over and over again or stole kisses to remind themselves that they too were human, and that "there is on this earth what makes life worth living," as Marco's favorite Palestinian poet once wrote of women, war, and a lost homeland.

But even Mahmoud Darwish's poetry was eventually not enough to remind the refugees of the life worth living and fighting for. Regardless of who would win in Syria, Palestinian refugees had nothing to reap but countless tears and continued exile. As if this were not enough, Marco would never have left Yarmouk if a discontented militia leader had not accused him of theft. Sure, Marco had taken the liberty of salvaging and repairing a few broken batteries from a bombed out military barracks, but it was only to keep the hospital generators running longer. One of the nine men who paraded Marco through the center of Yarmouk, declaring him a "thief" and threatening to execute him publicly, had been a patient in Marco's surgery ward seeking urgent care. It was Marco who extracted the bullet from his left thigh a few months earlier. "Khaled Abdul Ghani al-Lubani is a thief and all thieves deserve to have their hands cut off," declared the militia leader from the Free Syrian Army.

More humiliated than terrified by the public spectacle and feeling ultimately betrayed, Marco decided right there and then to escape Yarmouk. He escaped with his hand intact, but he was gutted by the futility of the entire fight and the depravity of those behind it. The decision he thought he could never make was cemented by the grisly sight of a sixteen-year-old Palestinian girl who was forced to "confess" her crime. After the bullet ripped through the palm of her right hand, she made her tearful "confession" of allegedly spying for the regime and was instantly executed with multiple shots to her face by a satisfied commando. The street verdict claimed she had placed GPS coordinators into areas where the Free Syrian Army operated, yet the street talkers paid no heed that the government had no "smart bombs," only barrels of explosives that shattered every corner of Yarmouk many times over with no precision or technological savvy. Logic and facts did not matter when the goal was intimidation.

A quick visit to his house in Sa'sa and a fervent hug from his father was all that Marco needed to commence the journey he would face with Maysam by his side. One thousand American dollars, most of the cash they had kept in their family home, was stuffed into his pockets, while Maysam took nothing but the reasons for her escape from Yarmouk: primarily her love for Marco, but also an accusation by the regime of treason for helping treat members of the Free Syrian Army and consoling their families. Most of her Red Crescent peers had already fled, and it was now her turn to follow. Within a few weeks, soon after they finalized their paperwork and prepared for the journey ahead, she had divorced her husband and married Marco, the savior refugee, who had spent most of his life confined to a single street that now stood in ruins. Free to imagine the world in any way he desired, Marco needed to reach the other side of the sea, even if he swam and walked a thousand miles. He did, in fact, walk that and a great deal more.

* * *

The first attempt to cross the sea was with Abu Dandi. There was something about his intimidating looks that seemed shady and not to be trusted. In his fifties, he was heavy, with a large, protruding belly, and short white hair. He was addicted to overcooked black tea, and spent most of his time at the Syrian Club playing backgammon, oozing the crude confidence of an unatoned gambler. His blank stare would follow the dice as they rolled onto the table, but he was always aware of who was in his presence. Having spent most of his life taking chances when the stakes were high, he remained oblivious to outcomes; 1,300 euros per person was the fee to deliver them safely to Greece. Marco agreed.

Other Palestinian refugees, accompanying them, also pledged their faith in finding a new life via this no-guarantees trip. One was Zakariya Zuriki, an in-your-face thirtysomething who took pride in being "rude" and didn't hesitate to speak his mind regardless of the consequences. A Che Guevara-type beret gave him the authoritative image he wanted in spite of his short and thin stature that was exacerbated by his long, soft hair. He had a strong voice that surged from his gut. Its depth was alluring and gave him a persona of coolness that, according to him, drove women mad. Zakariya hailed from the Palestinian Deraa refugee camp and he knew many songs about Palestine, though he almost never spoke of his family or their whereabouts. Never a coward, he was a good man to have on a rickety dinghy. He had joined the Syrian uprising at its onset and was one of the very first to carry a rifle, driven not by political ambitions for Syria, but because he just could not bear the sight of Deraa fighting and dying alone. He insisted that no one who was a bystander could "call himself a man," and many friends who died in that war were "like brothers," he added, taking a deep breath and shifting the conversation to another topic whenever their memories invited unwanted tears. "Men don't cry," he believed, but when they cannot overcome their grief, they should sing about death and women.

Isam Awad was another Palestinian refugee who claimed to have worked as an officer in a Syrian mukhabarat prison. In this no-man's land, human rights laws were meaningless writings on flimsy pieces of paper on some bureaucrat's desk. Intelligence, whether true or not, was gathered by torture. Women were raped and humiliated, and men's genitals were electrocuted while large sticks were pushed up their anuses. But he was one of the first to defect and join the opposition, or so he claimed. Be it a café or Marco's shabby flat in Ucyol, Isam's eyes shifted from side to side, surveying his immediate surroundings and because they seemed too close together in his bony face below dark protruding eyebrows, this added to his air of being in a constant state of suspicion. When in the company of women, his confidence immediately vanished and he would shrink into a silent wallflower, incapable of conversation. Even when he tried to be social in a male-centric chat, it was impossible to listen to him for too long without being distracted; being boring was a trait he had mastered. Although a chunk of his left leg had been shaved off by a bullet, it did not stop him from literally limping his way out of Syria, walking four kilometers at a time, stopping for the occasional quick rest or to drain the trapped blood in his nasty festering wound. He often spoke of his past valor, little of which could be verified. Only his stubborn unhealing wound was a testament to some tragic and mysterious past. His wife and daughter also fled Syria in a small dinghy; she left him as soon as she made it to Europe. For Isam, making it to Greece would be the first step towards seeing his baby girl.

There was also Mohammed al-Bahri, the guy who seemed to be the most "normal" of the group, but he shared very little or perhaps was not asked to share much. He had a photographic memory and wore a childlike wool hat. Marco avoided contact with him on the advice of the former mukhabarat officer with the shifty eyes. And that was fine by him, as Marco did not want to know what Mohammed's past entailed. What each of them used to be did not have any weight in the here and now: saint, devil, teacher, or torturer, all that counted was who paid the fee to get on the boat.

At merely twenty years of age, Abdulrahman Abu Alia was the youngest in the group. He believed that life was one long battle. A cigarette rarely left his pursed lips and dizziness overcame him if he did not smoke for more than an hour at a time. There was more to him than a cloud of billowing smoke that followed him wherever he moved. He had once been a promising volleyball champion and his sturdy athletic build was noticeable beside the small frames of Zakariya and Isam.

The inseparable brothers Muaz and Muntasir Abu Shilla joined the small band in the first leg of the journey. They had been through tough times together and were positive about turning another page in the new chapter about to unfold. But in their naiveté they didn't really understand the danger of the voyage ahead. Back in Syria, they had lost their Syrian identifications, and instead acquired Palestinian travel documents that were given to them by the Palestinian Embassy in Damascus, along with 1,200 American dollars, when the brothers staged an angry protest blocking the entrance to the embassy for days with a few dozen Palestinian refugees with no IDs.

Marco couldn't understand why Abu Dandi charged him 1,300 euros, about twice as much as each of the other passengers was asked to pay. But asking questions and stirring up problems would not have been wise, even though Marco's funds were drying up quickly after a similar amount was exacted from him for Maysam's share of the journey. Frantic calls to his wealthy aunt in the Emirates was the daily routine. Her promises to send extra money when her professor husband was paid at the end of the month gave Marco little confidence.

An hour after their journey began, the dinghy's small engine came to a complete halt, most likely due to the covering of algae and rust so thick that it looked as if it were part of the engine's structure. Without any warning, in one single, heavy choke, it expired. As alarm suffused Marco from head to toe, he knew going back was not an option. Adding to the acute drama, Maysam's fears and anxieties were culminating into mumbles about the menacing sea, the motherless children she left behind, and a future that was hanging by a thread. No longer was mere dizziness and nausea her nonstop torment, but stomach-churning heaves and violent gags of seasick companions could be heard in the background. "No, we are not fucking going back, you son of a bitch," was Marco's immediate reaction when Abu Dandi resolved that they should paddle back to the Turkish shore. Ignoring Abu Dandi's aimless gaze, Marco took on the oars of leadership and confidently urged his comrades to row forward towards

Greece, falsely claiming that he could see the lights of Lesbos. Fatigued and sickened by Maysam's retching, afraid to go back, yet unable to move forward, demoralized by Marco's weeping and eventual defeat, the men gave up after pushing every muscle and every bone in their physically exhausted, hungry, cold, weak, and shaking bodies. Surrendering to destiny, they watched as the boat drifted in one direction, only to be tossed back and forth.

Left without options, Abu Dandi conceded and called the Turkish coast guard. When they beamed their lights onto the tired faces of the passengers, the human distress didn't faze them and they coolly hauled them to an Izmir prison as if the midnight excursion was mere routine in a mindless job. There the Abu Shilla brothers discovered that their Palestinian documents were a cross to bear when they were kept in jail for twenty-five days. To avoid the same fate, Marco ashamedly denied his identity, claiming to be Syrian. When they were freed two days later, he and Maysam were transported by a prison vehicle to the center of the town. They made a pact to try once again.

They had met the captain of the second boat, Abu Salma, while in prison. Captured freshly after his own failed expedition, Abu Salma promised them safe passage or their money back, guaranteed. Fortunately, their previous payment was not cashed by the miserable smuggler with the protruding belly. To maximize the use of their money, the refugees invented an insurance system with the help of a trusted Gazan man. They would individually deposit the money with the Gazan man, who would only deliver it to the smugglers in Turkey when the refugees arrived safely at their Greek destination. Trusted by all parties for his famed honesty, the Gazan man would charge a small fee, and the refugees would retain the hope that they could try as many times as was required to escape. His was a rare virtuous element in the devil's den of human contraband.

Abu Salma asked for a thousand American dollars per person, with the ninth travelling for free. To fill the quota now that the Abu Shilla brothers were in a Turkish jail, a Somali woman and an Iraqi man were brought on board. They all agreed to the price.

Abu Salma loved hashish. Not only did he smoke cannabis like Abu Alia smoked cigarettes, he also adopted the character of Bob Marley by wearing the same multi-colored hat, long braided hair, and speaking in a Jamaican accent with a bizarre Egyptian Arabic twist. He often carried his three-year-old daughter on his shoulders, and whenever he wanted to assure others of his honesty, he swore on her name and pointed at her as she held on tightly to scruffy patches of his facial hair. She was an innocent who seemed unaffected by her daddy's bad character and substandard parental skills. But Abu Salma's compulsive lying was even worse when he was half awake or half baked. Luckily, he was not the captain of the tiny boat, but the facilitator of the trip. A Moroccan migrant wanted to get to Greece too so he agreed to steer the boat in exchange for being the free-travelling ninth person. He was also a smoker and surreptitiously took puffs from the "great" hashish to calm his nerves. By comparison to the first trip, this one was practically hassle free, but as the Moroccan fired up the engine, he immediately steered the boat into a massive rock on the beach. Soaking wet and bewildered by the few-meter journey, they disembarked from the damaged boat and headed back to the beach.

One day later, Abu Salma facilitated another expedition with the Moroccan who was given a second chance. This time he drove the boat much further following his promise that he would ease up on cannabis and be fully mindful of any rock that could halt their progress. The engine did not abruptly stop, but nervously made ticking sounds before it quickly hemorrhaged a line of dark diesel fuel into the crisp blue Mediterranean Sea. Then the pathetic dinghy suddenly stopped, on reaching Greek waters. When the coast guard intercepted them, they threw out a rope from their large boat so that they could haul the unwelcomed passengers to safety. The Moroccan began to yell relentlessly: "Don't touch the rope, men. They will push us back to the start. We are only a few hundred meters away from the beach."

Trusting his knowledge of how the smuggling business worked, the passengers paddled frantically with all their remaining energy to circumvent the Greek boat. It was as if it was the last remaining task in their epic struggle to feel human again. But the dinghy was stopped and the crushing emotions of defeat weighed heavy on their slouched bodies. Frustrated, a Greek coast guard officer hit the teary-eyed Moroccan on the head with the wooden paddle. His loud howl warned the passengers that the Greeks were not playing around.

"Baby, Baby," screamed the Iraqi man in a desperate attempt to elicit sympathy. But there was no baby on board, and when one of the officers inquired: "Where is baby?" the Iraqi pointed to the round belly of the Somali woman. Unable to understand the broken-English dialogue, the Somali migrant was bewildered and frightened by the sudden interest in the belly fat she had always felt uncomfortable about. Folding her arms on her stomach in a tight squeeze, she ignored the ruckus. Having little interest in bringing the refugees to their side of the sea, the Greek coast guard paid no mind to the travelers' distress and disgrace, and efficiently telephoned the Turkish gendarmes who hauled the dinghy away, holding its passengers prisoner for two more days. This time around, no one repeated the folly of declaring to be Palestinian. The Abu Shilla brothers were still in jail, still paying the price of their gullibility.

Swearing in the name of his three-year-old daughter once more, Abu Salma insisted he was the best smuggler in the business, and if it were not for their damn luck, they would have already reached Greece and would have been dining like kings while the Greek gods watched from above. Promising the group a bigger and faster engine for their fourth try, Abu Salma once again led the passengers back to the familiar designated spot where the dinghy was supposedly tucked away; but the boat was nowhere to be found. It seemed like a sick joke he concocted under the influence of the smoke he could not live without. Pledging his word of honor yet again, he vowed the "technical error" would be sorted out by morning, and asked his passengers to find the patience to sleep at the beach overnight. To their continued heartache and in spite of his final performance, he was never seen again. Emotionally and physically drained, they walked back to the main road, only to find the gendarmes waiting for them. When they were eventually released, the Abu Shilla brothers had also been set free, Palestinian documents in hand. "This smuggler is solid," they insisted referring to someone they had met in jail. "He has a sturdy boat with a massive engine that can take us all the way to China," one of the brothers animatedly declared.

On the fifth attempt, the group of nine had grown to twenty war refugees. To avoid suspicion, they split into two groups and walked to the beach via separate roads. No one spoke along the way, and no one dared ask questions. This boat was slightly larger than the last one and the engine was smaller than the first. The men yelled and roared in anger. The women cried out, some grabbing their hearts, some dropping to their knees. Maysam broke down and buried her wet face into the sand. "I cannot do this anymore. Death in Syria is better than this torture," she wailed.

Most of the passengers just walked away and stood in the sand trying to form a new plan. The Palestinians, along with

Marco and Maysam, stayed as their will was too strong to give up after all they had been through. Assuming the role of leader, Marco, hiding his insecurities, assured the group that they now were experts in sailing, and they could steer the boat to Greece. "Just go that way," the smuggler pointed his stubby fingers in a vague direction in the darkness. And that is exactly what Marco did. He challenged the darkness in the final push towards freedom. For the entire journey, Maysam quietly sobbed and held onto his arm for dear life. With the moon as their only light, Isam Awad's weaselly eyes fretfully surveyed the black skies and black water for gendarmes and the coast guard and other real or imagined dangers. At last, the much awaited lights of the Island of Mytilene glittered in the distance. "*Ya Allah, Ya Allah, Ya Allah,*" muttered Maysam, quickly reciting as many prayers as she could to help the dinghy reach the shores, bringing an end to the Syrian and Turkish nightmares, and freeing them from the abyss of the condemned.

A small jar of crunchy peanut butter was all that remained in Marco and Maysam's small duffel bag when their feet touched the sand of Mytilene late at night. The exhilaration of their success exploded in cries and leaps for joy that were soon subdued by a haunting, unforeseen, and unexpected fear of the future. The water soaking through their trainers suddenly felt like a cold omen.

* * *

It was a two-hour walk along the main road until a police vehicle captured them. Excitedly relieved but exhausted, they had been waving down passing cars, this time seeking the police, not evading them. They had never been so happy to be taken in by armed men in uniforms, as this was a first step in obtaining the coveted pieces of paper confirming their presence on Greek soil. The official document would also indicate that they had only six months until they had to leave the country. Expectedly, they had to be kept in detention before being released to a refugee encampment, if they chose to do so a few days later. With bigger plans in mind, they wanted no part of the refugee camp. They knew Greece was a dead economy and real opportunities were rare. Wasting no time at all, they left their prison cells and headed directly to Athens in a large ferry, Hellenic Seaways, costing 50 euros each. Once there, Marco and Maysam stayed in the Hotel Sparta, a humble inn in the neighborhood of Omonia, at the cost of 7 euros a night. They were grateful to God, but with no money left for the next leg of the journey, they anxiously awaited more funds from Marco's aunt, who in turn waited for her husband to get paid at the end of the month.

In those days, being smuggled out of Greece to the ostensibly hospitable Fortress Europe was not an easy feat compared to later years when the refugees were galvanized by their large numbers and the despairing philosophy that there was nothing to lose. The lengthy and costly process included ever-changing smuggling arrangements with dodgy characters, requiring fake identifications and, most importantly, sufficient funds. Nameless faces dictated the rules and you had to abide by them.

Some of Marco's friends from the dinghy departed a week after arriving in Athens. They paid no heed to warnings of the strenuous passage they would face if they opted to travel by foot. The enterprising few who opted to chart their path on land returned with nothing to report but utter failure and humiliation. The cost of the journey, shouldered mostly by Isam, was stolen by the creepy smuggler who disappeared with the backpacks that held every belonging still precious to them and their last reserves of vital money. Without even a dime for a taxi to take them back to their starting point in Athens, the powerless men were a pitiful sight.

Marco and Maysam could not tolerate the idea of travelling overland, and decided instead to fly to their destination using fake passports. As soon as his aunt's cash arrived, Marco quickly sought and found a smuggler whose name was Jamal al-Sudani. Originally from Sudan, he claimed to have French residency and was always accompanied by a fashionably dressed girlfriend who spoke bits and pieces of several languages, including Arabic. To avoid his friends' earlier mistake of handing over their money to the smugglers at the start of the journey, Marco sought another "insurance" office, where he deposited the smuggler's fees on the condition that the funds would be released to the Sudanese man whenever he and Maysam arrived at their next destination. He underwrote all of their money, nearly 4,600 euros, which was guaranteed to pay for the couple's trip and related costs.

The early preparations for the next phase of their journey meant that the Palestinian and Syrian couple had to take on another identity: Bulgarian. Lining up at the airport security check on their way to Rome, Maysam held a passport identifying her as Sofia, while Marco was John. They were told that the key to success was to avoid raising suspicion by behaving normally in this totally abnormal situation. Maysam, with fair skin, western-style clothes and captivating eyes, made it through the security check without a glitch. With her boarding pass in hand and her heart throbbing in her chest, she waited for Marco to join her.

But Marco did not look Bulgarian, nor did he know what behaving like a "normal" Bulgarian entailed, and his fake ID was spotted even before his passport was thoroughly examined. After he was held back by airport security, he was rigged up, futilely interrogated then tossed outside the airport despite his insistence that he was a fully fledged Bulgarian citizen. Whether the passport was forged or not did not matter, what mattered was that he had to play the part and believe that he was Bulgarian, at all costs. A few hours later Maysam called to inform him that she was in Rome and would have to proceed to another country without him. She took the next plane to Copenhagen, then to Oslo and finally to Stockholm where she stayed.

Marco remained hostage to the Sudanese smuggler's trickery, changing the identity in the counterfeit passport to a man with a "less suspicious" shade of darker skin: Portuguese, to be exact, with the name of Eduardo. When this ID failed, he became the Spaniard Antonio, and then another European, and another, and so on. After all of these failed and embarrassing attempts, it became clear to Marco and his Sudanese smuggler that the airport route was no longer viable. Marco was just not a good con man. Every time Marco attempted to find his way through the security check at the airport in Athens, he was singled out and asked to join a line of other refugees who were also caught red-handed, fake passports and all.

Marco was now convinced that journeying on foot was his only option. After braving the sea in a rickety vessel, he felt certain he'd survive whatever hell awaited him. Others readily joined in. The new expedition included Isam, Zakariya, and Abu Alia from the sea voyage, and Omar, Thaer, and Hussein, all newcomers, all Palestinians. A Sudanese land smuggler instructed them to meet him up north in the city of Thessaloniki, called Saloneek by Arab refugees due to the impossibility of pronouncing it in Arabic. The easy part of the trip included a night at the house of the smuggler with a "last supper," followed by a five-hour journey to Saloneek and a bus ride into the city. Marco took in the visual beauty and historical buildings, but even his Marco Polo spirit had dwindled to almost nothing. The real journey began at the railroad tracks with each of them carrying essentials like blankets, food, extra jackets, and plenty of water. Accompanying them were two old Somali women who sought the road to Macedonia as well. The man in charge was a Bangladeshi by the name of Mohamad Saed, who was soon nick-named Sméagol, after Tolkien's corrupt fictional character.

Sméagol, a diminutive, bald man in his thirties, had discolored teeth, with a few missing and others separated by gaps visible from a distance. He was perfectly skinny, except for a round little pot-belly that made him look as if he had swallowed a small animal, yet to be digested. He looked and smelled filthy, his pants had no zipper, and his belt was replaced by a contraption made of plastic bags, rolled and tied together to form a rope that he needed to carefully disentangle every time he had to relieve himself. He led the gang of nine, including the two Somali women, as they walked along or beside the tracks so as not to lose their path.

On their first day of the journey, they walked for twenty long hours. On the second, they walked from eight in the morning until three the next morning. No matter how carefully they tried to ration their water supplies, they were running out quickly, and the food was completely gone. Fear of dehydration was at the back of everyone's minds, coupled with constant hunger pangs as they walked along the tracks. To Marco, hunger was nothing new and his expertise in suppressing mounting anxieties came in handy. Macedonia was finally getting closer and the numbness in their bleeding feet was proof that they were alive and had made it that far.

They listened carefully to Sméagol's ominous final instructions: cross the street, jump the fence, climb the hill, walk for one hour and cross a river to their destination, a small village with giant windmills. What the treacherous Sméagol failed to inform them was that the river was not a natural body of flowing water but an open sewer, and to cross it, even on its most shallow parts, they would be covered by human feces up to their navels. Moreover, the distance between the shit river and the village was much further than Sméagol estimated, or perhaps the distance seemed further because they were weighed down by dried excrement hardening and cracking on their clothing, whose stench was unbearable as they climbed up hills and crossed valleys.

It was about midnight when the small village with the giant windmills finally appeared in the distance. The brief moment of ecstasy instantly vanished when two sets of blinding police lights flashed in the group's faces, and another set illuminated their shadows behind them. After some days in Macedonian detention lacking basic human needs, they were sent back to Greece. Unfazed, they restarted their hellish journey again the following day walking for twenty hours, then twenty more, then crossed the street, jumped the fence, climbed the hill, walked a distance and once more crossed the vile shit river, only to be apprehended by the same police unit at the outskirts of the small village with the giant windmills.

It was for the best when Sméagol eventually abandoned the group, for they discovered that the journey did not really require so much walking, and that he had dishonestly mapped it out to minimize his costs and maximize his fees. Half-jokingly, Isam fantasized about ways to murder Sméagol, the man no one would miss. His replacement, a Bangladeshi called Nasser, had a more human dimension and was better dressed. He managed to find an alternative route that was less tedious, although it still demanded the ritualistic baptism in the shit river. But instead of carrying on to the village to be greeted by beams of light, they would jump onto a moving cargo train that was known for slowing down in that specific area before gathering speed once more. Old metal screeching on metal, diesel fumes burning in the exhaust and a wide-open side door beckoned them to enter; they all managed to accomplish the feat that seemed to be out of a Hollywood western, except for the two poor Somali women whose heavy bodies fell on top of one another, with them shouting of hurt limbs and disappointment as they watched the train pass by.

The Palestinian refugees gathered in one corner of the wagon, while almost sixty other hapless men and women watched in silence as the new arrivals scrambled to make sense of an absurd situation. The others were black Africans, or brown Arabs and Asians. Some of the women wore traditional scarves over their hair, others did not, while some had pulled them off for fear of being noticed during their travel—but they all reeked of shit. When the train came to a complete halt, many hours later, nearly a dozen police officers stood outside poised in aggressive military positions, toting shields and commando gear, and accompanied by barking dogs on leashes, ready to stage a massive arrest of which compassion was no part.

It was not clear why some refugees managed to evade the police and escape successfully across the border. Perhaps they were vitalized or sickened by their collective smell and hopelessness, or encouraged by the police's inability to contain such a large number of men and women fleeing with force and determination. Unlucky yet again, Marco was apprehended. Handcuffed along with some others, they were taken to Gazy Baba prison in the capital, Skopje. "You have to wash," he was told by a Macedonian officer with a straw-colored moustache. The officer, in his forties, was covering his mouth and nose as he pointed at Marco's feces-defiled body. "But we are hungry," Marco pleaded to the guard, and was told with a snarky grin that it was Ramadan and he should be fasting anyway.

It had been four days of grueling travel wherein Marco had not eaten a single meal. After they were sent back to Greece, the gang ate whatever they could find at the smuggler's house, mostly dried bread and stale cheese, then showered before embarking on yet another attempt, this time with a person by the name of Trilla. His smuggling tactic was simple. He snuck people into the back of trucks manned by drivers who were unaware that they were transporting war refugees. When the trucks stopped across the border, the refugees would flee and seek asylum.

The Palestinian group had diminished to three: Marco, Zakariya, and Abu Alia. After a fairly short journey to the border, the driver parked the vehicle in an empty lot to try his luck at a border-point casino between Greece and Macedonia. In total silence, they peered out from the rusty holes on the side of the large truck. Border police stood around bored while both countries' flags waved above the casino and lawfully transported passengers walked around in complete ignorance of the truck's human cargo. Feeling caught between two worlds of time and space, the refugees saw no reason to worry as they waited anxiously for the next border crossing. But when the trucker returned, he opened the truck's upward sliding door and found the three men hopelessly staring at him. There was simply no point in running and they were all at a loss for words. The police mission this time was easy. They took the three by the hand and threw them back across the Greek border, where they were once more detained.

* * *

Luqman was the gentlest of all the smugglers. He was an Algerian man in his early 20s, who offered the Palestinians a special price due solely to the fact that they were Palestinian: 200 euros each from Greece to Macedonia, and the same amount from there to Serbia. This time the smuggling was by a train that carried sand for construction. The train arrived once every few days, and the adventure would require the refugees to bury themselves as deep in the sand as possible, leaving only their faces exposed to breathe precious air. While waiting for the train, the three men fed on a cheap but pleasant meal cooked in a small family restaurant located across the street from the point where Marco and company were meant to plunge into the sand trucks. Images of quicksand and being swallowed alive rushed through Marco's mind as he chewed on a meal that resembled Palestinian cuisine. As they made it into the train, the men realized that they had been afflicted by food poisoning, leading to repeated and excruciatingly painful bouts of diarrhea.

It was a very long journey before the sand train arrived at its final destination. There was no point keeping track of time or distance, or counting the hills along the way as Marco used to do. They knew, however, that they had finally made it to Macedonia, and it would be a matter of time before they found a safe house to plan the next leg of their route to Serbia. As they walked into a local train station to purchase their tickets to the big city, a giant officer was on their heels and in a righteous tone asked the three to line up and show their papers. As they went into their pockets to pull out the tattered IDs, Zakariya and Marco whispered to one another:

"Do you want to make a run for it?"
"Fuck it. Yalla."

They took off running down the stairs as fast as their worn-out feet and diarrhea-ravaged bodies would allow, an act of courage that inspired other refugees, who appeared from every corner of the station, to follow suit. A scene of chaos unfolded as the enormous officer dispiritedly tried to catch them all. Running sideways, running backwards and leaping forwards, he grabbed at any refugee he could, failing to catch any of them.

* * *

The following week was eventful. Maysam discovered she was pregnant, yet within days she lost the baby. In an emotional sermon over the phone, she accused Marco of being unfaithful to her, although he explained to her that no self-respecting woman would want to sleep with a refugee who reeked of shit. Some of the Palestinian refugees who accompanied the couple on the dinghy trip showed up, each with a story stranger than fiction. Isam had torture marks on his back but refused to speak about his agony. They were all penniless, and had no stamina to move past the refugee accommodation provided to them. Marco cashed whatever money remained in the "insurance" office, repaid the little sums he borrowed from his friends, filled a small bag with bottles of water and decided to finish the journey alone to silence the tremulous chatter in his brain.

His destination was Lojane, an Albanian town that bordered Serbia. First he needed to reach Kumanova by bus, then take a taxi to Lojane, then walk north to the Serbian border. Whether he was purposely misled by cruel villagers, or his fatigue had impaired his sense of direction, Marco found himself, after a day of continuous walking, back in Lojane. Starving and his raw feet burning, he obtained a warm meal to refuel and try his luck once more, but was ambushed by seven men who stole his last 200 euros and his dinner. Lost and confused, Marco's disorientation was clear even to the thugs, who were courteous enough to orient him toward his destination. They told him to walk to a village called Vaksintse, before reaching Lojane, then cross over to another small village, Miratovac and carry on north. They also spared his passport, his only claim to coveted asylum.

He followed their directions and occasionally stopped to wipe the blood pouring from his toes and the back of his heels. He walked for twenty-four kilometers before collapsing outside the village of Cukarka. When he awoke, he could barely believe his eyes as he found himself a guest in a small mosque looked after by a kindly imam. The Muslim clergy, whose salary was not provided by the government but donated by the poor residents of the small village, knew more about Palestinian history than Marco did himself. As the Imam recounted some of the tragic history of the Palestinians, he softly wept along with Marco.

The imam reoriented Marco again, gave him 50 euros and directed him to the city of Bujanovac. From there Marco could take the bus directly to Belgrade. Although the journey was coming to a conclusion, the risk was real that he could still be apprehended by the Serbian police and because his legally allowed stay in Macedonia had expired, Marco also risked being sent back to Greece. Having been on the road for nearly three months, he could not consider such a dreadful possibility.

The imam of a second mosque in Biljaca, where Marco stopped to rest after many hours of walking through forests and on unpaved roads, was not kind and seemed well-versed in judgment rather than compassion. Sternly, he told Marco that guests were welcomed in the mosque for only one day. Marco stayed for exactly that long, but before leaving he felt a strong urge to pray. It had been a long time since Marco had kneeled, and as he rested his forehead on the ground, he sobbed uncontrollably. The weight of everything he had experienced came tumbling down. There was no one there to console him or to explain to him why three generations of Palestinians were still enduring the same legacy of dispossession and Nakba after all these years; or why a Palestinian is cursed with displacement even if he changes his name, denies his identity, carries a fake passport and claims to be Bulgarian.

Soon after he boarded the bus to Belgrade, his nightmare of being caught came true. Two officers waved to the driver to pull over and stop. Determinedly, they walked towards Marco, nabbed him, handcuffed him and took him back to the border. Marco put up no fight. He simply stood there. He was not angry, or sad, or despairing, or confused, or experiencing any precise feeling that he was familiar with. He felt no fear, in fact no feelings of any kind. He just started walking to Serbia again, as if he were walking to Kakwab Elementary School in Yarmouk, no deviations, no talking to strangers, just keeping to what was familiar to him, one straight line.

* * *

Just before he died, Mohammed Abdul Ghani al-Lubani had transferred the deed of his Yarmouk home to his son's name and also left him with another small plot of land in Al-Mujaydil, the original village in Palestine from which he was expelled before walking to Jobar. The old man, a proud man, who paved roads in Nazareth and scooped cow dung in Syria, also left his family with his most prized possession—a large, old, rusting key that had opened the door to his cherished Palestinian home. The house no longer exists, but the key was kept in the family home in Yarmouk as a testament to their right of return—and now the Yarmouk home no longer exists either. The legacy of that original refugee, who once walked to Jobar, with his whole family, in one straight line, is still fully observed by his grandchildren—all of them.

And Khaled Jamal Abdul Ghani al-Lubani, also known as Marco, is still walking to his next resting place, in one straight line.

Each step that Marco's bleeding and muddied feet took was not only his own. To the Palestinian refugee, escaping Syria's inferno was resuming a journey made by countless others. Crossing dangerous borders, evading police and snipers, and walking like the undead in the throes of starvation and dehydration is the high price they paid to find their last earth.

Ahmad al-Haaj now takes us back in time to when he was just a boy. In his escape from his village nearly seventy years ago, he was given a huge responsibility. When his father was presumed dead, his mother was left with an impossible choice while they were trapped in the siege of Al-Faluja. She wanted to save one of their children and she needed it to be Ahmad. Because he was the oldest and most educated, the heartbroken mother thought he would be able to preserve the family legacy with all of his knowledge in hand. Surviving Yarmouk or surviving Al-Faluja, one was no less brutal than the other.

2
Abu Sandal—The One with the Slippers

It was not the end of Ahmad's tormented journey but what would happen next was too much for his disoriented mind to comprehend, and he dragged his tired body onward to an uncertain destiny. He lay down on a patch of unscathed green and slept under the shadows of a gloomy sky. But the lifeless sound of raindrops soon awoke him to streams of water gushing down his dusty face. Layers of dried mud that had amassed on the long road fell away like chunks of earth from his once polished shoes. He was the only child in his entire village to ever enjoy the comfort of a pair of shoes, earning him the moniker "Abu Sandal"—the one with the slippers.

In this state of displacement and numbness, nothing mattered anymore. He just wanted home. Since he had left, moving in one straight line, all that he needed and all that meant anything to him was for his family to be reunited around the warmth of a winter fire in that same old brick house with a tiled roof. He could still see his father standing proudly in the center of the room with the high ceiling, skillfully subduing the flames of the fire-pit before placing the favorite silver teapot laden with loose tea, *maramia* (thyme) and cane sugar. And how he missed waking to the chickens cackling in the stable next door. It was so cold here, so wet and unwelcoming, and the gusts of wind coming from the sea were relentless in their fierceness and velocity.

So he stood up, took a deep breath, wiped what remained of the mud off his face, and carried on south. Two large, shabby-looking suitcases held everything he could carry: school uniforms, ordinary clothes and cherished books that were evenly distributed so as to balance out the weight in order to carry as many as possible.

But how was he to continue when the road seemed so bare and infinite, and the horizon ahead was the darkest shade of grey he had ever seen, promising misfortune and nothing else? And when the ones he had left behind might stay behind forever?

The towering figures of two women with strangely formed bodies arose slowly in the distance. As they got closer, their shapes became clearer and clearer, and soon he realized that two large wicker baskets, perched impeccably on the women's heads, had appeared as if they were extensions of their bodies.

"Where do you come from son?" inquired one. "Where is your family? What is your clan?" inquired the other.

"I am from over there. I walked across the border."

Ahmad needed to say no more, his sullen eyes told a thousand stories. The horror stories of the war, and the obstruction of the main roads that linked Gaza to the coastal frontier were known to many in these parts of Palestine. These ladies with their motherly gazes knew it was nothing less than a miracle that this fifteen-year-old boy managed to slip by the guns of the Jewish militias, dodging every violent ambush and evading every landmine, and finally escaping death by the skin of his teeth.

Sympathetic to the young boy, the two women, who were on their way from the town of Jabaliya to the Gaza market, handed Ahmad six oranges and six lemons, carried his bags all the way to the Syed Hashim Ibn Abdul Mutalab Mosque, and directed him to the closest road that led to the heart of the city where he could find shelter.

Ahmad al-Haaj had been here before, but certainly not in this terrible state of hunger and enervation, and certainly not under these tragic circumstances. Gaza had always been kind to him. Here he learned how to be his own man, how to think for himself, and how to challenge all dogmas, religious or otherwise. Gaza was the place that offered him formal education and bestowed upon his family untold pride. At long last, the al-Haaj family had the exceptionally educated and culturally refined son that they had always dreamed of, who even regularly wore shoes and deservingly earned the title "afandi."

Perhaps it was his perceptive instinct, or a true understanding of the tragedy that had befallen his country, for Ahmad knew that this time was different and that many others still had not really understood how deep this scar would be. No matter how hard he tried to shake off the disturbing notion that shook him to his core, he knew he would never see Al-Sawafir again.

He finally oriented himself to the areas of Gaza that he was familiar with, and carried on walking to Imam al-Shafi'i High School with his bags, oranges, and lemons. At the back of his mind, he wondered with sorrow if his father was still alive, or if his body would ever be recovered; and if it were, would it have the dignified burial he deserved; and if the family cow that ran away during the haze of the last battle would ever be found. To the loving family, being attached to an animal as if it were a member of the clan did not seem odd in any way.

It was 7 a.m. when he walked through the main gate of his school. Though its walls were the same and the familiar morning bell chimed and greeted him like it always did at that time, every day, even on Fridays, he was no longer the same person he was a day earlier when he left Al-Sawafir, and walked all night, covering a distance of at least twenty-five miles.

He arrived in Gaza on November 16 in that fateful year of 1948 when the world watched a crime happen and looked the other way. By then, on the other side of the border, north of Gaza city, men with superior arms, speaking foreign tongues and with war stratagems that were conceived many years earlier, had all but sealed the fate of Palestine and that of the al-Haaj family.

* * *

Ahmad al-Haaj was born in 1933. His father, Khaleel al-Haaj was a fellah, but unlike the rest of the Al-Sawafir clans altogether numbering around 1,000 fellahin peasants, Khaleel owned his own land, one hundred dunums or so. It was a fortune that appeared as an unintended sudden consequence of his family's misfortune, that of his four brothers' untimely demise in the First World War. Like thousands of fellahin, the brothers were dragged into foreign lands to fight the Ottomans' war, aimed at prolonging the empire's reign in the eastern Mediterranean. But they lost, and their defeat ushered in the age of the British Mandate over Palestine.

Khaleel raised his family in Al-Sawafir al-Sharqiyya. In fact, there were three different Sawafir villages in that region, all located about thirty kilometers north of Gaza, along the Southern Coastal Plains of Palestine. There was eastern Sawafir, where Khaleel raised his kids and cattle, and western and northern Sawafir, where his land was more or less equally distributed.

But much of that land was lost to the encroaching influence of large families whose wealth and status had been handed down from one generation to the next. For a peasant to own so much land was an aberration, and with his brothers no longer by his side to support him, Khaleel had to labor alone to fend off the constant attempts of the large clans to deprive him of his land and strip him of what was rightfully his, dunum by dunum, using every trick they could think of. At times they resorted to the unfair tax system once espoused by the Ottomans and later faithfully applied by the British, to ensure that the nonconforming peasant returned to his proper place, poor and subdued.

But Khaleel was a fighter, and his commitment to the honor of his brothers and love of his ever-shrinking land had nothing to do with greed or lust for power. Most peasants, himself included, had developed an intimate relationship with their rich and fertile land, for it was their only sustainer, after God, of course. Without land there could be no food and all would perish.

With time that relationship to the earth symbolized something that was worth more than anything tangible. Al-Ard, one's land, was central to the fellahin's unassuming discourse that centered on Al-Ard, al-'ard, and al-walad—land, honor, and offspring. This was the ultimate priority of the fellahin, who did not comprehend the complexity of their unraveling world.

Some of the villagers of the three Sawafirs traced their origins to bygone nomadic tribes that once lived in the vicinities of Damascus, called Arab Al-Sawafir. It was never truly confirmed whether that was true, or why the tribes would have left Damascus centuries ago in the first place. But the southern plains were a rational choice for a balanced existence. Many Palestinian clans lived there, generous and welcoming, some tracing their history back to the ancient tribes that settled in Palestine before books were written in which ancient deities promised real estate to warring nations.

The plains were about fifteen miles wide with low rising hills. Most of it was flat arable land with mineral-rich soil that insatiably absorbed the nourishing winter rain, then eagerly awaited the next season's crops. The winter rain was the fellahin's only respite, keeping them in tune with the changing seasons, telling them when to spread the seeds, when to harvest, when to grind the wheat, and when to huddle in mudbrick homes for protection, make more children and pray for rain.

Al-Sawafir had also lived with war and was never shattered by it. When the soldiers of Mohammed Ali Pasha, the self-declared monarch of Egypt, experienced a bitter defeat at the hands of the Ottoman army in 1840, they retreated from Acre and other parts of the eastern Mediterranean to their Egyptian province.

But some remained in Palestine and this is how the western Sawafir came about. It was the soldiers' and their descendents' newfound home for the next one hundred years and more. With time the newcomers took on Palestinian Arab identities, habits and accents, and were gradually integrated into the modest world of the fellahin who, unlike large and powerful clans, had no class system through which people were filtered, and when necessary, alienated.

Back then most of the fellahin wore no shoes, thus strengthening their ties to their land, binding them eternally and intrinsically, and keeping their lives humble. But this was by no means a sign of lack of interest in education or improving their lives, as schooling, however limited, was coveted by the peasants who were mostly illiterate. So they built a little school, made of mud bricks like the rest of the village.

Education was offered until the fifth grade, and it attracted pupils from eight different neighboring villages, making it the heart of life for many children. Ahmad al-Haaj began his studies there, and also attained the nickname Abu Sandal from his fellow classmates who were less fortunate and could not afford such luxurious slippers.

To say that fellahin children were eager for opportunities would be an understatement, for life for the children of fellahin was not easy. They began to work the land at the age of five or six, and when there was no land to be worked, they were offered as cheap laborers on land owned by larger families, in exchange for a single sack of wheat at the end of the harvest season.

Fifth-grade education offered more potential than the near-slavery experienced by the fellahin. Aside from the prestige derived from knowing how to read and write, the fellahin craved the possibility of receiving a dependable fixed salary, however meager, through some government employment. Government jobs which only required basic literacy were not controlled by the direction of the wind, winter rain or organized mass prayers beseeching God to look down kindly on luckless peasants. No mother wanted to watch her child suffer the consequences of not knowing how to spell his or her own name.

To the pride of his parents, Ahmad was a particularly fortunate child, and a good one. Though at the age of five he worked his father's land like everyone else, his keen intelligence made him the smartest of all of Khaleel's children—some would even say all of Al-Sawafir's three villages combined. Curiously though, it was a single verse of poetry that changed the direction of his career and life forever. And none of it was planned.

Mr. Ferrell's British accent was unlike the accent of Ahmad's other teachers, and his odd clothes were like some he had seen in the pictures of his history books. He was the English language inspector in the region's schools, and he happened to be visiting Al-Sawafir Elementary on that decisive day.

Entering the classroom in a confident march, he quickly quizzed the pupils in front of the visibly nervous teacher who was intimidated by his authoritative demeanor. Not five minutes passed before the educator was reprimanded for not enforcing more love for poetry in the children. Feeling sorry for his beleaguered teacher, who stood frozen, Aḥmad declared his fondness of poetry to Mr. Ferrell, falsely claiming that it was fostered by the teacher who in reality knew very little of the English language altogether.

To prove his claim, Ahmad stood up and recited a verse from *Horatius at the Bridge*. His exaggerated manner even stopped his fellow classmates from staring at his slippers, and to the complete bafflement of everyone involved, he exclaimed:

> *"O Tiber! Father Tiber!*
> *To whom the Romans pray,*
> *A Roman's life, a Roman's arms,*
> *Take thou in charge this day!"*

Unable to understand how genius could blossom in a village where shoes were a vanity, Mr. Farrell raised his hands high in the air, clapping loudly, and gesturing and urging the students to do the same. And with uncontainable jollity, he wrote down a few words on a piece of paper and handed it to Ahmad after indicating to the little ones to stop their applauding.

It was a scholarship—or, to be exact, 120 Palestinian pounds which amounted to half of Ahmad's future high school tuition, in addition to room and board in the al-Amiriya school in Yafa. The cost of attending this dream school was all to be shouldered by the Mandate Government functioning under the authority of Her Majesty the Queen. The only problem was that the school had no hostel, and according to Ahmad's father, the distant relatives who lived there would have been a bad influence on him, so he was told that it was not for him.

Due to the interest that the peculiar child garnered, the scholarship was re-assigned to Imam al-Shafi'i High School in Gaza, where a few years later, Ahmad would walk carrying two heavy suitcases, muddied shoes, six oranges and six lemons.

* * *

Khaleel married three times, and Ahmad was the first child of the third wife. The first of the wives, Fatima, had died in childbirth, a common occurrence in those days of limited medical expertise and equipment. Her only legacy was her daughter, Ahlam.

The second wife was the outcome of a barter between the al-Haaj and Hourani families. Poverty during those days made a dowry of gold, silver, and Palestinian pounds an unsurmountable obstacle for most fellahin, for the British had linked the Palestinian currency to sterling as early as 1927. So they made a deal: widowed Khaleel married Zakiya, whose brother in turn married Khaleel's sister. Zakiya's father and all of her brothers, save one, died in the First World War, and marriage was the only way out of a lonely life. She would go to bed at night dreaming of her prince and praying he would be good to her. Though she had never seen Khaleel before, she was happily surprised to find a remarkably handsome man, with giant shoulders, strong hands and dark chest hair that seemed to overflow through his shirt, waiting for her to consummate their marriage when the zaffah and local band arrived from a neighboring village.

To the contrary, Khaleel was not captivated by Zakiya's plain looks, sole eye, and the deep cystic acne marks covering her face and body that could still be seen through the expensive makeup imported from Yafa. But, still, a year later they had a daughter whom they called Utur—Perfume.

It was not the pockmarked skin or displeasing looks that caused divorce between them, or the stress of making ends meet. Irreconcilable conflict arose between Khaleel's sister and the Hourani brother, which naturally meant that Zakiya's barter marriage had to end as well. Heartbroken, she had to leave her attractive husband, and took Utur to live in Beit Daras with her uncles from her mother's side.

Zakiya was eventually redeemed once again and married into the Ashur family, had three children whom she also adored and who all grew up to become leading members of an Arab nationalist party in Jordan. Peculiarly enough, they would become close friends to Ahmad who grew up to be a communist and a very radical one at that.

For his third marriage, Khaleel wed his longtime neighbor, Zaynab. This marriage was a blessed one, and their love got them through all the wars that followed. From their union, Ahmad was the first born and then three sisters followed: Maliha, Fatima, and Safiya; then came Mohammed, and Mahmoud, who soon died from malaria, followed by another Mahmoud, also taken away by malaria. After that Abdul Jawad arrived, and then the little star Maysar, the only one of all the daughters to receive proper education in Beirut.

All the names given to children held some kind of emotional value to Khaleel, and when he first said their names, a big smile would beam across his face. Some were named after his brothers killed in the Great War, after his deceased first wife, or whoever left a void in his heart. It was his way of keeping them alive. But after the sequential losses of both Mahmouds to the same disease, he swore any future offspring would never bear that name. Khaleel was a strong believer in heavenly signs and bad omens, as were many in the ancient land.

As the bountiful family grew, their home grew as well. They first settled in a humble mud-brick house of three rooms and a bakhsheh—an open area where chickens freely roamed and picked at whatever bits of food were thrown their way. The detached latrine was the only place where one had some moments of privacy; and a tabun, an oven made of hardened mud and fueled by dried branches and wood, was the epicenter of intimate family gatherings when steaming hot traditional Palestinian dishes were brought out and admired like a treasure.

In the center of the bakhsheh, a one-meter wide and ten-meter deep hole in the ground stored much of the harvest and the family's livelihood to be consumed or shared judiciously throughout the year, until the next harvest. Although the roof of dried tree branches was fastened skillfully together forming an almost waterproof ceiling, the winter rain of the Mediterranean downpours often tested it.

The largest plot of what remained of Khaleel's land was located in northern Sawafir, where the man eventually built a new house adjacent to his forty-five dunums. The new house constructed with bricks and a tiled roof was meant to guard the land, but with time it became the family's favorite shelter. The spacious animal's share nestled the cows, camels, horses, and donkeys in a roofed corral ten meters long and five meters wide. Between the two brick rooms and the stable, there was a relatively large open space that was not fully sealed, and was strategically positioned so that the family could benefit from the natural warmth provided by the breathing of the animals. The family often gathered there, around the fire pit, where Khaleel told fibs and stories of past grandeur, of family's lost fortunes, of disobedient spirits that haunted the village, and of the heroism of lost uncles who died in a conflict they hardly understood.

Ahmad spent most of his childhood in that new home which he truly loved, devouring whatever school books he had or cleaning off the books left by British soldiers in the garbage heap near Al-Sawafir. He could not understand how anyone would throw away such life knowledge. And in that house he read all the books he could until the massacre of Beit Daras, whose frightening outcome drove the fellahin of Al-Sawafir and fifty other villages into an exile that would refuse to end.

The geography of Al-Sawafir was essential to the political awareness of Ahmad al-Haaj. To the east of the village, built mostly on privately owned land of another Arab village, Joulis, a British military compound had existed for as long as Ahmad could remember. To the west of Al-Sawafir, also built mostly on privately owned land of another village, Beit Daras, a Jewish settlement known as Be'er Toviya was in slow but constant expansion.

The fellahin were perhaps unsophisticated in their understanding of politics which mostly consumed educated Palestinian elites in near and far cities, yet it was becoming clear to them that the British army and Jewish settlers had developed a particular kinship, and that the constant robbery of fellahin land by both was being mirrored in other parts of Palestine as well. It was unfolding in front of their very eyes. There was no need for political analysis.

Be'er Toviya's identity also changed throughout the years. When it was first constructed from funds provided by Baron Edmond de Rothschild in 1887, it was called Qastina, after the name of a nearby Arab village. That original Jewish settlement was destroyed by angry fellahin during the riots of 1929 when many Arabs and Jews were killed, starting in Al-Quds, then throughout Palestine. It was rebuilt, looking more like a fortress the second time around. It carried the name of yet another Arab village, Bir Ta'abya, a name which was altered to a more Hebrew-sounding variant, Be'er Toviya. The topography of the Jewish village, however, was dissimilar to the surrounding nearby villages of the fellahin, which had no walls, no fences and no defenses.

The road between the British military camp and the Jewish settlement was noticeably busy with much traffic. The settlers crossed the outskirts of Al-Sawafir to provide food to British soldiers, who trained Be'er Toviya residents on the use of their British war technology. It was clear that Al-Sawafir, which had stood the test of time, famine and wars for centuries, was in danger of being erased from that geography altogether. As Khaleel and his children worked on his land, a political transition was taking place, one that aimed at changing the ownership of Khaleel's land, and all the land owned by the fellahin and even the larger clans as well.

* * *

The Jewish Agency operated in Mandate Palestine as if it were a government. Even Jews wishing to obtain a driver's license from British authorities had to first apply to the Agency, which was in fact the central and only form of official contact between Jewish settlers and the British rulers of Palestine. The fellahin, on the other hand, had to undergo several forms of control mechanisms, not just that of British and sanctioned Jewish institutions, but also from large Arab families who owned most of the land and subjugated the peasants to near-slavery work conditions. It was a complicated and well-planned "conspiracy", and Ahmad, who traveled between Al-Sawafir and Gaza quite often, began to unravel its many threads.

Large Palestinian families obtained their authority by several means. They were coopted by and consequently cooperated with the British as soon as the Ottomans were overpowered and routed. These clans also obtained some of their political legitimacy from nearby Arab states, who sought influence amongst the people of that area. These Arabs had themselves already fallen under the control and spell of the colonial powers, be they British or French.

Even when the British encouraged or allowed Palestinians to develop their own political parties, for after all, the Mandate was supposedly a temporary transition to some form of Palestinian independence, the parties were formed around familial and clan lines. The Husseinis in Al-Quds launched their Arab Party, and later took it upon themselves, without the consent or consideration of a single fellah, to form the High Arab Committee. The Abdulhadis launched their own Independence Party in Jenin and Nablus, and the Nashashibis helped offset the growing influence of the Husseinis, not just in Al-Quds, but in other urban centers as well. That was the British-sponsored "democracy" that was needed to fulfill the terms of the Mandate. Yet despite declared hostility towards Britain's colonial intrigues, the large families-turned-political-parties acquired their validation from the very same colonial power that had already promised Palestine to the Jewish settlers.

Whatever small patches of land that were sold to private Jewish institutions were mostly sold by these very families. They barely cared about the fate of the peasants who were both expelled and made homeless, or were forced to agree to work under even worse working conditions.

The fellahin, on the other hand, were left with few dismal options. Some subscribed to the self-imposed moral, political or religious authority that the presumptuous clans granted themselves. Others, fueled by dignity, rebelled. And their rebellions, in what was a three-year uprising starting in 1936, began as a strike declared by Arab parties. The strike was meant to send a message to the British without crossing the line of what was permissible, which might risk alienating the Mandate Government.

The fellahin had no such qualms, and quickly escalated the strike to an armed rebellion. Some sold their harvests, others leased whatever little plots of land they had acquired. Others even sold their women's precious gold and went to war. Expectedly, it was a vastly disproportionate war, for no fellah who ran around mostly barefoot, using a machete or even an outdated Turkish rifle, could stand against the army of His Majesty the King.

The fellahin were excruciatingly crushed. Their bodies were dumped in mass graves and their homes were burnt, along with their harvests. Vile deeds were done to their women that no fellahin would dare speak about, preferring to die a thousand deaths before reliving that trauma. With every strong-willed rebellion, their leaders fell in droves, and those unlucky enough to be caught were tortured and executed. They were ready to die for their cause, and Farhan al-Sadi, Izz al-Din al-Qassam, Mohammed Jamjoom, and Fuad Hijazi met that somber end. And with each falling martyr, a song would resonate in the mouths of the fellahin and across the picturesque olive groves, immortalizing the names of the dead, and mobilizing the living to rebel even more.

By the end of 1939, the British agreed to end land transfers from Arabs to Jewish settlers, but the decision came too late. That year Europe exploded into unprecedented fury. If the First World War led to the demise of the Ottomans and the advent of British rule over Palestine, the Second World War ushered in the end of British rule and the demise of the fellahin.

When British forces officially left Palestine on May 15, 1948, many in Al-Sawafir and nearby villages raided the army compound, hoping to salvage anything that could be eaten or sold for badly needed supplies. But the well-trained militias of Be'er Toviya had already seized the facilities and its small airstrip, and greeted them with machine guns. That was the start of a bloodbath that Ahmad refused to forget for the rest of his life, and he described it in no other terminology than this: the Crime where British and Zionist designs over Palestine were finally coming to fruition.

The Jewish settlement in Palestine began in earnest in 1881 when the leaders of the Zionist Movement in Europe eyed Arab Palestine as an exclusive home for Jews, paying little heed to the indigenous inhabitants of the land. These early ambitions translated into a bloody, but well-orchestrated action on May 15, 1948.

Between these two defining dates, Palestinian actions were also evolving, and largely united around three schools of thought. The dominant semi-intellectual, affiliated with large families that obtained formal education first under the Ottomans, and then the British. This lot seemed to constantly hover around whatever dominant power ruled over the Palestinians and did little to challenge the status quo. Another group subscribed to religious dogmas, and were at times rebellious and at times coopted by those exploiting their naiveté. Some among this innocent bunch genuinely believed that the feudal families were descendants of Prophet Mohammed, giving them a compelling enough reason for their blind obedience. And a third group sought answers from sources other than the British or those who spoke on behalf of God. This third group was the smallest, largely found in urban centers, and near institutions of learning.

Ahmad was a proud member of the last group, declaring his loyalty to communist ideals. Perhaps it was the fashionable thing for a fourteen-year-old to do, but a year later, at fifteen, his progressive, critical thinking allowed him to see the world with painful clarity when Al-Sawafir was lost. This laid the foundation for the rest of his life.

* * *

When the war was about to start, Ahmad al-Haaj was in his second year at his Gaza high school. Much of the fighting was taking place in other parts of Palestine, mostly near areas where Jewish settlements and towns held military sway over largely disorganized local fighters.

When Arab fighters attempted to cut off the few Jewish settlements in the south from the rest of the Zionist command, several fighters were killed and their actions instead resulted in the blockading of the main Arab roads. This meant that Ahmad, along with seven other students, could not return to their villages north of Gaza, a predicament that compelled the school's headmaster to appeal to a responsive British officer who managed to sneak the frightened students in the back of a congested supplies truck back to Al-Majdal, but not further than that.

Dropped in Al-Majdal, they still had to walk five, eight, twelve, and in the case of one student, fifteen miles through dangerous terrain to reach their villages.

When Ahmad arrived in Al-Sawafir on April 8, 1948, he learned that Arab fighters under the command of Abdul Qader al-Husseini lost Qastal, west of Al-Quds, and that the Zionists attacked the village of Deir Yassin and slaughtered almost half of its inhabitants. All the roads that led to Al-Sawafir were subsequently closed; the one between Al-Sawafir and Masmiyeh, the one near Qastina, the one close to Be'er Toviya, the road between Masmiyeh and Al-Quds, near Khalda; even Al-Quds itself was nearly isolated now that Deir Yassin was conquered.

Word of mouth brought news of similar massacres in the following days. The neighborhoods in Al-Quds were falling one after the other, starting with Sheikh Jarrah. Yafa itself fell later in April, followed by Haifa. Many of the terrified residents managed to flee as they were chased out with nothing but the clothes on their backs. But many were killed, or fell prey to execution by gunfire or grenades. And not all of those who rushed to the open sea were lucky enough to jump into stable vessels or the fishing boats that remained afloat. Entire families watched each other drown, their screams swallowed up by an unforgiving mother nature.

To buy his German rifle and 125 bullets, Khaleel al-Haaj sold a cow and four dunums. Laughter roared across his village as some found his action hasty and excessive. The

Arab League had promised to send its armies to liberate Palestine, but it did not take a young communist like Ahmad long to realize that the rag-tag Arab armies, mostly operating under the command of the same colonial powers that handed Palestine to the Zionists in the first place, were not capable of fighting a liberation war. Only when the Arabs did not arrive did the fellahin understand the depth of their crisis, prompting some to follow suit and obtain rifles in a crazed rush.

Just as the large Palestinian cities were about to fall to the militias, Arab paramilitaries were sent to aid Palestinian fighters, as a first step before the anticipated arrival of the official armies. But with time, it was becoming clearer that the Arabs were belatedly joining the war with the understanding that they were not to venture into areas designated for the proposed Jewish state.

Egyptian units arrived through Sinai, reached the Gaza district, and moved towards Iraq Suwaydan, hoping to reach Bir al-Sabi, and as far as al-Khalil, Beit Jibrin, and Bethlehem. As for the Arab Salvation Army, led by a French-trained Lebanese officer, Fawzi al-Qawuqji, it entered Palestine through the Galilees, ostensibly to reach Yafa, Haifa, and Nazareth. The latter paramilitary units were quickly routed and regrouped back in the Galilees once the main cities fell and their inhabitants were killed, expelled, or fled.

* * *

Al-Sawafir itself had ten fighters, one of whom was Khaleel al-Haaj. While Arab militaries were losing the war, the fellahin were winning small battles in the south. Fighters with old Turkish rifles would gather from the nearby villages and move towards whichever village was likely to be attacked. In the second battle of Beit Daras, when Be'er Tuvia mounted another failed attack, the villagers held their positions yet again, still hoping that the Egyptian army would arrive soon and defeat Be'er Tuvia once and for all.

Ahmad was shaken by the sight of the dead bodies collected by the Red Cross as Arab fighters were celebrating their victory. But he did not dare show any sign of weakness and held back the emotions engulfing his fledgling manhood. His father Khaleel also took part in that battle where he used twenty bullets, and, by the end of the fight, had nine to spare. Beit Daras, whose inhabitants were known for their oddly large heads, generosity, and impatience, had twelve rifles and a total of 967 bullets, all equally distributed among the toughest men in the village.

When the triumphant Al-Sawafir fighters returned proudly to their village from Beit Daras, holding up their rifles and chanting their cheers, the immensity of the victory was overshadowed by the understanding that the Zionist militants were likely to return with bigger guns and more fighters.

The fellahin fighters had no time to lose to formulate a strategy, and met in Ahmad al-Haaj's new house, the one built with bricks and a tiled roof. Their humble leadership was composed of three mukhtars and elderly men representing the most esteemed families. They were all men who had never imagined they would be drawing up war plans. Using nothing but their intuition as their guide, their decision was for the fighters to secure the main road, and others to join in using knives and clubs once a call for help was issued through the chants of "Allahu Akbar" should the village be attacked. And it was attacked.

Zionist militants moved in large numbers, all traveling in fortified military vehicles. Some of these were gifted or abandoned by the British and others purchased for the purpose of this war. Each military convoy consisted of anywhere between forty to fifty cars, with operations based on a set of military strategies that was aimed at isolating large areas before moving in to empty a besieged village of its inhabitants, exacting whatever price was required in blood and destruction.

In many cases, once the population of a village was banished, the remaining residents who did not leave due to pride, ill-health or an elderly body were pitilessly murdered and the village then looted and burned to the ground. Yet despite their defeat in Beit Daras, the militias seemed to direct their focus elsewhere, far away from Al-Sawafir and its ten fighters. That was the case until the Egyptian army officially entered the war on April 15, 1948, the same day the British formally left their positions, thus relinquishing Palestine and leaving the Zionist militias in control of most major cities.

But even then, Ahmad skillfully moved about between the villages, guardedly but with relative ease, using side dirt roads and avoiding the main road where the ten fighters and his father hid warily in the bushes, dreading the return of military convoys. Miraculously, Ahmad even went to Al-Majdal to sell harvested and milled wheat to purchase bullets for his father's German rifle.

A feeling of hope and relative stability began to return when the Egyptians deployed some army units from Sinai, through Rafah, to Gaza City, which they designated as their headquarters and then moved north. Upon their arrival in Gaza, they were joined by many volunteers, including Ahmad Ismail, the physics teacher at Imam al-Shafi'i High School.

The first full-scale battle fought by the Egyptian army was a success. On May 17, they surrounded Yad Mordechai kibbutz, a few miles to the south of Asqalan, for four days and finally conquered the fortified settlement with the help of local Gaza fighters who were later assigned fixed salaries from the Egyptian army for their bravery. On May 19, they reached the town of Al-Majdal, where they met with various volunteer forces who also enlisted in the Egyptian army. These volunteers, under the command of Mostafa Hafez, were the core of what was later known as fedayeen, Palestine's freedom fighters.

The Egyptians continued their drive further north to Iraq Suwaydan, then curved slightly to the east to Al-Faluja on their way to Bayt Jibrin in the direction of Al-Khalil. Their intention was to remain within the borders of the proposed Arab state, and not to go beyond the boundaries of the coastal area of that state somewhere between Rafah and Isdud.

The state set aside for the Palestinian Arabs per the United Nations partition plan of the previous year, was less than half of the original size of Palestine, even though the Arabs then constituted the vast majority of the country's population.

The Zionist militia convoys eventually returned, with a vengeance. They made their expected move against Beit Daras on June 5. Striking at dawn, they charged against the village until the early afternoon hours. By placating the stubborn Beit Daras, they knew the entire structure of local resistance was likely to fragment and collapse, so they proceeded to surround the village from all directions. All roads leading to it were cut off to ensure that fellahin fighters could not come to the rescue. By then the fighters in Beit Daras had acquired up to ninety rifles, but the invading militias had amassed an arsenal of modern weapons including mortars, machine guns mounted on top of fortified vehicles and hundreds of fully armed troops. The fellahin did not stand a chance.

Within the first hour of fighting, Beit Daras was on fire. Those who could not fight attempted to quell the flames of treason, but to no avail. Those who managed to escape ran to the Egyptian army, stationed only three miles north. But their frenzied calls for help and the destruction they described was not enough to implore these comrades to help them. The commander told the beseeching locals they could not intervene as they had not been given the orders to do so. Worse still, they even refused to supply the villagers with weapons or ammunition to defend themselves, for that also required a signature from the general command in Gaza.

It was too late anyway. By then the militias had moved in, and executed survivors of the initial onslaught, civilians and all, whoever they were—men, women, children—it made no difference. There were neither rules of war nor rules of engagement. Some escaped running through burning fields, tripping on one another while chased by sniper bullets. The few who remained alive arrived in Joura, Al-Majdal, Hamameh and the other nearby villages. The demise of Beit Daras had crushed the spirit of the smaller and less defendable villages. The massacre instilled fear and horror, especially as the death toll reached three hundred in a village with a population that barely totaled two thousand.

The mukhtars of the much smaller Al-Sawafir met again and resolved that Be'er Toviya was likely to continue its attacks now that the heart of resistance had gone up in flames. They urged the people to sleep in open fields for fear that their homes would be burned in the middle of the night while they were inside. Terrified and unsure of the plan that guaranteed nothing, hundreds of families walked late at night to nowhere in particular, hauling whatever food they could manage, and pushing along their cattle and donkeys. They all slept under the open sky, with the intention of returning in the morning to salvage whatever else they could carry—their chickens, the remaining flour, bottles of olive oil, small stacks of corn, and lentils.

* * *

Khaleel's other plot of about twenty dunums was located near Jsir. When a truce between the new State of Israel and reluctant Arab army units was declared sometime in mid-June, Khaleel felt safe enough to mill his wheat. Though he no longer had access to his land and homes in Al-Sawafir, he found the perfect alternative to make that life-giving ritual happen again. On the outskirts of Jsir, a small four-room elementary school had everything he needed. The classroom walls were still adorned with a noble map of Palestine and verses from the Quran that inspired the children to believe in their homeland. And the perfectly even courtyard where the children once freely ran about during recess was now the place where the wheat of the al-Haaj family could be milled. Ahmad, now no longer an afandi with a Turkish fez and pressed school uniform, was the one entrusted with the sensitive mission of hauling the wheat on top of the family's old steed to the Jsir Elementary, along with his two sisters, a cow, and a donkey.

That village was close to Al-Faluja, where the Egyptian army was still stationed. Even though the state of truce declared between the Arabs and Israel still applied, the al-Haaj family and the rest of the fellahin were surprised to discover it did not apply to the local resistance. As a consequence, Jsir became an easy target like the rest of the villages in that region, and their seven rifles and 250 bullets would be no match for keeping the encroaching army at bay.

Just as Ahmad began the exhaustive process of milling the wheat by hand, and just as he started to feel a slight sense of safety, the odious firing began once again. Jsir, with its humble houses of mud bricks and roofs of dried branches, went up in flames like those that had engulfed Beit Daras. Caught between their mounting fear of the unexpected battle, and worry about disobeying their father's strict orders, the children panicked.

They all started to run faster than they ever had. The donkey was somehow leading the way, while the steed trotted alongside the siblings in a display of loyalty. Their cow, Baraka, the wonder-animal able to produce boundless quantities of milk, lagged way behind. Maliha tried hard to rescue her Baraka whose gluttony had kicked in as she found herself in an uncharted meadow. She chewed on the green grass without a worry in the world. "Just leave her behind and save yourself," yelled Ahmad. But Maliha would not let go until finally Baraka, determined to set her own agenda, edged closer to a cliff that verged onto a steep valley below. She was never to be seen again.

The kids kept their shaking bodies hidden in the tall green grass until the late afternoon. Unnoticed by the soldiers who were shooting to kill, they witnessed the slaying of the remaining inhabitants of Jsir and the turning of Jsir Elementary into a mini military base where machine guns were mounted on the school's rooftop. The once perfect spot for Khaleel to mill his wheat was transformed into a perfect place for their enemy to kill.

No one survived the Jsir battle, not even Baraka was spared. As an antidote to the pain, Khaleel's children gave Baraka's young calf much love and affection. But the greatest loss came when Khaleel's wife, who was pregnant with Maysar at the time, learned that Khaleel was presumed dead. The girls sobbed as they watched their mother slap her own face and pour dirt on her head, in keeping with the traditions of women's mourning in those days.

Only a few teardrops escaped Ahmad's eyes after abruptly being told by his uncle to 'not cry in front of the women' or even cry at all. Whatever sense of security was felt by the al-Haaj family vanished along with Khaleel. The new-found man of the house, Ahmad had some big shoes to walk in, despite still being a boy at heart.

Following the Jsir battle, the people who slept in the open fields with hopes of finding protection from harm no longer had trust in the safety of their numbers. The mukhtars instructed the vulnerable and traumatized inhabitants to march north, inching closer to where the Egyptian army was stationed. Although they knew the army had watched the battles from afar and did nothing to honor the truce, they prayed to God for guardianship.

Most of the villages were deserted by then, ghost towns left to rot among the cadavers of war. The few fellahin who remained were too tired from their hard lives to even think about moving. Yet their advanced age or debilitating ailments did not spare them the end that met most of their fellow villagers. Among the dead was Aziza, Ahmad's grandmother from his mother's side who was executed by the militias; as well as Fatima, his grandmother on his father's side. Fatima never knew that her son, Khaleel, was missing and possibly dead. Maybe it was better that way.

The al-Haaj family, like many others, tried to make their way to Al-Faluja just before the truce ended on July 9. Fifty villages, once teeming with life, around Beit Daras and Al-Sawafir were completely evacuated, if not burnt to ashes.

But as soon as the truce ended, and under the broad daylight of the warm summer sun, the vitalized Israeli army moved to attack the disorganized Egyptian troops in Iraq Suwaydan. The fellahin watched the calamitous battle unfold right before their eyes. Defeated Egyptian soldiers wearing bloodsoaked uniforms came running through the crowds, asking for water and directions to Al-Faluja, which was easy to find. They simply had to follow a road dotted with hundreds of families escaping in horror, and marked by the dead bodies of soldiers and fellahin alike.

Hope resurfaced as quickly as it was quashed when the Egyptians retaliated, for they were soon to discover that they were being led into an ambush. Many young Egyptians were killed on that day. They too were mostly fellahin, as poor as the Palestinians, and equally ill-fated. Other Arab volunteers were in an even more miserable state as highlighted by their torn and mismatched uniforms, some walking barefoot, others wearing old Ottoman jackets, or discarded British army trousers, while still others used ropes as belts to keep oversized clothes in place.

The distance between Al-Sawafir and Al-Faluja was about three miles long; long enough to feel like forever under such insecurity. So just before the al-Haaj family started off on their final escape plans, they passed by the village of Hatta where Khaleel's old friend, Mohammed Lafi, still remained. Upon learning of the reported loss of his courageous dear friend at the battle of Jsir, Mohammed insisted that the distraught family stay for lunch. Hoping to bring some kind of closure to Khaleel's memory, he slaughtered a sheep in his honor.

The listless mother and her children slept that night in Hatta and would resume the journey at dawn. But those few peaceful hours were once again interrupted when the sounds of war exploded through the village and screams echoed in their familiar rawness. The host and his guests, along with all the inhabitants of the village plus their animals, began scattering in all directions, not knowing where to run or where the bullets were coming from. Recently born Maysar was cradled in her mother's arms. Maysar tried to comfort the baby whose face had become red from screaming. She knew no baby should ever emit those blood-curdling sounds, which seemed unhuman. She ran, praying that her direction was the right one. Ahmad held his brother Mohammed's hand, little Jawad held onto Maliha's cotton dress, and they all fled while crying their father's name, knowing he was nowhere near them and would not come to their rescue.

Among the dead that day were the wife and son of Mohammed Lafi and Baraka's only calf, whose killing deepened the grief of the al-Haaj family. The family was fortunate enough to take shelter in an old British army stable. Many others were not so lucky, such as the entire family of eleven who perished under the weight and flames of a collapsed building. Though the attack that night targeted the village of Karatiyya, the plans required the destruction of Hatta as well. By dawn the al-Haaj family finally made it to Al-Faluja, officially becoming refugees. Not knowing it at the time, they would hold onto that status forever.

* * *

Ahmad and the entire al-Haaj family were trapped under siege in Al-Faluja for months. The small town that had tripled in size by hosting thousands of refugees from neighboring villages was cut off from the coastal road when the newly formed Israeli army sullied the second truce. Trapping the defenseless refugees, nothing could get in or out except the buzzing warplanes swooshing over the town for many days and nights. Their disappearance would only last a brief instant after dropping their cargo of barrel bombs or other exploding projectiles to create as much carnage as possible. Villagers ready to risk their lives for the benefit of their fellow men would anxiously wait to cover chemical explosives with blankets as soon as they touched ground before breaking down into hundreds of bits of inflammable shrapnel that set many homes and people on fire.

Faced with the prospects of starvation or death by exploding bombs and scorching fragments, thousands began to flee yet again while vigilant troops loomed in tanks of steel and snipers dotted the distant landscape surrounding the town in every direction.

The ones who made it across the several lines of defense believed that God was on their side. Some reached the areas that were still controlled by the Arab Legion near Al-Khalil, and other refugees made it safely to Gaza. But thousands remained, immobilized by fear or apprehensive about leaving whatever little wealth they had stored in the town. Unsure of what to do, the al-Haaj family decided to stay, until one day in an emotional outburst, Ahmad's mother pleaded to him: "Ahmad, my son. I had my heart broken too many times in only a few weeks. We have lost everything, and I cannot afford to lose all of my children."

She thought of Khaleel, and wondered again what end her dear love had met. She could not bear to watch a gun, shrapnel, or flames take away another cherished piece of her heart. So she urged her son to flee during the night: "Escape, son. You are the only one educated amongst us. If you live, and we all die, at least I would die knowing that my first-born was saved, and I would have a smile on my face as I depart this earth."

In those days Al-Faluja was a quasi-socialist utopia that suited the young communist well. No one seemed to own anything there, or really cared to. Everything was shared in a spirit of genuine camaraderie: tea and sugar, wheat, cloth, garbanzo beans and lentils. Even the collective agony on display in the many funerals all around town was a shared burden. Despite the death squads hovering in the sky and all over the main roads, Ahmed was hesitant to leave behind that feeling of unity, and his family. But he knew he could not go against his mother's wishes, so he prepared his escape.

After selling the family's remaining calf and harvests, Ahmad stuffed his earnings of 180 Palestinian pounds into his pockets, along with some coins given to him by kind-hearted fellahin. Initially refusing to accept their money, he eventually succumbed to their wishes when they explained that cash no longer had any value, and that they might not live to harvest their land another year. A distraught neighbor even invited him to marry his young daughter so she could run away with him rather than possibly being raped by the militias, as had occurred throughout those conquered lands.

Word of the escape plan traveled fast among the villagers, prompting the kindly Sudanese commander Syed Bik Taha to summon the young man to his headquarters near the frontlines.

Syed was a strong, sturdy man who fought in Al-Faluja to the very last bullet. He understood the extreme danger that an unarmed young man would encounter in the dark of night, and did not approve of Ahmad's intent to leave on his own.

Ahmad stared at the commander's intense gaze as he drank the mint tea offered to him. Taha informed him that army men would join him during his escape. Besides surviving, Ahmad's only task was to hand a letter to an Egyptian army commander who would likely meet him towards the end of his journey. The brief encounter with the commander had a lasting impact on Ahmad. For the rest of his life he spoke of how the Sudanese were the bravest of all men; simple and honest like the fellahin, and of untold courage, like the fellahin. Ahmad would never forget him.

The escape party totaled fourteen. Most of the others who joined in with the four military guides were the village's few educated young men, all barefoot except for Ahmad. The first leg of the journey sometimes required the group to walk on all fours, and to slide their bodies like snakes on the ground. The twenty-five miles in territory controlled by the enemy was the longest walk they would ever have to endure. The slightest sound could have meant the death of them all, so there was not to be a whisper, and at times not even the sound of breath.

As dawn began to show its early signs of light across the sky, the group was ordered to run as fast as their naked feet could take them. The hope was that they would outpace the sun, and avoid being seen and possibly killed by army units patrolling the border lines. As Ahmad sprinted through the mud, his once polished shoes reminded him of a life he would never see again.

After the grueling journey, they reached the border line on the other side of Gaza. Relief charged through their wobbly bodies as they all crossed the first Egyptian army barracks. Handshakes and manly hugs were shared by all as they bid their goodbyes to the military guides who, without a moment's hesitation, went straight back to the besieged Al-Faluja.

Staring into nowhere, Ahmad stood alone trying to process all that he had seen and done. Hoping that he had just enough energy left to reach the school, he continued to walk alone, but he collapsed from sheer exhaustion into a deep, ill-timed sleep. It was then that the two kindly Jabaliya women found him to give him the six oranges, six lemons, and carry his bags all the way to Syed Hashim Ibn Abdul Mutalab Mosque. And it was then that Ahmad al-Haaj became a refugee in Gaza.

When a permanent truce was eventually reached, Palestine was no longer called Palestine. Nothing would be the same ever again after the fellahin were forced into refugee status, the Arab troops left in shame, and the militias they fought against wore new uniforms and new hats and began calling themselves an army.

The first generation were assigned the "refugee" title and were forced to keep it until most of them died in exile. Never given a chance to see their homes again, they hoped their children would heal their wounds one day, so they passed on keys to homes that no longer existed, deeds to lands that were harvested by strangers, and memories that were too heavy to bear. They grew old speaking of the loved ones they left behind, and the deceased whose fate left scars in their hearts, and how they would do anything to go back to sit under those roofs made of branches that never quite kept the winter rain away.

The al-Haaj family followed their son to Gaza on February 27, three or four days after the Al-Faluja siege was lifted and the dead and living were diligently counted by United Nations observers. The Egyptian army evacuated its positions after the Arab defeat was made official. And for a reason unbeknown to Ahmad, the Arabs celebrated what they imagined was a victory.

When the Egyptian army passed through Gaza on the way back to their original positions, their military convoys were joined by ceasefire observers as well as a convoy of fellahin families who had remained trapped in Al-Faluja. As they entered their new lives, the weight of becoming refugees, without their humble wealth of wheat, garbanzo beans, and lentils, tortured their minds.

Ahmad, and thousands more, stared at each tired soul as they walked past, looking for familiar faces or recognizable gestures as they stood near the border to ascertain who remained dead or alive of his family, friends, and acquaintances. When he was finally able to wrap his arms around his mother and all of his siblings, gratitude rushed through him, especially on learning that his sister Maliha, who was almost killed trying to save the gluttonous cow, was alive and well.

Not everyone was that lucky, of course. So many familiar faces were assigned a place in memory, as their journey in this life would end in Al-Faluja and not in Gaza's refugee camps.

Ahmad lost many people dear to him, including his uncle and his family from his mother's side, and a teenaged Egyptian soldier he had befriended in the early days of the siege. The two friends would talk every night into the early hours of the morning, about poetry and an ideal world where all the fellahin of the world were united against imperialism, Zionism, and the feudalistic families that spoke of revolutions but chose to escape before the battles even commenced. These missing faces would haunt Ahmad in the back of his mind, yet many fellahin thought that perhaps there was some mercy in not coming back at all.

Like many other families, Ahmad was quarantined in a military camp in Buraij for three days to prevent the spread of disease. While they endured this last obstacle, Ahmad thought it opportune to rent them a home in Gaza's Al-Tufah neighborhood, and start some semblance of normalcy. Though he had the best of intentions in protecting his family, it would later transpire to be a mistake he would always regret. Since they dwelled outside the confines of what later became the official refugee camps, they were denied access to much-needed food aid, blankets, and donated used clothes.

As they finally rode together on the back of a horse cart from Buraij in the central parts of the Strip to Al-Tufah in the north, Ahmad's shirt was soaked with his mother's tears. But none of them had any idea of the hardships they were yet to endure.

But one very good thing did happen: they learned that Khaleel had not been killed. He reappeared when a prisoner exchange took place between the warring parties in June 1949. Caught fighting in Jsir, he was forced into hard labor along with hundreds of other prisoners, after surviving torture. When Moshe Dayan interrogated him, Khaleel had little information to offer:

"Why did you buy a German rifle to kill Jews?"

"I needed to defend Palestine."

"But this is our land too, no?"

"You came from Russia, Bulgaria and Poland."

"How many Jews did you kill?"

"I don't know."

"Where did you get the money to buy a rifle?"

"I sold my land."

"You had bullets on you. How did you pay for the bullets?"

"I sold my wheat."

Khaleel's first job in prison included restoring Beit Daras's old airstrip so that it could be used by the Israeli army to bomb Al-Faluja, where the al-Haaj family was taking shelter. The mechanical, repetitive motions of his manual labor were not enough to keep his mind off the irony of his existence. So, while imprisoned in Tel Aviv, he took on the habit of smoking and forgot the judgement of right or wrong. A Jewish prison guard gave him his first cigarette and told him that "smoking exhaled the pain away." When Khaleel was freed, he walked out of his three-day quarantine in al-Sarayya military camp in Gaza—which was once a British jail, later became an Egyptian jail, and then an Israeli jail—and chucked away his last cigarette, never to smoke again.

Khaleel lived in Gaza's Al-Tufah neighborhood where he often spoke of his family's eventual return to Al-Sawafir. Yet Khaleel never returned to the village he cared so deeply about, and died there in Al-Tufah where he never felt at home.

Ahmad wanted to be a physicist, so he studied science in Egypt. But he became a teacher instead. Eventually he was relieved of his duties due to his political activism, and his strange ideas about socialism and why the Arabs lost Palestine. Time in jail was another price he paid for being true to himself and what he believed, not for any crimes that he committed. In Egypt he was imprisoned twice, each period lasting three lonely years. Israel too incarcerated him when the Gaza Strip itself fell under Israeli military occupation twenty years later.

"There is so much difference between the torture inflicted by Arab and Israeli jailors," he would say with pain masked in anxious humor. "The Israelis' torture is based on tried and proven scientific formulas; the Arabs beat you up with batons and release hungry dogs to maul your naked body."

Through all this, Ahmad remained as strong as the unity and hope that pushed Gaza forward. Resourceful and never broken, he aged as did many other fellahin. When forced out of work, he drove a truck for a living, and took every chance he could find to speak about Al-Sawafir and its barefooted fellahin, who were pure and true socialists because they shared tea, lentils and ragged clothes.

* * *

"Have you ever seen a ghost roaming the corridors late at night?" Ahmad was once asked by an Egyptian prison guard sometime in March 1955, soon after the schoolteacher and sixty-five others were arrested at night and transferred to a prison camp in the heart of Cairo. The Gazans, all descendants of fellahin-turned-refugees, were incarcerated and routinely tortured for waging a popular uprising against an American proposal that had initially been accepted by the government of Jamal Abdul Nasser. The plan was to settle the refugees in the Sinai desert, far away from Al-Sawafir and the other five hundred villages from which they were exiled. The Gazans' relentless opposition prevented this, but the leaders of the Intifada still paid a heavy price for their indiscretion.

"I don't believe in ghosts," Ahmad said.

"I do."

The ghost in question was that of Syed Bik Taha, the brave Sudanese commander who fought in Al-Faluja until the last day of the siege. Although he made it out of the Palestinian town alive, it was in Egypt that his battle ended. Some say his crime was refusing to heed orders to surrender the town to the Israeli militias. But whatever the reason, he was not one to give up. His last days were spent in the very jail where sixty-five Gazans were later tortured and imprisoned for four years, starting on March 15, 1955.

"They kept stuffing loaves of fino bread down his throat, until he suffocated," said the guard softly. He was a fellah hailing from the south of Egypt where peasants used to wear no shoes, and he believed that land and honor hold priority over everything else in life.

It was never corroborated that the ghost of the Sudanese commander roamed the dark halls of the central Cairo prison. Perhaps he was checking on the morale of the troops, urging them to fight until the last bullet or last breath. But Ahmad survived in Syed Bik Taha's former prison cell, abandoned to his thoughts for four years, resting his tired head on the same cold, damp, grey wall where Taha wrote his name and that of a woman he once loved, next to a map of Palestine; all of Palestine.

Tamam Nassar was of similar age and refugee status to Ahmad al-Haaj. Known as Umm Marwan (Mother of Marwan), she was a friend of my mother's back in the Gaza refugee camp where I was born and raised. Like most women of that generation, she was illiterate. Yet she possessed the heart of a self-aware rebel. While the men were off working as cheap laborers for Israel, these women did everything necessary in order to persevere. Not only did they raise children and make ends meet in dire circumstances, but they also protected their families by fighting with soldiers, and labored to build communities in overcrowded and impoverished camps.

When I was a child and teenager, I had the pleasure of meeting Umm Marwan on numerous occasions. Twenty-five years later, she could not help but weep into her white scarf when she spoke of my parents, now buried in the Martyrs' Graveyard in the camp. Her tears transformed into laughter as she recalled my father's antics and my mother's love for him. Here I tell the story of the long path she endured. 'Would you want to go back to Palestine, Umm Marwan?" I asked. "Oh son," she answered. "If I can only breathe the air of my village one more time and die, I would die happy."

3
Spirit of the Orchard

His writings on the prison walls denoted all that was certain to Kamal. When he carved the names of everyone he was devoted to, there was not enough untouched space on the concrete surface to keep his own scratchings separate from what had been engraved by other prisoners. So he found the most faded of all the memories and over them he imprinted his own. First he etched the name of the woman he loved most: Umm Marwan, his mother. Weeks earlier, when the soldiers with their angry dogs showed up at his home in the middle of the night to throw their weight around, and began dragging his weary, injured body out to the street, his sisters cried like any siblings would. But his mother, fearing an overwhelming loss, shrieked in indescribable pain. Her screams pierced the calm of the night like a fractured arrow that somehow managed to travel miles in all directions—even beyond the Matar Orchard. Some say they heard her howls past the dark Hirthani Orchard from where only masked fighters and soldiers ever emerged, and where others disappeared, never to be seen again. He was hardly conscious throughout most of the ordeal, and though his mother's cries were reminiscent of ones he had heard all too often since childhood, they were still vividly different this time. Each bloodcurdling scream resembled the cries of a wounded beast, seeking mercy yet finding none. He would never forget the pain inflicted on his beloved mother, whose wailing echoed in him like a broken record. In a ring of small flowers, her name would be the first to be immortalized on his prison cell wall.

In traditional Palestinian culture, parents are given titles that carry the names of their first-born sons. Umm Marwan simply meant "the mother of Marwan." Tamam Nassar was her birth name. A few years after Marwan, Kamal arrived and her love was plentiful for her second-born too. The many sleepless nights he spent inscribing names on prison walls was a testament to this. Later on another boy, Jamal, appeared, followed by three girls. All were born in the same refugee camp in Gaza. Having boys always meant more prestige for a mother in a peasant society. It did not matter that all the peasants and landlords had turned into refugees living a squalid existence, some things never changed. But Tamam was different from her sister Palestinians in one regard. In her heart she desired daughters, for the absence of her mother Hamda who was long gone, and the sisters she had always dreamed of, left a loneliness inside her that she felt could only be quashed by the female spirit. So she asked God for girls, and her body responded to her prayers with three baby girls each separated by only one year. Iman, then Asmahan, and then Manal came into the world and Umm Marwan was satisfied.

During the dark nights, when memories of Nuseirat Refugee Camp would come alive, Kamal would envision a beautiful flower. It grew sparsely through this second most populated camp, and though it had only three delicate petals, its intense red color exploded in simple beauty. On the wall of his cell in Khan Younis, he decorated each of his loved ones' names with a ring of these flowers, and stared at his creations when pangs of pain would resurface. That same intensely red and usually odorless flower also grew in the Hirthani Orchard, but some said that the Hirthani strain had an aroma so powerful, it was almost intoxicating. Since masked fighters and soldiers were the only ones who dared enter the enigmatic orchard, no one could attest to the claim. One fateful day, many years later, the camp residents woke up to find that the orchard had been completely destroyed. It was a puzzle how an undertaking so brazen and violent could have happened when no one heard the sound of bulldozers carrying out the evil deed. All that was seen that morning was a cloud of suffocating dust hovering above the camp, while the orange and lemon trees lay lifeless on their sides next to dead flowers that had once perfumed the now heavy air. Alas, it would not be the only orchard in Umm Marwan's life that contained within it both tragedy and mystery, hand-in-hand. Her earliest memories were attached to another orchard that existed many years ago.

* * *

Tamam Nassar's memory of Joulis, the Palestinian village where she lived until the age of five, was hazy. By the time she was born, the British had already colonized Palestine for decades. The few memories peeking through the naïveté of her innocence were largely about racing after military convoys pleading for candy. Once, upon returning to the family mud-brick home with a whole bar of chocolate and a big smile on her face, her older brother Salim confiscated the prize and claimed it as his own. Had it not been for Ismail, the oldest of the three, Salim would have devoured the bar in one or two bites. Though he was barely twelve years of age, a strong sense of responsibility pushed Ismail to play the role of the father at times, since Yousef was gone most of the day, either working hard on the family's land or offering his labor to other landowners whenever his small property grew tired of yielding the same crop year after year. Hamda, the mother, was not afraid to put in her share of manly work, never hesitating to shoulder some of her husband's grueling tasks while still tending to the children, loving them as best as she knew how and doing everything else in between.

Back then Tamam did not encounter Jews, or perhaps she did. But since many Palestinian Jews looked just like Palestinian Arabs, she could not tell the difference or even care to make the distinction. People were just people. Jews were just their neighbors in that southern village, and that was all that mattered. Although the Palestinian Jews lived behind walls, fences and trenches, for a while they walked freely among the fellahin, shopped in their markets and sought their help, for only the fellahin knew how to speak the language of the land and decode the signs of the seasons. Tamam's house was made of hardened mud, and had a small front yard where the little girl and her brothers were often confined when the military convoys roamed their village. Soon this would happen more and more frequently, and the candy that once sweetened the lives of the children was no longer offered. During those tense days, Yousef spoke often about the betrayal of their Jewish neighbors and a conspiracy between the Zionists and the British. Though each day she hoped for another chocolate bar, young Tamam knew deep in her heart that the days of candy were gone forever.

Then there was the war that changed everything. The battle around Joulis crept up all too quickly and showed little mercy. Some of the fellahin who ventured out beyond the borders of the village were never seen again. To ensure the safety of her children, Hamda told her kids about a terrifying ghoul that lived inside the orchard adjoining their home. Instilling fear in them, she insisted they should never walk past the dirt road outside Joulis, for crossing in the monster's path would be a risk too great to take. But the ghoul, despite her occasional nightly raids on Joulis and the devouring of a sheep here or there, kept largely to herself. With time, Hamda told them, the villagers learned to respect the ghoul's boundaries and believed that she meant no harm.

As the legend goes, when the ghoul gave birth to her first child, she wrapped it up in warm sheep's wool, then hid it among sheep as she went to fetch water from the nearby creek to quench her thirsty body. The flock of sheep belonged to the household of Abu Ghanim Abed. While the ghoul was away, a thunderous storm suddenly erupted, compelling the shepherd to herd the sheep back to the safety of the village. Unsuspectingly, the shepherd also herded the newborn ghoul child along with them. When Abu Ghanim's wife discovered it among the sheep, she cared little whether it was a baby human or a baby ghoul. Motherly instincts compelled her to breastfeed the little creature as if it were her own, hold her tight throughout the storm and nourish the tiny ghoul, Zalibiya, with cinnamon and nuts. Gripped with worry and rage when she returned to find the baby missing, the mother ghoul pursued the scent of her little one. Soon relief came over her, when she finally arrived at Abed's home to find her baby safe and warm in the arms of a loving mother. Her anger turned to elation and gratitude. The startled Abu Ghanim stood in disbelief when she appeared and asked him to extend the palm of his right hand. She clasped it between her furry palms and whispered in his ears:

> "I give you my word before Allah, and if I ever betray you, I betray Allah. Hard times are ahead, Abu Ghanim, but you and your family shall pass this safely. You shall all survive, and with time you shall attain wealth and boundless offspring; many boys who will carry your name and bear you many grandchildren."

The ghoul's prophecies came true. When many fellahin were killed in Joulis during the war, Abu Ghanim fought a brave fight and somehow survived. And when many houses were blown up by the invading militias, the Abed family home remained intact. The prediction of hard times was certainly true—Abu Ghanim became a refugee in Gaza, a destiny he had never foreseen. But fortune was on his side when all was considered, and this was shown by the gift of nine children from the same wife, who in turn eventually each bore between seven and ten children, mostly boys. These all married too and had flocks of their own children. The Abed family even had enough abundance of wealth to allow Abu Ghanim and his wife to embark on a pilgrimage to Mecca when they were still relatively young and strong enough to bear the harshness of the journey, and then come back to a loving house with rooms over three floors which let in Gaza's warm sunshine through more than twenty windows.

Tamam never met the ghoul, though. At the age of five, she left the village with her family because it was Joulis's turn to be destroyed. She sat on the back of a cow along with Salim, as Ismail, their mother Hamda, and their father Yousef all walked the long way to Al-Majdal. Anticipating a return once the war was over, they stopped in an orchard along the way to hide their treasured harvest so that they could retrieve it upon their coming back to Joulis. But the road from Joulis was mostly one straight line that never ended and hardly ever curved or deviated from the onset of the nightmare, and the Nassar family's exile became a permanent one. As the family crossed the dirt road outside Joulis on that fateful day in 1948, Tamam wondered if the mother ghoul would meet the same fate as all the other villagers whose dead bodies dotted the dirt road, barefoot, bloodied and half naked. Salim whispered in her ear not to worry as they both perched on the back of the cow. He had heard from trusted sources that the mother ghoul was seen entering the orchard that bordered their village just as the war began, so it would be forever safe from the British and the Zionists. They would never capture her or her baby, nor the spirit that kept them both fervently alive.

* * *

Salim himself would disappear into an orchard, leaving no tracks and very few clues. Some believed he was locked up in a prison deep underground somewhere. That was in 1956 when he was just a teenager. By then the Zionists had a state of their own and took over Gaza for a few months. Salim was around sixteen years of age when the Suez crisis culminated in the Suez War. The two great powers, Britain and France, allied with Israel to defeat the Egyptian army and conquer Sinai. The Egyptian army was, in fact, ordered by Jamal Abdul Nasser to withdraw, but even that decision did not guarantee the invaders an easy victory. Under international pressure, they were compelled to pull their forces out of the Egyptian desert. Britain was hoping to regain political influence in the region, years after its army left Palestine in the hands of the Zionists. Yet it was too late, and neither the Americans nor the Soviets had much patience for Europe to stage a comeback, so Israel and its allies were ordered to leave the newly taken territory. The Israelis dragged their feet for months, refusing to withdraw from Sinai, and by extension from the Gaza Strip, which they had conquered for the first time since Palestine's great Catastrophe.

Salim followed their every move. He obsessively wrote in his journal everything he saw and heard. Whether it made sense or not, he tried as best as he could to piece it all together. Everything was in ink: the names and ages of those killed and wounded by the army, the types of military vehicles they used, and his thoughts on what he perceived to be detailed information about their daily conduct. No one knew if Salim was spying for anyone, or if he just took it upon himself to document the short-lived occupation of Gaza. Although Tamam was illiterate as were most refugee girls in Gaza at the time, she observed Salim and his edgy body language intently. She was certain that his constant writing was not school work, as no schools were open during that period. Gaza was shut down in anticipation of a looming defeat.

Following the war of '48, Gaza had fallen under Egyptian administration and military control. Initially, Gazans welcomed the role that Egypt played in the Strip. This was based on the assumption that sooner or later, Egypt, along with other Arab countries, would liberate Palestine and send the refugees back to their villages. Soon it was evident that Gaza would not be free, and the Egyptians grew harsher with time. Gaza's true defenders were the fedayeen who ventured into the newly established Israel to ambush soldiers near border areas separating Gaza from the new state. Many lost their lives and were celebrated as martyrs with symbolic coffins and the chant: "With our souls and our blood, we shall avenge our martyrs."

But Salim was not a freedom fighter. He did not wear a khaki uniform, brandish a rifle or wear a kufiyah around his neck before delving into the dangerous orchards north of Gaza. He just wrote down everything he witnessed in his journals. Perhaps it was a humble attempt at coping with the loss of his childhood in Joulis, a defensive move to take hold of whatever remained of his youth as it was ripped away in the rawness of Gaza. Life was never easy for the Nassar family. The Strip was hardly welcoming towards them when they first arrived. Squatting wherever they could and pitching a UN-supplied tent here or there did not allow vulnerable refugees to feel what it was like to have a home. Security, warmth, and protection were rare commodities, especially when the more powerful had their way even within what little shelter was found. A rich Gazan, who owned much land in the town of Deir Al-Balah, complained to the UN agency responsible for the welfare of the refugees to remove the squatters from his land or else suffer the consequences. So in a truly dismal moment, humanity did not prevail and the refugees were forced to pitch their tents elsewhere. Their numbers grew, and Yousef and his family became permanent residents of the UN-run Deir Al-Balah Refugee Camp, located somewhere between the center of the Strip and its southern corners.

Survival was all that Yousef aspired to achieve for his children during the war of '56. The risks were too high to ask for more. Many were killed when Israel took over Gaza and the Israelis became its new masters. The whole ordeal happened so quickly when the Egyptians pulled out, but the one thing that remained consistent was the will of the fedayeen who fought alone and died equally alone. Their famous battle in Khan Younis, a town located a short distance south of Deir Al-Balah, was to be remembered for generations for the fedayeens' refusal to surrender. They knew the terrible fate that would become of them, yet they chose to be veiled in a shroud of honor and fight until the bitter end. When the resistance was crushed in Khan Younis and in the nearby town of Rafah, the Israeli army moved in and executed men in their homes in cold blood, and lined up young men and children against walls, mowing them down—they fell like dominoes. Hundreds perished and thousands more were left with the kind of pain that never lessened with the passing of time. This was how Khan Younis earned its title, the Castle of Resistance, a designation that stipulated a price of blood that was exacted from its sons and daughters from that day onward.

This all took place starting late October and ended abruptly in March of the following year. Soon before the Israeli withdrawal, sometime in February of 1957, Salim ran away to the orchards as did scores of other young men who were fleeing in the hope of finding safety by crossing to Jordan through Israel. They naively assumed the orchards extended further than the furthest horizon they could conceive, and would at least offer them shelter all the way to Amman. But when they walked north for a few miles, the trees grew sparse, and the soil underneath their tired feet succumbed to the light of the bright Mediterranean sun, and to the vigilant eyes of the Israeli military that was hovering above and clustering below in strategic points. The soldiers waited patiently for Gaza's fedayeen to embark on their hopeless journeys.

Salim held tightly onto his journals with a sense of great importance and prestige as he walked into the orchards on a mission divinely self-constructed. Nothing could change the way he felt about the earth-shattering information he had so patiently gathered in Deir Al-Balah, so he held onto them even tighter after realizing that the orchards did not extend beyond the first horizon. As Salim and his friends emerged guardedly from the other side, an expanse of empty space met their disappointed gazes. Before them stood a land once rich with greenery which was now a sad shadow of its former self. It had been leveled within months after the fellahin were exiled, to make room for Israel's agricultural settlements. As the group quarreled about whether to continue their march to Jordan or return to Gaza back through the same orchards, bullets flew all around them and bodies began to fall.

Salim never returned, but his loved ones kept him alive in their hearts. No one could irrefutably confirm whether he was living or dead and Tamam grew old searching for him, despite the fact that he once stole her chocolate bar. Ismail and Tamam followed every clue and every rumor about the disappearance of their teenage brother, yet every time they would come back empty-handed and broken-spirited. The Red Cross told the Nassar family that Israel was not holding anyone by the name Salim Nassar, and from Deir Al-Balah all the way to Amman, no marked grave carried that name in all the cemeteries where young victims rested in peace. One of the young men who survived the orchard massacre told the family that Salim was shot just as he surfaced outside the orchards, and that he had hauled his injured body into the safety of the orange and lemon trees where he bled to death alone. But how could he have known if Salim died alone? Tamam was never convinced, or perhaps she did not want to believe that she no longer had a brother. So she sought the help of a reliable psychic, an old nomadic woman with a hundred tattoos and a thousand wrinkles on her face that told stories older than she was. She could offer Tamam no more than a single line: "Your brother is locked up in a prison deep down underground and can never be rescued."

Tamam married five or six years after Salim disappeared, and five or six years after the Israeli army left Gaza, at least for a while. She married her cousin Mahmoud al-Assar, still with a heavy heart as her mourning for Salim never truly ended. She refused to dye her palms with henna as tradition dictated, and insisted that the celebration remain private and small. But Mahmoud wanted all of Deir Al-Balah to know that he was to marry Tamam, a modestly beautiful woman who had just turned twenty years of age. When she met him, he was a soldier with the national guard, wearing a mismatched old army uniform, and carrying a rifle and his most prized possession: he kept a single bullet in his right pocket at all times. Tamam's mother Hamda and several elder women of the family first met to arrange the wedding details. Mahmoud was to provide ninety-five Egyptian pounds as a dowry, a bottle of hair cream, a handkerchief, a bar of soap, a bottle of perfume and a quality comb. Thanks to the women's expertise, the whole wedding was organized in a matter of days.

Once Al-Fatiha was read out loud by representatives of both families to formalize the agreement, modest festivities ensued and a feeling of happiness was felt by all. Several trays of tasty couscous, smothered with cooked vegetables and meat, were prepared to perfection and shared joyously as was always done at Gazan weddings. The celebration was made even more special when Suleiman Daud, a member of the fedayeen, fired some bullets into the air with his prized pistol. When the main festivities came to an end, as many members of both families as possible were crammed into the back of a pickup truck. Tamam and Mahmoud sat next to the driver as they pondered the new phase of their lives and listened to the jubilant crowd cheer them with wishes for prosperity and many children. After a trip of less than half an hour, they all were dropped off in Nuseirat, close to Mahmoud's family house which was made entirely of mud-brick rooms and tucked somewhere between two orchards, Matar and Hirthani.

* * *

Tamam's stay at her in-laws lasted for only one year and a few months, long enough for her to give birth to Marwan and become pregnant with Kamal. She was then kicked out with her husband and first-born for reasons that she did not care to remember, or perhaps wished to forget. Her father, Yousef, the hardworking man of Joulis, bought the couple a new home not far away from the in-laws, a single mud-brick room with no toilet or kitchen, for the price of fifty-four Egyptian pounds. Luckily for them, the refugees were largely left to their own devices back then, expanding on their mud homes as they found fit. Mahmoud spent most of his days shattering rocks near the Gaza Valley and selling them to a local quarry by sunset. At night he joined Tamam in fashioning mud bricks and slowly expanding on their single-room home which was not big enough for their expanding family. Soon there was a bathroom, a kitchen, and a tiny front yard. It was finally feeling like a real home when another room was built, and then a third. But then Israel returned to Gaza, this time staying for decades. When Israel defeated the Egyptian army and conquered the Strip and Sinai in 1967, most of the refugee camp was demolished. It was rebuilt by the refugees with their own hands and by the UN, mud brick by mud brick. The status of the refugees did not change. The Israeli army needed to widen some roads so that its tanks would be able to move through the streets of the camp unhindered, hunting down the remaining fedayeen and quickly subduing any rebellion among the poor refugees. The roofs of the houses of the new camp were made of grey tiles, and in winter were covered with large sheets of plastic and speckled with small sand bags to prevent the rain from seeping through.

When the war of 1967 concluded in Israel's favor, Mahmoud simply ran away, leaving Tamam, then pregnant with Jamal, to fend for herself and her two children. He never meant to disappoint the wife he loved, but Mahmoud was terrified of the Israelis beyond rationality. He sought shelter in the Gaza Valley, not only because he knew that his single bullet, which he carried in his pocket, was not enough to repel an advancing Israeli army, but because of a deep-seated trauma that had haunted him since he was a teenager. During the previous brief occupation of '56, Israeli soldiers who raided Mahmoud's house were bored and wanted entertainment, so they ordered him to dance in the street like some sort of puppet owned by a perverse master. Fearing the worst, the petrified teenager obliged and was eaten away by degradation. He danced a little, twirled a little more and ran back and forth between two patches of soldiers who were laughing from their bellies. He ran as fast as he could between the vile jokesters, while yelling obscenities in Arabic that they ordered him to repeat over and over. Fearing another episode of humiliation as a grown man, but this time carrying the title of Abu Marwan—father of Marwan—he timorously fled in such a way that earned him even more humiliation from his unimpressed wife and amused neighbors.

Umm Marwan, on the other hand, ran away with her children to an orchard known as Izbat Al-Majanin—orchard of the crazy people—somewhere between Nuseirat and Deir Al-Balah. Along with thousands of others, she waited there with little food and water, trying her utmost to protect her children. The events of the war were transpiring before their eyes as they peered outside the orchard desperately seeking good news from beyond the tree tops. But there was little good to be reported or observed. First, Egyptian military vehicles swished by expediently, as if in a state of urgency or panic, heading back south to Sinai. Then the few soldiers who were abandoned by their units ran south as well, some even in their undergarments after having ditched their military uniforms in case the Israeli army would stop them and execute them, as was their practice. Then the fedayeen followed, some heading south, others running in the opposite direction, and still others not knowing where to go at all. Many were bleeding, screaming, crying, and befuddled by a crisis that was later named Al-Naksa, the Setback—but it was more than a setback. The Israeli air force had already won the war when it blew up Egypt's seventeen airbases before a single aircraft had even taken off.

That was not the only battlefront that went awry. Syrian and Jordanian armies desperately fought back encroaching Israeli forces, which pounded them from the air, land and sea. Israel was determined to expand its territorial control throughout the region and had copious amounts of western arms to do so. Gaza was then a killing field. Palestinian fedayeen units lost all communication with their Sinai and Egypt superiors and chaotically fought using light arms and pistols which were no match against the superior weaponry of the enemy. But the outcome of the battle was no happier than in 1948. Egyptian soldiers, mostly fellahin inspired by Nasser's revolutionary rhetoric and promises of social justice and equality, fought and fell in droves. Many were killed or captured, and the rest fled into the open desert, often being left to the miserable fate of being gunned down by the Israeli air force that roved through Sinai uncontested. The bitter fighting on the outskirts of Gaza soon ended with a thorough defeat as well. There was nowhere to run to but the sea, the desert and to Israel itself, and they were all equally lethal.

Despite her own exhaustion, Umm Marwan carried her children, now filthy, hungry, and fatigued, back to her mud-brick home three days later. When she was finally reunited with her husband, her first task was to dig a large hole in the ground that would serve as shelter for the kids if the conquering army began blowing up homes and lining up people against walls to be gunned down. But even defeat can offer moments of hope and respite. As soon as Gaza was occupied by Israel and things calmed down enough to offer a veneer of normality, Tamam and her brother Ismail began venturing out into the once inaccessible territories looking for Salim. They walked through the orchard where he was said to have disappeared and then walked the same path that they hoped Salim might have crossed. They stopped in every graveyard and read the names of the dead on simple tombstones, and wherever they failed to find the name Salim Nassar, they were nonetheless overtaken by the hope that he was still alive. Meanwhile, Abu Marwan was consumed by the fatherly duty of feeding his children, especially since the rocks of the Gaza Valley had all been smashed and pulverized years ago by refugees like him trying to survive by selling them to quarries. So he joined many thousands of hapless refugees who returned to Palestine as cheap laborers in what had become Israel, tending to the same land that was once theirs, offering their services as manual laborers in factories, as janitors, street cleaners, or carrying out any menial employment that Israeli Jews found crude and beneath them.

When most of the men disappeared into the gorge of grueling labor in Israel, the refugee women reigned supreme and rose to the demands of every task. They took care of household chores, raised children, repaired leaks in their roofs, mended raggedy clothes, lined up to collect meager supplies from UN feeding centers, scuffled with occupation soldiers, ensured that their children were doing their homework, upheld fellahin traditions, and celebrated, mourned, danced, and cried. This was all done without their men by their sides—men who would return on the weekends to plant their seeds and levy upon their families either love or physical abuse, consoling their own sense of emasculation and dishonor.

The unkindness of life made Umm Marwan the strong person that she became, while her husband existed largely on the periphery of their complicated existence. He provided income, and occasional guidance and discipline, but not much more. She embodied all that was needed to feed the soul by being the epicenter of love and authority, serving the role of both parents in a family that was rarely blessed with easy times. But Umm Marwan was human too, and sometimes the trials of life were too much even for her to bear, so she would delve into the Hirthani Orchard to converse with a woman who many in the camp doubted existed.

* * *

The woman of the orchard was Fatima. She was rarely seen in the camp itself, but her presence in the Hirthani Orchard was always felt, as if it were a spirit or a wandering ghost entombed between a life she loathed and a death she feared. Her family members died one after the other soon after they were expelled from their Palestinian village to the Gaza refugee camp. No one really knows the cause of death. Some say it was a plague that fed only on her family and spared everyone else. First, her mother died, followed by the death of her father a few months later, then two brothers and finally two sisters. There was little medicine in the local UN clinic, and the few aspirins that were readily prescribed for every sickness simply held no sway before the mysterious illness that struck the tiny, insignificant family. Fatima was left alone at the tender age of nine, defending herself in a shrinking world of refugees and military men. The last that people had known of her was when she lived in the house of distant relatives in Buraij Refugee Camp, serving their elders and putting up with the abuse of their young. Then she disappeared for years. Not a soul knew of her whereabouts and some rumored she had committed suicide, a taboo which guaranteed her eternal existence in hell. One day rumors about her resurfaced again, this time suggesting that she was the invisible guard of the Hirthani Orchard.

At first very few believed them because refugee women did not serve as guards of orchards, or of anything else for that matter. To be the guard of an orchard meant constant chasing after thieving kids, facing up to drug addicts and hunting down fornicators who sought cover in the darkness of the orchard to carry out their wicked deeds. Yet the rumors persisted and some even claimed to have actually seen Fatima. They said she wore a traditional thoub (long robe), donned a thick belt on her waist where she kept a knife on her right side, and a small machete on the other. People said she was as ugly as a ghoul, and that her hair was a wild mingling of black, white and henna-dyed colors. But whenever the accounts of those self-proclaimed witnesses to her existence were examined, the stories seemed to fall apart. For one, the traditional dress she allegedly wore seemed inconsistent with the pattern of embroideries affiliated with the village of Adas where her family came from. Those who hail from southern villages like Joulis, Beit Daras, Al-Sawafir, Adas, and Falouja wore thoubs with different patterns and colors from those who come from villages further north such as Mighar, Qatra, Akir, and Zarnuka. Fatima's thoub, as it was described, seemed to have been embroidered with a pattern that challenged all the traditional designs and even the entire social hierarchy that separated the refugees. Moreover, if Fatima guarded the Hirthani Orchard, where exactly did she live? And why is it that she never ventured out to the camp to buy groceries? And how did she survive the many Israeli raids at the camp when the Hirthani Orchard was used as finishing staging ground? How was it possible that none of the fedayeen ever encountered her presence?

The fellahin can be merciless in their gossip, especially some of the brazen refugee women whose husbands spent their entire week collecting Israeli garbage and erecting houses for Jewish families. Sitting in front of their homes just before sunset, these women would talk and talk about all kinds of nonsense, spreading rumors about infidelity and whatever else was the juicy topic of the day. If the rumors about Fatima were true, and she was indeed as ugly as a ghoul, she would have been thrashed beyond mercy and chased by unruly children in the camp who would have pelted her with pebbles and foul words. Not even the chastising of a kindly old man or woman would have been enough to keep those little vultures away.

Before the Intifada started in 1987, Fatima's existence was confined to occasional rumors and unconfirmed encounters. When children would sneak ever so cautiously into the Hirthani Orchard to collect wild berries or pick its coveted oranges, they would feel a presence: a spirit, a being, an animal of some sort that would violently charge but never approach. Gripped by fear, they would run away without being touched in any way, but somehow they were certain that something had been there with them. These stories were not taken seriously by most, until one notoriously unruly child returned home one day with marks on his body. It was as if someone had swung at him with a heavy belt, and branded him once or twice on the back, and a third time on his legs. The little boy was so terrified that his mother sought the help of Umm Marwan and other neighbors who all rushed to the Hirthani Orchard and dared to go inside. But yet again, there was no one and nothing except the eerie stillness of the trees, interrupted by the occasional splash of rushing water from somewhere deep in the orchard.

From that day forward, Fatima, or her ghost, or whoever the spirit was that guarded that orchard, was referred to as the ghoul. Bedtime stories were quickly spun to send numerous little children to bed, petrified but at the same time entranced with excitement. The ghoul stories represented a folkloric tradition that went back hundreds of years, and was rife in the fellahin culture until the year of exile to the refugee camps. In that year, the Palestinian ghoul was presumed dead, killed in the war perhaps, or vanished into an infinitely dark orchard where even military men did not dare enter.

But the ghoul was summoned again when the Intifada broke out. In fact, were it not for the ghoul of the orchard, Kamal would have bled to death, and Umm Marwan would never have retrieved his body. She loved Kamal very much, although he was a rebellious, skinny and strange child who always mumbled about socialism and a utopian world where the fellahin united and liberated their land from oppressive landlords and the armies that protected them.

* * *

When the Intifada broke out, Kamal also emerged from his own solitude. Baffled by his father's choices, he never understood why his own father would offer his services to the very Jewish landlords who stole his land. He loathed the smug, confident looks on the soldiers' faces as they walked through the humble dwellings of the refugees, brandishing their guns, barking orders, harassing girls, and commanding boys to dance, sing, and slap one another for no reason other than to validate whatever voids they felt inside. All these violations filled him with rage and he hated the soldiers beyond words. He hated school as well as his teachers. To him they seemed so docile, adhering to the rules of the occupier which decreed that Palestinians not teach their own history, so that the fellahin were denied even the right to remember who they were or where they came from. As a young boy he quickly learned that self-respect demanded that one defy orders and stand out from the rest. While he was still just a child in elementary school, he colored a Palestinian flag using UN agency-supplied coloring papers and crayons and taped the small flag to a pencil, raising it in the market on his way back home. The soldiers were resting in the shade of Abu Ayman's bookstore and caught him red-handed. They slapped his face repeatedly, and then held him for days in the "tents," where the soldiers established their military camp near the road separating Nuseirat from Buraij.

It was not until high school that his fighting spirit truly materialized. With an unmatched obsession for reading and writing and a sincere persona that grabbed the hearts and minds of everyone he encountered, he was the obvious choice to lead the youth unit of the Popular Front for the Liberation of Palestine. A brand of revolutionary Marxism was all that the refugee camp needed to throw these occupiers back to whatever European hell they came from. Kids sat in total fascination when he lectured them about how the refugee camp was not their Palestine and that the real Palestine was a land so fantastic and beyond the furthest horizon they could possibly conceive. In their young minds, he instilled the sense of mission that it would be they who would lead the masses home. His new recruits were told how most of the factions were defeated in Lebanon, not just in the battlefield itself, but, maybe more importantly, psychologically as well. The lesson was that it was now up to the fellahin to rise again, and redeem the sins of a generation that was dishonored beyond redemption. Indeed, Gaza rebelled, not because of the urgings of Kamal, but because of a thousand such youth who took on the responsibility of forming a new leadership that challenged the Israelis and also the traditional order in Palestine itself.

The uprising did not start in Nuseirat, but in the Jabaliya refugee camp in the afternoon of December 6, 1987. Nuseirat was the place, though, where thousands of youth took to the streets and vowed to avenge the innocent blood of the Jabaliya victims of the previous day. They swung large flags made of silky fabric that swayed beautifully in Gaza's salty air and as the momentum grew and they became intoxicated by their own collective chants, they marched to the "tents" where the soldiers were uneasily perched on the tops of watchtowers, hiding behind their binoculars and automatic machine guns. Within minutes, a war had started and a third generation of refugee-camp-born fellahin stood fearlessly against a well-equipped army that was visibly gripped by fear. Rocks were hurled in all directions by the children, although most never hit their intended targets. The Israelis hit many that day and several children were killed. Among deafening chants that freedom was coming, the remains of the dead were carried to the Nuseirat Martyrs' Graveyard and laid to rest. Though these ones paid the heaviest price, there were still many wounded children who needed tending to when the UN clinics declared that they had run out of the cure-all aspirins and had no available operating rooms. Fortunately, resourcefulness was not lacking in the medical staff of Gaza's Al-Shifa and

Mamadani hospitals which treated many wounded children from Nuseirat and other refugee camps in the Strip, with whatever humble equipment they had. Within days Gaza was the breeding ground for a real revolution that was self-propelled and unwavering. The chants of Palestinians in the Strip were answered in the West Bank, and echoed just as loudly in Palestinian towns, even those located in what became known as Israel proper. The contagious energy was emblematic of children and young adults wanting to reclaim the identities of their ancestors which had been horribly disfigured and divided between regions, countries, and refugee camps. Even refugees exiled outside Palestine yelled back from across borders and fences, desperate to regain a collective sense of self: "With our souls and our blood, we shall avenge you Palestine," their voices thundered across the heavily militarized borders of Syria, Lebanon, and Jordan.

Kamal was no longer tucked away in a dark room reading the works of Marx and Gramsci, waiting for things to change. He was in the streets of Nuseirat fashioning his own utopia. The fastest of the children with the strongest arms were placed on the front lines to taunt the soldiers and throw rocks when they drew near; those in the back lines were ready with raw onions to supply the "troops" with tools to survive the tear gas; the most able-bodied were placed in the middle in order to charge against the soldiers when the frontlines needed aid, or when the wounded needed to be carried to safety. Yet no revolution is complete without art as a source for emotional and political power. Poets molded words in the most articulate of ways to communicate the message of the revolution to the masses. Graffiti adorned every available space on every wall throughout the camp and those with the most roaring of voices led the marches, rallies, and funerals. The unity was palpable and the undying thirst for expression was channeled through creativity.

It was Kamal's world, one of solidarity, camaraderie, and wild youth who needed no one to speak on their behalf; no faction leaders with large mustaches and big egos, wielding machine guns to articulate the aspirations of the people. These youth, born in a place that was never truly perceived as home, reared by a submissive generation that was fed from the bosom of defeat, did not offer their uniformed obedience. Although Kamal's small build and introverted demeanor did not necessarily qualify him for tasks requiring physical robustness, his astute emotional intelligence and ability to connect with the children of the fellahin propelled him into an almost accidental leadership from the very start. With time, he walked confidently in those shoes and earned respect from his fellow Palestinians. His brother, Marwan, would proudly carry him on his shoulders, echoing the words of the thousands of marchers behind him: "Revolution until victory … Revolution until victory." No task was too large or too small when it came to pushing the rebellion forward. Kamal threw rocks, carried the many wounded to blood-stained ambulances, and brought the dead to their final resting ground, all with the same amount of conviction. He even led prayers for the souls of martyrs when childhood friends were shot in the head or throat, as being an avowed socialist did not mean a lack of faith or a world without God. Hundreds fell, dead or wounded, throughout Palestine in a matter of weeks. Yet the more they bled and died, the more determined the living became, and the faster they again mobilized, regrouped, and recharged. Their chants grew louder: "No east, no west, this is the uprising of the people."

But then they caught him. Kamal was home watching the news during one of the many military curfews imposed on the camp, when the Israelis came looking for him. The beating commenced as soon as he was in reach of the first soldier who entered the house. "Ya Ibn Asharmouta!"—they immediately branded him a son of a bitch as they began punching his emaciated face. One soldier twisted both of his arms behind his back, while another kept kicking him in his genitals. Unalloyed pain erupted through his guts, as blood violently gushed out of his brow and mouth. The naturally protective instincts of his mother instantly rose to the scene as she wedged herself between him and the soldiers to absorb as much of the beating as possible, only to realize that Marwan was being targeted out as well. "Iman," she screamed at her eldest daughter, "shelter your brother!"

Iman was a rebel at heart, or maybe her moment of rebellion arrived at that juncture in time. She was not detained, but her jaw was broken with a single punch. That beautiful, sensitive child of fourteen years shrieked in pain both from her body and her heart. 'Kamal! Marwan! My brothers!" she yelled. Hearing the screams and fearing the worst, neighborhood women transformed into warriors of justice and descended upon the house. Suddenly, defenseless, powerless, and illiterate women found their voices and their calling. It was the microcosm of a battleground of a war much bigger than them. The women attempted to lessen the pain of the two boys, by enduring as much of it as they could. They cried to God for mercy and He answered when more and more women, both familiar and unknown, arrived from everywhere. Broken limbs and bruised faces did not hinder Marwan and Kamal from escaping in the midst of the chaos which, in the end, served a greater purpose. From this darkness came forth the birth of a movement from the women's collective power for the first time since they became refugees. And it was led by Umm Marwan herself.

Kamal escaped, but a limping and physically weakened Marwan was eventually caught trying to cross the Gaza Valley at the southern border of the camp. He was sent to Khan Younis to serve six months in jail for his role in the Intifada, and when the military judge sentenced him, he was told that he would not be released until Kamal was caught. Marwan had no qualms about serving jail time on his brother's behalf until his last day on God's rebellious earth. Committed to his credo, Marwan would not divulge a single name of any of the other activists, not even when they hung him naked, with his toes barely touching the cold prison floor; or when they repeatedly punched him in his genitals or sent electric shocks to his penis and nipples. Yelps of agony were all that escaped from him and nothing more.

Marwan was older than Kamal by only a few years, yet more mature in many ways. When Mahmoud was laboring in Israeli factories for weeks on end, Marwan's strong sense of family compelled him to play the role of the father. But this feeling of responsibility was not limited to his blood relations; he was just as devout towards his fellow Palestinians, neighbors and friends. This duty and a need to protect his younger brother was what drove him during the Intifada. When the Eid holiday massacre took place, their neighbor, a young boy named Raed Muanis, was killed and Marwan carried him to safety, trying to hold back the blood gushing from his face. As he looked into the dead boy's eyes, he pleaded to his brother Kamal to escape to the valley and spare him the pain of possibly losing his brother too. "It is a massacre brother. I kiss your hands, run away." Kamal did not listen, forcing Marwan to charge back towards the soldiers so that he could stay close to his brother and be his guardian. And whenever Marwan could not restrain Kamal from leaving the house during military curfews when snipers occupied the camp's tall buildings, including the famous water tower inside the Martyrs' Graveyard, Marwan always had to follow suit. Kamal lived in his own world where revolution was the only escape from his family's permanent misery. When recruiting youth in the camp, besides galvanizing their ideals, he ensured there was always a balance in numbers between sons of peasants and sons of laborers. True socialism demanded both.

As soon as the curfew was lifted, Umm Marwan went searching for him when he disappeared in the orchards. Yelling his name, she crossed the valley, and fought the current to reach the furthest orchards. Heartbroken, finding no sign of him, she went back home to her family after having dried all of her tears. She told them Kamal was safe and sound in the Hirthani Orchard and that the soldiers would never find him, no matter how hard they tried.

Every day her son was the object of her prayers. Dawn prayer in particular could not be missed because Allah loved the most faithful who would kneel for his mercy when everyone else was still asleep. Now that both Marwan and Kamal were not able to play their roles in mobilizing the camp, Umm Marwan was overtaken by a duality within her that she had never known before. Two opposing forces lived within her: an unfamiliar sense of responsibility towards a revolution that she hardly understood and her cultural socialization where women were taught that their place was in the home and not the battlefield. Never weak or docile, her strength was expressed in withstanding the longing to go back to Joulis, the daily exhausting torment and humiliation placed on her by the soldiers, the anguish of Gazan life, and the confining expectations of society. These were all battles in and of themselves, and once she found her truth, there was no going back on her choices.

Being on the frontlines of revolution brought her closer to her children and gave her newfound strength. She was too weak to throw rocks, and her chants were muted by her inability to remember the slogans. But there was something that she did well and which she did fearlessly. In wedging herself between screaming children and angry soldiers, she found her calling. So she led a group of women, and roved the streets of Nuseirat looking for soldiers even during curfew, for the presence of soldiers meant that children would soon be lined up waiting for their bones to be broken, their faces to be smashed against the sidewalk, and their teeth to be crushed by cowardly fists.

When Wael Abu Safieh was about to be taken to the "tents" where the soldiers rested, drank alcohol, spoke Hebrew and punished little kids, Umm Marwan led the women's protest by leaping inside the back of the jeep where Wael was handcuffed and blindfolded. Holding as tightly onto his feet as possible and pulling as much as she could, she refused to let them have their way. To deter her, the jeep driver drove off at full speed hoping that she would let go and fall onto the sand, but she tightened her grip even more. The soldiers pulled her hair, punched her in the back and kicked her in the stomach, soon discovering that she was more relentless than them. When she could not endure any more, she screamed at the top of her lungs, as she always did, so that women of the neighborhood would come out of their homes ready to throw themselves into harm's way and help whichever victim was she was trying to free. Wael was eventually taken to the military "tents" and Umm Marwan to the local clinic. She returned the next day and repeated the routine as if every boy was Kamal and every teenager Marwan.

* * *

Nuseirat extended from the sea to the highway and was divided between various blocks that each carried a number. It bordered Buraij to the east, Deir Al-Balah to the south and the Gaza Valley to the west where the sea quietly breathed hope and offered respite to the refugees. But when the Intifada started, the sea became off-limits, and the giggles of happy children were never heard anywhere near the beach for almost seven years. Buraij was smaller than Nuseirat in size and population, so when the small camp that also bordered the eastern orchards of the Strip was besieged, Nuseirat came to the rescue. The Israeli military encampment, which began with a few khaki-colored tents, and then grew to a hundred or more during the Intifada, was positioned precisely between the two camps. When an army blockade on Buraij reached a point where the refugees began to starve, or were killed while trying to break free, almost all of Nuseirat walked in one massive rally to Buraij. "We live together; we die together" was the slogan, and Umm Marwan was once more on the frontlines ready to shield the first line of youth who carried flags and chanted for Buraij's freedom and the freedom of all Palestinians.

The snipers stood motionless, in awe of the crowds whose masses extended from the army tents to the sea. It was the furthest horizon the soldiers on the watchtower could view. Even if they had wanted to fire, there were not enough bullets to take out everyone. Young and old, weak and strong, they all walked in unison. Marching in front, women led the way as icons of female power while children carried crayon-colored flags. The soldiers hid behind the towers and trenches, not firing a single bullet. The refugees of the camp who had been trapped for weeks, came out of their homes in disbelief when the masses started arriving in Buraij. Thousands hugged random thousands in a scene of solidarity never witnessed before in the history of the two camps. As the Nuseirat refugees celebrated their victory upon their return, Umm Marwan felt the tug of two arms embrace her from behind and fold gently upon her neck and chest. "Mother," said a voice that had grown hoarse from insistent chanting. It cradled her very being.

Kamal's cheekbones had sunk in to highlight a perfect skull merely covered with a layer of whitish, pale skin. But his spirit was as charged as ever, like that of a commander of an army, although beset and starved, who still believed victory was at hand only if the troops held strong for just one more day. He had been gone for many weeks, living in thick, dark orchards that sheltered him and many others. But when he heard that Nuseirat had risen to break the siege of its neighbors, Kamal could not tolerate remaining in hiding while the most historic moment of his life was unfolding, and he returned to the camp. Against his mother's wishes, Kamal promised to stay for only one night, and then run away back to the orchards first thing after the dawn prayer. Of course she wanted nothing more than for her son to be with them, but home was too risky and Umm Marwan knew the Israelis would come looking for him sooner or later. He had missed his family, Iman's endless chatter, his mother's warm touch, and the comfort of his floor mattress with its perfectly fluffed pillow. She promised to make him all the food he desired, and proudly spoke of the many kids she had liberated from the hands of the soldiers during his absence.

Abu Marwan was home with nothing to do. He had lost his job in Israel when the fruit factory owners received a police memo that the man's two children were involved with the fedayeen. With no income and with Marwan still in an army prison in Khan Younis, the family grew even poorer. Few, if any, urgent supplies had made their way to them in the recent months. Later they were smuggled to the camp through the Gaza Valley by young men sent by Kamal himself. But the fresh vegetables and fruits collected from nearby farms and orchards were not meant for the family's own consumption. Instead they were to help the neediest of the refugees regardless of clan or faction. One of Kamal's notes to his mother, read by Iman, stated:

"Dear Mother,

I know how great our need is, but I hope you understand that my moral duty compels me to help others who are in greater need than us. Please distribute this food equally among those who need it most, and make sure that no member of our family, or even al-Assar clan receive any of the shares. Start with the house of Umm Raed Muanis. Hug her for me and tell her that Raed's blood was not in vain, and that we are all her children.

Your loving son,
Kamal.

Kamal wanted to break all the divides that stood between the refugees, and confront even factional hierarchy. Although Umm Marwan understood his intentions, her frustration was fueled by the wants of her own family and her innate predisposition to protect them. She was only human after all. Still, she honored her son's wishes starting with Umm Raed's house in Block 5. Exhausted both mentally and physically, having knocked on many doors that day, she did not return home until after midnight. Kamal's pride was nothing less than exceptional when she told him all about it upon his return for that single night.

Yet on that very night, the soldiers reappeared. Their collaborators among the refugees informed the army that the young rebel was back. Without wasting any time, they went to Umm Marwan's home an hour before Kamal was to be awakened and readied for his escape. When Kamal understood the scenario about to unfold, he jumped to the roof of the house by climbing on top of the large blue container where the family stored water. But the soldiers had anticipated his move and he found them on the roof, ready to fire at will. Surrendering was the only option. All that Umm Marwan could hear from the living room below were Kamal's muffled screams, and the sounds of heavy pounding.

She beseeched God for help, but the neighboring women were kept locked in their homes as the army had already anticipated their rebellion. In sync like a chorus, they accompanied the mother's screams in the early hours of dawn in a last desperate attempt to help. Minutes later, the soldiers were dangling Kamal from the roof of the house, as if he were a slaughtered animal suspended on the hook of a butcher shop, bloodied and pacified. At that exact moment she howled, producing a similar sound to the one that emanated from her gut when Salim went missing in the orchards many years earlier. Kamal was unconscious and despite the fact that the battle was lost, she still charged vigorously against her attackers, fighting for her child, unmindful of the blood which was oozing from her face and mixing with his.

Along with Iman, she ran into the street trying to track the army that had stolen her son. But when they disappeared into the main road connecting the camp to the Gaza highway and eventually to the army tents, she could no longer run, or even walk. All the strength that refused to abandon her since the day her family left Joulis evaporated. Kamal was gone, and she felt it would be the last time she would ever see her precious son. Falling to her knees, she softly wept, crying "Kamal, my son" over and over.

When Kamal regained consciousness, he found himself in a small cell, with thick, unwashed walls that felt so cold and foreign. His blue jeans were torn, scuffed and terribly bloodied. Staring at his exposed pointy shoulders and the bones of his ribcage, he wondered where his shirt had gone and how he had become so skeletal. He picked up a tiny little pebble and began leaving his marks on the wall. "Umm Marwan," he wrote, around which he drew a ring of small flowers. He had never anticipated that the odorless red flower of the camp actually sometimes had an intoxicating fragrance until he reached the Hirthani Orchard. While he was there, camping under a tree, hiding from the army, he calmly picked a flower and brought it to his nose. Instantly the world around him was no longer cold and dark. The trees grew taller, and the grass was like that of a green, endless meadow. The hunger pains disappeared, and the victory of the revolution that he had unleashed with his young friends in the camp seemed assured.

He also saw her, Fatima. She was an old woman, but hardly ugly or a ghoul. Visiting him often, she would gaze at him like a loving mother without exchanging a single word, and bring him bread, feta cheese, and fresh tomatoes. Her thoub combined the embroidery styles of all the fellahin villages into one and the wrinkles of her brow mimicked the carvings of the soil of the Hirthani Orchard.

Kamal spent most of his prison time in the torture chamber. After every long and harrowing session, he would be tossed back in his cell where he resumed his artwork on the walls. He did not reveal to his tormenters a single name, and denied any recollection of them even when they questioned him about the activities of his own brother. With the option of releasing him or renewing his stay, the army instead decided to beat him senseless. They broke all of his limbs, and every single rib in his chest. They pounded his genitals with their guns, and cracked his skull by bashing it repeatedly against the wall, on his writings and homages to his family and all of those he loved. Blood splashed color on the petals, now a vivid red, of the small etched flowers, their fragrance smelling of his blood.

* * *

When Umm Marwan opened the door to her home, she came face to face with a woman she had never met before. "I am Fatima," said the woman, who was old but hardly ugly or a ghoul. "Come with me. Kamal is in the orchard." Without seeking any answers, or even wearing her slippers or throwing a cover upon her hair, Umm Marwan ran behind the woman, with a sense of urgency that invited the curiosity of others in the camp. Many joined her, forming a large crowd that delved into the Hirthani Orchard. A few minutes later they all emerged and returned to Block 5, carrying the young man who was covered in a vivid redness and had a glow unlike the color of any blood the refugees had ever seen. The young man, nearly lifeless, was expected to be drained of his last drops of blood in that orchard, but a mysterious woman hovered above him, caressed his hair and washed his face before daring to leave the Hirthani Orchard in search of his mother.

Kamal died years later. He made it to Amman using a different path from the one that his uncle Salim had chosen for himself in 1956, when he was probably shot dead and buried under a lemon tree in a faraway orchard. If his grave existed, it still remained unmarked. No one knew the fate of his journals filled with all the details of the suffering of the refugees in Deir Al-Balah. In Amman, Kamal had just embarked on his graduate studies in economics when after a visit to the doctor he was told that he had brain cancer. Considering his frail body and the many ailments that he had accumulated from his times in prison, he was said to have only six months to live. In keeping with his fighter's spirit, he returned to Nuseirat with a plan to defy the doctors' grim verdict, and began teaching young people at a local university economics and the history of a homeland that was meant to be kept secret. When he finally died, thousands from the neighboring Buraij refugee camp descended upon Nuseirat. The massive crowd mourned him as a martyr and buried him in the Martyrs' Graveyard, near the large water tower, not far away from Raed Muanis.

Umm Marwan's rebellion never ceased. She took every opportunity possible to spread the message of her revolutionary son, standing in the frontline of every protest and every funeral of the camps' many martyrs; all sons of fellahin who believed that a utopia was possible. And during her weak moments, fearing that others might notice her tears, she would go to the Hirthani Orchard and converse with Fatima, where the two women cried together, surrounded by little red flowers with an enchantingly beautiful scent.

The spirit of Umm Marwan represents an entire generation of Palestinian refugee women. In their enduring of harsh lives, these women raised a new generation who would sustain the fight ahead. Hana al-Shalabi is another legendary embodiment of this spirit. She withstood the longest hunger strike ever undertaken by a Palestinian woman in Israeli prisons. Accused of planning to avenge the death of her brother, who was killed by Israeli soldiers in the village of Burqin in the occupied West Bank, Hana suffered imprisonment, torture, long interrogations, and untold humiliation. When I first spoke to her, I initially felt apprehension, knowing that she had been kept in an underground dungeon for many months and was tied to a hospital bed fighting starvation. But my anxiety dissipated and I found myself speaking to a kind, calm and charming person. At times, she laughed when recalling the folly of her Israeli interrogators. Other times she was angry, feeling as if she had been betrayed by her own brethren. And then sometimes, she would pause and held back tears when she uttered the name of Samir, her martyred brother.

4
Death Notice

When the two women were alone together, the stern, stubborn, and impermeable façade she displayed to the outside world dissipated into thin air, and she embraced her own vulnerability. Not even the drunken soldiers and filthy guards, so good at breaking people, would bring her to her knees. Even when they took every opportunity to humiliate her, strip her down in the name of security, slap her face until her entire body weakened, or kick her until she was completely numb, she stood her ground. But when the door sealed shut, she would breathe a sigh of relief and let out the many tears of bottled-up pain that had accumulated since the last time she met her friend. Memories of her beloved brother's fondness for flowers and the short time he walked this earth would roll off her tongue like a bedtime story without a happy ending. Images of her mother and father waiting angst-ridden for her release cut into her already feeble body, famished from being denied basic nourishment. Talking and crying intermittently, she would sometimes fall asleep or faint in mid-sentence, only to awaken with her body convulsing in pain and nightmarish hunger, signaling that the end was indeed near.

Hana was as strong as human beings come, but without her friend Lina, her resilience to withstand starvation during those protracted weeks would have been greatly compromised, not least by the pressures inflicted on her by those determined to see her fail and remain captive forever. Lina was no stranger to the inner workings of Israeli prisons or the means by which her captors obtained what they wanted. She had lost her freedom when she was sentenced to seventeen years in prison after being accused of transporting fighters to targeted areas inside Israel. Though she denied all charges to the bitter end, through many long days and nights of extensive torture, her interrogators insisted on her guilt, and they won.

When Hana met her, Lina was forty-eight years of age, and had three more years left to serve. At first, the two seemed to have little in common: Lina was from a village that became part of Israel when that state was established on the rubble of hundreds of Arab villages, and Hana was from Burqin, a village in the north of the West Bank. Lina was older, wiser, fairer, taller, and had green eyes. Hana was rapidly shrinking since starting her hunger strike, and her dark and healthy skin grew pale, translucent and covered in a rash that slowly invaded her body, eating up whatever signs of vitality it once exuded.

With time, Lina's maternal instincts took over and she assumed the role of Hana's caregiver. She bathed her, combed her hair, negotiated with the prison administration on her behalf, tucked her into bed, and covered her gently as if she were her child. When Hana was about to be declared dead, Lina even sang for her, and whispered a few last jokes into her ear. "If you ever agree to end your hunger strike, please, please add this to your list of demands: a shawarma sandwich for your loving sister," Lina told Hana once, as she gently massaged her arms, trying to keep the blood flowing for a while longer. Then Hana would smile, leaving her dearest friend with the hope that the defiant woman of Burqin still had enough energy to live and fight one more day.

Throughout her forty-seven-day hunger strike, Hana al-Shalabi never slept for a consistent number of hours. In the first few days, she would doze off and suddenly wake up with gripping fear that someone was trying to hurt her. Then after a week of striking, taking nothing but a few sips of water a day, her body ceased to function normally.

Instead of sleeping and possibly finding a moment when she could shut down her mind and feel somewhat human, she would fall into a state of delirium, overtaken by frenzied hallucinations where memories and persistent fears coalesced into a sonata of night terror. Yet every single time, Hana would wake up and manage to find the strength to mumble a few verses from the comforting words of the Quran. Then, just as fast as the tears fell down her face, her body would delve back into a state of restlessness. Once in a while, she would chance upon a vivid dream where she would be back in her love-filled home with Amer, Amar, Samir, Salam, Huda, Zahira, Sahir, and everyone else who meant something to her. In those sweet dreams, she was never shackled, never tied down to a bed and never hungry. And whether they were delusions or messages from beyond, Samir would be happily walking around the village wearing his favorite denim shirt, adorned with a bright red flower pinned to his pocket. In Hana's mental picture, he tenderly visited the elderly women of Burqin and bestowed upon them a sense of peace via an illusion of youth which made him live on forever. But Samir's body was no longer of this earth.

It was Hana's turn to follow. Barely aware of her surroundings, but fully conscious of her past, she opened her eyes one more time. Without warning, a whole sequence of events, taking her from Burqin as an elementary school girl with a checkered uniform to this overpowering dungeon where eternal death was a welcomed respite from the revulsions of life, flashed before her.

* * *

She was born on February 7, 1982, the same year that Palestinian factions were driven out of Lebanon and the refugees of the Sabra and Shatila camps were slaughtered en masse. "When one dies within a larger group, it is much easier," her mother said back then, trying to mask the grief that eventually hardened into the larger collective Palestinian suffering. "There is no will but the will of Allah," muttered her father as he shook his head and rolled another cigarette, cramming in more tobacco than usual. Burqin was located in the Jenin district not far from south Lebanon, but was certainly, at least in those times, much safer. When her father, Yahya, and her mother, Badia, were finished having children, the final tally was ten. Of the six females, Hana was somewhere in the middle, after Najah, Salam, and Huda, and before Wafa and Zahira. Samir was the youngest of the brothers, and only two years older than Hana. Carrying the legacy of their father and his father before him, the other three boys, Omar, Amar, and Sahir became farmers.

Yahya's dark skin did not reflect old age, but was marked by wrinkles on his neck, face and forehead that conveyed a hard life and a chronicle of heartbreak. Badia's fair skin, blond hair and coveted green eyes were enough to classify her as beautiful, and the children were divided more or less around the same traits. Hana took her father's dark skin and brown eyes, and deeply loved him and everything he did or stood for. Though she was the rabble-rouser of the girls, and Samir of the boys, she always received what she wanted and she liked it that way. Her security was strengthened by the fact that Yahya unabashedly loved his girls more than his boys. The only aspect of life she feared in the midst of this grounding love were the Israelis because they were the only people she had ever laid eyes on who carried guns. Maybe her father's preference for the girls was driven by protectiveness, or fear, or compassion, knowing that boys would grow up to be men in a society that privileged them over women, and assigned them not only greater rights, but also greater responsibilities.

The brothers all went to school and when they would return each day, following a quick lunch of whatever the earth had to offer, they took their tools and descended upon the land—to break boulders, level soil, plant seeds and monitor the direction of the wind through the early whispers of a promising storm.

The account of how Yahya and Badia met was repeated often and lovingly by her father for as long as Hana could remember. He was a young horseman, who strolled across the village hoping to solicit the envy of his peers and the admiring looks of the teenage girls. One day he noticed Badia fetching water from the well on the outskirts of the village. It was love at first sight. When they married they lived in the Burqin Valley, not far from Safad in the north. They were proud of the land and Yahya's father, Sabir, was a farmer who raised sheep and horses. Feeling affinity with his craft, his skills became his certainty and he was one with his earth. But there was a truth he spent his entire life trying to mask: Sabir was a refugee.

Sabir hailed from the port city of Haifa in Palestine where he owned much land and a fine rifle. He escaped to the Jenin orchards with his immediate family a few months before most Palestinians were dispossessed of their land and forced out. Locals would hail the artistry of his horsemanship and some said Sabir was the best shot in Haifa. When the fervor of revolution was festering as Zionists were gaining more powers and Palestinian peasants and workers were growing penniless, crowding the port city in search of jobs that were mostly available to Jews not Arabs, Sabir took his horse and rifle and vanished. Following several raids by British troops on various Shalabi homes, it became well-known that Sabir had killed a member of a Zionist militia. It was a single bullet that he fired as a Zionist gang was on its way to plunder a village not far from Haifa, to raise their flag as a sign of another successful conquest. The bullet shot through the air while he was on horseback, then he promptly galloped beyond reach and disappeared into the horizon.

The war and Nakba followed, but when Sabir settled with his family in Burqin, he adamantly refused to be identified as a refugee. For he had not been driven out by war, but by his own conscious decision to join the resistance and shield his family from the vengeance of the Zionists and their British benefactors. Yet without any document recognizing him or his family as refugees, Sabir received no aid of any sort. Going back to the land and focusing on everyday survival was not only about fulfilling his physical needs to obtain food and nourishment, it was also an attempt to resurrect hope.

Burqin was heaven and no place matched it in beauty or charm. It was located in the Beisan area, at the juncture of two of the most fertile plains in Palestine—the Jordan Valley and Marj Ibn Amer, at the foot of the Mount Carmel range. The Shalabis were wedged in this new paradise, amid the valleys and the mountains, and between the memories of an unreachable perfect world that was once theirs, not so far away. The newly formed state had a country and an army, but they still eyed Beisan and whatever remained of the Palestine they intended to claim wholly as their own. It was only then that the faultless canvas of Burqin was ruined, cluttered with fighter jets and the scarring tracks left by the heavy chains of army tanks and soldiers' boots. When the first strike took place, Yahya and Badia were in the fields that were owned by Sabir. During the panicked rush to find shelter, Badia's first-born, Najah, had fallen out of her mother's loving arms to the ground, and her mother only realized that she had lost her baby after running a significant distance towards her home in the village. Returning with the same panicked haste, and oblivious to the menacing army that had invaded her once serene horizon, she wailed between the stocks of wheat, yelling the name of her infant. Around her, the smoke of burning villages gathered like a dark cloud that promised no rain.

Hana was born in that lost paradise. In the first few years of her life, she would hear of "the Jews" but would hardly ever see them. Somehow she knew that they meant her harm, but as long as she burrowed into her mother's side, or was nestled in the arms of her father, no one could spoil her happy childhood. When she began her studies at the school that was just a short walk from her home, she found endless possibilities for relishing life. The innocent joy of being with other girls her age, harvesting wild flowers, chasing birds, and discovering the world around her made her feel like all children should feel. And her rebellious attributes of being wild, loud, feared, and loved made her the queen of a perfect universe populated by little girls with budding personas wearing checkered school uniforms. Then one day she saw him, and he changed her life forever. "Please, help me," he said quietly. But she froze, and he fell on his face and died.

* * *

She was eight years old when a teenage boy named Mohammed dashed towards her as fast as he could while she was chewing on a hearty sandwich of za'tar and eggs. At that time, he should have been in school, not running around without a purpose in the streets of Burqin. Just as he reached her, only a few feet from where she stood, he fell on his knees as though he were about to pray, held silent for a moment, and then whispered to her gently without the slightest sign of despair or pain: "Please, help me." Hana did not understand what kind of help he sought or what was going on. So she remained motionless, still holding onto her sandwich, and gazing at his somber face with her eyes wide open. He had white skin, black hair and round brown eyes with long dark lashes that framed their warm idealism. As his body hit the ground, a gaping hole was revealed in the back of his head, and a stream of blood quickly erupted and created a pool of bright red gore. Seconds later, the soldiers arrived, barking in an alien language, drenched in sweat and screeching triumphant proclamations like predators looming over a lusted-after prey.

Over and over they yelled at her to go home, but her body was numb and her confused soul was in a trance. Her school bag fell behind her, and the sandwich crumbled in front of her. "Go home!" they bellowed angrily in broken Arabic. Snapping out of her hypnotic state, she started running and squealing unintelligibly about a boy, and death, and guns and blood. The real world was unmasked, showing that hidden between the meadows and lurking behind the mountains was a vicious and violent reality. When she reached home, she was unable to speak for many days. Sign language became her means of communication, but she could not muster up the skills to convey the brutal scene of the handsome neighbor boy with the lovely brown eyes dying right in front of her after a bullet penetrated his skull. At first, her unrelenting thoughts were disturbed by a burning feeling of guilt. "Please, help me," said the handsome boy, and she did not. She could not. She would not have been able to help even if she had tried with all her might, or had offered him half her sandwich, or all of it. Crippled by fear, six months passed before she went back to her school, overrun by soldiers who had pitched their tents there and who used the roofs as their watchtowers, aiming their guns directly at Burqin.

When the villages revolted, the kids in Burqin were on the frontlines. Wanting revenge for the deaths of their peers and to liberate their schools, they threw rocks at the snipers, and some even lobbed Molotov cocktails. By turning her fears inside out, Hana found the courage to be a part of this rebellion after she got over her initial shell-shock. The wild child with the indiscriminate appetite for fun would never be the same, and she went on a mission to avenge the handsome neighbor boy, and clear the road, from her house all the way to school, of the ugly, cruel men who spoke a strange language and wore military uniforms. Without her mom's knowledge, she emptied out the precious pure olive oil stored in the small bottles in her mother's kitchen so the youth could make Molotov cocktails. More than once she got caught by soldiers as she transported rocks in her schoolbag to the boys on the frontlines. As punishment the soldiers would smack her face and violently grab her by the hair and toss her around like a ragdoll. Though she would cry in pain and go home bruised, she would return the next day more determined to fight the vile enemies who had invaded her impeccable space.

She grew up angry, in a rage that was matched by many people all around her. Many sought a constructive way to offset their exasperation. Her brother, Omar, joined the Black Panthers, whose members were all sons of peasants and underpaid Arab laborers in Israel. They met in caves deep in the mountains and hid there for days on end before descending upon the villages, masked and armed, to declare strikes and mobilize people to rebel. Hana's mother, Badia, knew of Omar's dangerous endeavors, yet said nothing to discourage him or reveal his secret to his dad, Yahya, who continued to work untiringly on the family's land whenever the soldiers would permit him to do so. In a gesture of silent solidarity, every single night Badia would leave a large dinner on the table, made of cooked tomatoes, fried potato wedges, feta cheese, homemade bread and olives, and then unlock the backdoor and quietly slip into her bed. Whenever Omar and his friends slipped into Burqin in the middle of the night, they would sneak into the Shalabi house, eat Badia's predictable dinner, and carry out their death-defying plans.

But when Omar was injured during a nightly skirmish with the soldiers, the secret was unveiled to everyone, including an angry Yahya, who realized that his constant attempts to keep his kids out of trouble had failed badly. After the oldest child was caught and thrown in prison, Amar soon followed in his brother's footsteps and he too was imprisoned. Huda also joined them soon enough, when she was only fourteen years old, on charges of trying to stab a soldier in Jerusalem. Yahya's children had all grown up to have independent ideas and a sense of fearlessness.

Huda was madly in love when she disappeared from Burqin. Popular uprisings had liberated many young girls from the confines of family chores and tradition. So at the age of eight or nine, she joined the kids throwing rocks at soldiers as they passed by the village or at the checkpoints that had been set up all around it. She even fashioned her own slingshot which she used to target snipers on top of the school, and she began wearing khaki-colored pants and black boots like her brother and his comrades in the Black Panthers. It was only a matter of time before Huda fell in love with one of the boys with whom she shared such a complex existence. His name was Mohammed al-Sadi, a seventeen year old from Jenin. She even insisted on marrying him, though she was met by her parents' adamant rejection. But there was still hope, as the boy loved her back and promised her that he would wait for her until she reached a more appropriate age. He would do everything he could to win Yahya and Badia's approval. Huda only had to be patient and believe in their love.

Destiny had other plans for them. On the day he was killed, Mohammed al-Sadi was coming down the mountains with an assortment of wild flowers he had collected for Huda. The soldiers ambushed him and a few others, killing them all. When Huda heard the news she remained completely silent yet her anger boiled throughout her body as she proceeded to destroy her room, smash the glass windows, rip up all the pillows and tear out much of her hair, all without uttering a single word. Late that night she left the house and disappeared for a week. She resurfaced in jail. She was wounded and broken, but no longer silent. To avenge Mohammed, she had traveled to Jerusalem with a kitchen knife hidden in her bag, and attempted to stab a soldier. Before she could even strike her target, her young body fell bleeding to the ground. Months later she was released from her lockup only to face another "punishment" that truly broke her spirit, when she was forced to marry her cousin. After giving birth to three beautiful girls and two boys, she eventually learned to accept her life as it was. Happiness had eluded her, and she had no choice but to move on.

Her older brother, Omar, spent nearly two years in jail. When he was released, he had no reason to mask his face because the whole village knew of his affiliation. He spent most of his time in the mountains, although the soldiers returned to his family home every few nights, destroying everything in their way before leaving, only to return again and repeat the same deed. With time, there was nothing left in the Shalabi household that was worth destroying, and replenishing it was futile.

As early as the mid-1990s, Palestinian police began showing up almost timidly in the dusty roads of Burqin. At first Hana did not hate the police, she simply did not care for them or even notice them. In those days, they merely stood there, directed traffic, and attempted to solve family disputes and chase after petty thieves. But with time, they took on another role, one that situated them as a line of defense for the Israeli army. Sometimes they were sent to people's homes seeking answers about the whereabouts of fighters, demanding confessions and levying threats. It caused a lot of resentment in the village and it was then that Hana began harboring towards them the same anger she felt towards her enemies. Yet the masked fighters remained hidden deep in the mountains, rarely venturing out to Burqin or the adjoining villages. Their news was still passed on in the tried and true way, from one villager to the other, ever so discreetly through trusted allies. And when an Intifada erupted in 2000, they all descended upon the villages and the refugee camps to take part in what they considered to be a decisive battle.

The fighters arrived from the mountains and from the Burqin Valley, and from the orchards of Yabad, from Harsh Al-Saada, and other places. This time around, the odds were stacked against them. The Israeli army had treated the popular uprising as a fully fledged war and the Palestinian Authority, installed a few years earlier, was mostly concerned with its own survival and not with that of the Palestinian people. The last battle was in Jenin in April 2002, when fighters representing all factions united in a rare moment, and took on the Israeli army after it pounded the Jenin refugee camp and cut off the area completely from Burqin and all the surrounding villages. All the fighters were killed. The last was the daring Abu Jandal, executed in the square of the camp while his hands were tied behind his back. Every time they pushed him to the ground, he rose to his feet and stared into the mirrors of his murderer's soul. His body finally collapsed when he was shot right between the eyes. Then the entire camp was leveled and bombs made their way into people's living rooms. Hana's cousins Shadi and Nidal al-Nubani were killed when their house was blown up with them still inside.

When Burqin rose to protest against the long siege and the massacres in Jenin, Amar took a savage beating from the soldiers. They pounded his chest with the butts of their rifles and left him to bleed out on the outskirts of the village. Somehow he survived the internal hemorrhaging that nearly killed him, and he was soon able to return to working the land during the day, and protesting against the occupation in the evenings. But it was Samir who was slowly radicalized by the new Intifada and the lasting impression made on him by the gallantry of the Jenin battle when the fighters fought to the very end knowing their inevitable fate, and thousands of ordinary people refused to abandon the camp. While Omar and Amar were growing weary from imprisonment, occasional beatings and the feeling of betrayal by their own Palestinian leadership, Samir was about to take their place in the struggle, a decision that altered the course of Hana's life.

* * *

Samir looked different from his brothers and sisters, who each had distinct physical traits that were either similar to Badia's or Yahya's. He was neither tall nor short, and his skin was neither fair nor dark. Born in 1980, he was too young to care for or remember much of the Stone Intifada of 1987. Not even the Al-Aqsa Intifada, at least when it first started in 2000, seemed to affect him beyond the occasional protest, which naturally led to habitual roughing-up by soldiers. Compared to his brothers, Samir was pampered by everyone around him, a treatment that was explained by an incident related to a well.

When Samir's relatives were digging a well in search of underground water, the ten-year-old's curiosity got the better of him and he fell into the deep hole, landing on his not fully developed head and smashing his bones. The local hospital declared that he was fine, but his family's true agony started many months later when they discovered that a contorted bone in the front of his skull was causing swelling and almost claimed his life. A kindly doctor in Jordan did his best to save Samir. At thirteen years of age, after his brain surgery in Jordan, Samir was left with a massive scar that stretched across his head, from one ear to the other.

Nonetheless, Samir was a clever boy and he got great satisfaction from fixing anything that needed repair. Amar once accused him of damaging appliances for the sheer desire to fix them, an allegation that Samir vehemently denied. He disliked school with all of his heart for the sole reason that teachers had long sticks which they freely used to punish those deemed deserving of their wrath. Samir was a coddled young man, but that did not in any way justify the ferocious beating he once received from his math teacher for supposedly not paying attention to his words of wisdom. Not only did the teacher smack him across the face, he struck him with a stick on his legs, feet, back, and bottom. With each swing, the impact intensified until the grand finale when he made a point of hitting him on his head, right on top of the persistent wound that had almost ended his life.

Traumatizing him once again, that incident marked the last day of Samir's schooling and the beginning of life-changing introspection. With the help of his family, he spent months seeking practical alternatives to fill his days with meaning. He loved swimming, and was proudly remembered by his family for having saved a life at an Israeli beach just before he fell and damaged his skull. To his regret, becoming a swimming instructor was not an option. Doctors had warned of the dangers that water pressure could pose to his delicate head. Besides, West Bank Palestinians were not allowed any more on Israeli beaches, and the closest swimming pool was in the town of Jenin, which was too far away, too crowded and too restricted by military closures and repeated curfews. But Samir also loved to ride horses. Indeed, raising horses would have been an option if it were not for the fact that Yahya had sold all his horses when riding lost its sense of freedom after army checkpoints were erected around Burqin, slowing down or preventing movement altogether. And so it was settled, partly because of the lack of other options. Samir was to join his brothers laboring on their land, which had grown from three dunums to more than a hundred.

There were practical reasons behind the land expansion. When Yahya's father died, he made a business decision to quit animal husbandry altogether. By selling most of the animals, he was able to purchase new land. Then as soon as Omar and Amar finished high school, they acquired fresh skill sets that allowed them humble earnings in new professions. The older brother became a mechanic, and the other mastered the craft of carpentry. Though they were certainly more independent, whatever money they managed to save was invested twofold. Firstly, they reinvested in their father's land so they could continue to reap the benefits. Secondly, they acquired more land that was then collectively owned by the family. With time, they amassed one hundred dunums relatively cheaply because many farmers were driven out of their land by encroaching Jewish settlements and burgeoning closed military zones. Those who were lucky enough to be spared confiscation of their land by the army were not always lucky in obtaining the needed permit to care for it. But the Shalabis were not easily driven out; they continued to acquire as much land as they could and to support their village by hiring Palestinian laborers. Omar, Amar, their father, and now their younger brother, Samir, worked hand-in-hand with their neighbors and friends to keep bread on the table and the armed Jewish settlers, along with the army, at bay.

Since the land was secured in stages, the hundred dunums or so were not all located in the same area. The Burqin village, or town as some called it, was inhabited by around five or six thousand residents, many of whom worked as farmers. It was positioned in a most strategic location, at least in terms of its visual appeal and usefulness to those whose existence was intertwined with soil, wind, and water. The village itself was entirely situated on flat land, north of which was the lush green Beisan Valley and Harsh Al-Saada, which progressively merged into the massive and fertile plains of Marj Ibn Amer. In the pink-hazed dawn the ethereal call to prayer would echo across the horizon as the sun rose precisely behind the mountains that gently embraced the Jenin refugee camp. More mountains were located to the west, namely the Hashimi and Yamoun mountains, and yet more mountains stood to the south of Burqin known as the Qabatia mountains. Nearly fifty dunums of the family's land was tucked Between Burqin and the Qabatia, mostly safe from the capricious orders of land seizure issued by the army for reasons never explained. The rest of their land was spread in the area separating Burqin from Jenin, and some more near the Beisan Valley, across the creek where giant trees had grown unhindered for many generations.

Samir's reluctant attitude to his new profession slowly evaporated as he developed a strong relationship to the land. Rather than viewing his new life as monotonous, every time the young teenager rested, he was engrossed in nature's offerings. The beauty of its mountains, rivers, forests, plains, and bare soil surprised him over and over again. Times were still good then, and their family land could be shaped into whatever form the three brothers wished it to be. It was some time in the mid-1990s when he started pondering on the idea of being a farmer. The soldiers were still far off, but they drew nearer as time passed and the Intifada took off. And when Jenin was conquered, and all of its fighters in the mountains and the orchards were killed, the soldiers visited Burqin every night.

Something began lurking in Samir's mind and it seemed to take form almost independently from the revolutionary rhetoric that occupied much of the public space in Burqin, but especially within his family. He enlisted in the local branch of the Islamic Jihad and soon after that he placed a bomb in Martyrs' Street to ambush an Israeli military convoy. No one fully understood why Samir did what he did, or why he even joined the group in the first place. He had certainly changed dramatically since he was a child. When Samir was eight, Israeli troops confiscated his coloring books during a raid of their family home when they went through the children's school bags. Drawings of rifles of different shapes, along with pencil sketches of masked men and flags, were torn to bits. When the army left, he hid under his bed for the entire afternoon, insisting he was not afraid. On another occasion, when his brother Amar's chest was shattered by soldiers, Samir showed little emotion, only a puzzled look. Unlike both of his parents and all of his sisters, he did not scream, or cry, or faint at the sight of Amar gasping for air while blood oozed out of his mouth. Even when Omar and Huda were imprisoned, he did not say much, or even ask a single question, though it all weighed heavily on him. And whenever he failed to process profound emotions, he would walk to the family land in the Beisan Valley, hunch under a tree and scrutinize his world as the sky and towering mountains reminded him of everything that was consequential.

Just before he was apprehended for his militant activities in 2004, Hana saw her brother nervously hiding a rifle in his room. Insisting it was not his, he lied to her and said he was keeping it for a friend. But it was all confirmed when he was detained late one night, along with Ahmad Khalouf, a fighter whom the Israelis had been tracking for years. When they both stood before a military judge, Ahmad, with the poise of an experienced warrior, bore all the responsibility, partly because he knew that whatever he said or failed to say would not alter by more than a few years the life sentence he eventually received. Thanks to him, Samir was released nine months later. Yet despite much beseeching by his mother, on his very first day of freedom, Samir walked down Burqin's Martyrs' Street brandishing an automatic rifle and a defiant attitude.

There was no denying it—the student-turned-farmer was officially a fighter, and according to Israeli army protocol, it was a crime punishable by death. In fact, the soldiers returned to the family home on that same night looking for Samir. After destroying every chair and every table, pouring their olive oil on the ground, dumping sacks of flour and breaking every frame on the wall, they left Samir a death-note: "Your days are numbered."

The distressing pleas of Samir's parents to give himself up fell on deaf ears. "One or two years will be all, and they will set you free," said Badia. "You haven't killed anyone, son. They have nothing against you," said Yahya. But Samir had resolved that a short life in the mountains, even shielded by guns and bullets, was more liberating, and more dignified, than a long life in prison or confined behind the constant humiliation of military checkpoints.

In early 2005, Samir's visits to the village became more frequent. He made a point of seeing every member of his family. He hugged his brothers and their children with increased conviction. He snuggled his mother and kissed his father's wrinkled right hand, more than he had done when he was an affection-craving child. Even his generosity blossomed and he gave his small house, a place he had built himself and fenced with a thousand flowers, to his brother Sahir when he was engaged to be married. Samir knew that neither love nor marriage was meant for a man who lived mostly in the mountains with a promise of death hovering over his head.

No one could fool Hana. She knew that something was occupying her brother's mind from his sudden change in behavior and the exaggerated affection towards his family and neighbors. Having been so close growing up, she understood him better than anyone else. Together they had played, fought, threw rocks at soldiers, agitated their parents, and shared scary stories about ghouls that lived in the mountains and spirits of martyrs that wandered the orchards. Words were not necessary, they could read each other almost clairvoyantly. Thus he confided in her, as soon as she asked him why he gave away the keys to his home.

"I feel that my home is not the one east from here, but west," he said, pointing in the direction of the Burqin graveyard. "Hana, I intend to carry out a Martyrdom operation," he said somberly. Heartbroken, she refused to believe him. He gave her a piece of paper upon which was inscribed his last will: "Do not mourn me, but celebrate my martyrdom. Throw Hanoun flowers on my dead body, all around my coffin, inside the hallow earth before I am lowered to the ground and on top of my grave." That vivid red flower that grew wild and uncontained in the meadows encircling Burqin was Samir's favorite, though he loved all flowers; even ones that no one else cared for, because they did not exude an intoxicating smell.

It was on a Wednesday, at around ten at night, when Samir appeared at his family home, entertained a neighbor's child for a while, and then hurried inside for dinner. He looked particularly handsome that day, having stopped by the barber in the early afternoon, coming home clean shaven and smelling of cologne. He wore a new white t-shirt, with a red Hanoun flower pinned just above a buttoned pocket on his left side, along with black jeans, a khaki jacket and an army hat. Clearly preoccupied, he ate only a few bites of his cooked tomatoes, fried potato wedges, feta cheese and homemade bread before announcing that he had to leave and that important people were waiting for him somewhere. He tenderly kissed his mother goodbye, and for a few moments sat on top of the stairs outside the main door that was slightly ajar. He turned around three times, each time looking inside the house, each time smiling at whomever would meet his eyes. Then he slowly walked away. Hana chased him to the street but did not shout his name. She just stood there, and watched him slowly vanish into the darkness.

* * *

The first shot was not from a rifle but a pistol. It was exactly a quarter to midnight when the first bullet's crack woke up a startled Badia, who had just had a frightening dream where a bullet had pierced her chest. In actuality, a battle had just commenced and a rush of bullets was heard in the distance, only to be interrupted by the heavy sound of shelling. "Samir is dead," Hana muttered to herself, guided only by a sisterly intuition. The family stepped outside their home to find that the whole neighborhood was already in the street. The skies north of Burqin, where the Beisan Valley met Marj Ibn Amer, were lit up as if they were the northern lights. Then silence and darkness resumed and there was a palpable heavy feeling in the air. All the villagers looked at each other in distress wondering if anyone they knew had been hurt or killed or if there would be any consequences for them after what had just ensued. An hour later, Israeli soldiers entered the village covered in blood that was not their own. They stormed the Shalabi home asking about Samir, but arrested Sahir instead.

With her insides twisting, Hana ran to the roof where the family land was visible, and where she could clearly see ambulances rushing in and out of the area. Israeli helicopters were still circling, creating more confusion for the distant onlookers. "Samir was martyred ... Samir was martyred," announced a voice in the distance as is the custom when a youth is gunned down in Burqin. The village erupted in chants: "With our blood, with our souls, we shall avenge you, Samir."

Omar came rushing into the family home, exclaiming about the rumor going around that Nidah Khalouf, not his brother, was the one killed in the battle. He quickly called the local hospital but was told that the body of Samir al-Saadi had arrived, after he had tried to avenge the death of his brother who was martyred in the Jenin battle a few years earlier. Even though their son's death had not yet been confirmed, the dread of having lost their son was too much for the parents to take. The mother had already fainted by the time Omar came in and Yahya was no longer able to breathe without the help of local medics. When they were finally stable, they were assured that Samir was still alive and when dawn came all the villagers, including Yahya and Omar, gathered together spontaneously and began moving towards Beisan in their hundreds. The Shalabi family all stood outside for final assurance that Samir was safe.

When Yahya al-Shalabi finally returned, walking ever so slowly towards his house, he was joined by a thousand men all wearing grim expressions. His face conveyed intense emotions, but somehow he managed to control the tremors in his lips and keep the tears hidden for a while longer as his arms carried a khaki jacket, a discolored white t-shirt and a hat. Soaked with blood that was dripping through Yahya's fingers onto the earth, the small red Hanoun flower was still attached to the shirt and stood out in a vivid red.

"What are you carrying, dad," asked Hana, although already knowing the answer.

"Samir's clothes."

"Why are they drenched with blood, dad?'

"Samir was martyred."

"You are lying to me, dad. Lying is haram, daddy. Samir is not dead. Samir does not die."

Fighters from around Burqin descended on the village in droves. "God is great," chanted the crowds, but none of the family could hear them except for Hana. They had all fainted, one after the other, on hearing the final, heart-shattering news. The local ambulances that gathered Samir's remains after his body was blown up by a missile mounted on a military helicopter took them to the hospital. At the hospital Hana had her own intentions. "I want to see Samir." But everyone insisted it was a bad idea, for his body had been mutilated beyond recognition. "I want to see Samir," she repeated. But the dignity of the dead can only be achieved with a proper burial, a neighbor consoled, referencing Prophet Mohamed. Despite all the voices telling her otherwise, Hana knew she had to grieve for Samir in her own way and say the final words she could not say the last day she saw him. She walked straight to the hospital, followed by a stream of wailing women. Tears fell from her eyes, but she did not make even a whimper. Walking directly into the emergency room, where her brother's blood was still on the unwashed floor, doctors and nurses tried to dissuade her, but the determined look on her face made it clear that there was nothing they could do to keep her away.

What she saw was not exactly Samir, but the shattered remains of what was once a youthful body. Some of him still remained, forever to be part of the soil of the Shalabi land in Beisan. Hana huddled over his body, and whispered to him the words that would stay secret between them until they would meet again, as he had promised her they would just the night before. Her tears dripped gently onto his forehead, which she wiped off using the end of her scarf. Then she kissed him goodbye and walked out carrying the same poise with which she had entered the morgue, followed once more by the throng of wailing women who had not left her side.

On that life-altering night, not one but two young men by the name of Samir were killed. They were among seventeen who were assassinated by the Israeli army in those weeks. The fighters, representing several factions, including Hamas, Fatah, leftist parties and the Islamic Jihad, were meeting on Samir's land, receiving a shipment of rifles and were about to transport them to the mountains. Samir, along with two others, had been planning to launch an attack on the Israeli army on that same night. But a death notice listing seventeen names, including his, was handed over to the army by a Palestinian collaborator who also worked with the Palestinian Authority, and closely with Israel's internal intelligence service, the Shin Bet. The Israelis had trained him well in the art of treason, and had in fact imprisoned him for months in an effort to win the trust of the local factions. Alas, the traitor was only discovered when the seventeen, starting with the two Samirs, were killed in various ambushes. His body was eventually found in a garbage bin in Ramallah. Collaborators were often disposed of like trash.

All the factions proudly claimed Samir as one of their own. Graffiti and posters dotted the refugee camp for many months declaring him their freedom fighter. But Yahya refused to accept any such claims, and tore up the large banners erected all around the house and the funeral tent in the street. He also rejected financial support of any kind. "My son's blood is not for sale," was his typical, solemn reply whenever he was offered money. Before burial, Samir's coffin, adorned with a Palestinian flag, toured the entire village including the northern parts where he had spent most of his days laboring on the land, before finally resting in the west, in the Burqin graveyard. His body was sheltered with flowers, as was his grave, just as he had wanted.

Samir's love for his sister was undeniable. A year before he was killed, while he was serving his nine-month prison sentence, Samir called Hana to ask her about her tawjihi (final secondary school examination) scores. The results would determine whether she had to repeat the last year of school or move on to a local university. When she told him the good news, he promised her that he would use what little money he had to purchase sweets from the prison canteen for all the prisoners, regardless of their political and ideological affiliations. They both laughed so hard that day, but he still fulfilled his promise, uniting the inmates around baklava and Turkish delight. After Samir's death in 2009, Hana's enthusiasm for life faded. It was almost as if she had died with him. She wanted Samir to be proud of her so enlisted in the business school of the Arab-American University. But Hana spent a whole year there feeling as though she had no sense of direction or even the desire to have one.

Hana had so many questions, but not many answers when it came to knowing what she wanted or how she could fill the void in her life. She was compelled to run away from it all; maybe study law or even pursue a degree in nursing in Algeria or Tunisia. She only knew she had a desire for something else, something entirely different, yet that desire remained undefined. Her father wished for her to become a veterinarian, and imagined a future where the family would raise horses again. Yahya was eager to rekindle the past as best he could and resurrect the spirit of his dead father and son who had both loved horses. Although Hana listened to her father's sweet intentions, she was still plagued by doubt. Then, one day, the Palestinian Authority police came for her, as the Israelis had come for her brothers before her. A chubby officer with an exaggerated sense of self-importance who spoke Arabic in an accent never before heard in Burqin slapped her across the face, and demanded that she "confess." Instead, she sat in the interrogation room crafting paper boats with the pages on which she was meant to write her confession, and imagined a simpler time, before the handsome neighbor boy whispered to the eight-year-old Hana, "Please, help me."

* * *

Hana was visiting her cousin's house when they came for her. They had only a few questions, they told her, which she could answer over a cup of tea. But the few questions turned into a ten-day long interrogation. Every day she was grilled with the same single question, starting at nine in the morning until one in the morning of the next day: "Are you planning an attack on Israel to avenge your brother?"

Her Palestinian interrogator had an accent typical of Ramallah and his protruding belly did not quite match his muscular body which reeked of cheap cologne. The interrogation style was clearly modeled on an old Israeli method that Hana had been warned about. It felt like being on a roller-coaster. At first, he was soft-spoken using the friendliest possible terms, urging her to divulge information for her own sake and that of her family's. But when she told him that she had nothing to report, and that he should go ahead and reveal any evidence against her if there was any, his demeanor changed. Yelling in Arabic, and swearing oddly in Hebrew, he told Hana that he was no longer going to be nice and that she would come to regret her arrogant attitude. Then, once more, he calmed down, offered more tea and a large stack of white paper. "Listen, Hana," he said, "I will leave you alone. Take all the time you need, and write your confession on these papers. The Authority will protect you from Israel, no matter what plans you had in mind."

When he returned to the room, a sea of white paper boats greeted him. Every last sheet of white paper had been folded into a paper boat and filed neatly in perfect rows on his desk. Some were on the shelves under large framed posters of presidents wearing traditional scarves. The rebellious child in Hana had reappeared and was refusing to die. The officer did not like that child at all. He pushed Hana to the corner of the room and the paper boats began to fall to the ground around them. He fiercely slapped her face, as if possessed by a demon. But as soon as she fell on her knees, she stood up again, and charged at him, fighting to redeem her pride and innocence. So he hit her again, and again.

When the Palestinian Authority failed to extract the confession, the Israeli army came for her. They kept her prisoner for twenty-five months and accused her of joining the Islamic Jihad and of conceiving an attack to avenge her brother. They too had evidence, they insisted, but would never reveal it. She was kept in administrative detention, perpetual torture until a confession was extorted. There was no such thing as due process.

The family was still in mourning, though the forty days dictated by tradition had become months and years under the circumstances. When Badia lost her son, she also lost her hearing and most of her vision too, probably a consequence of all the stress and pain. There was no longer a reason for her to smile, and even the sight of flowers prompted silent tears that would flow down her face like a flooded Marj Ibn Amer after a sudden storm. When the soldiers came for Hana, Badia burst into tears, pleading to the soldiers to spare her child as the entire family was paraded down the street, the children in their shorts, their parents in their sleepwear and Badia and Yahya leading the pack and begging for mercy. The commanding officer was a Druze who spoke Arabic with a northern accent. He, too, claimed that he had just a few questions that could be quickly answered over a cup of tea.

When Hana was blindfolded and handcuffed, Badia fell on her back; and when Yahya tried to free his daughter from the soldiers' hands, they piled onto him, pounding his chest with the butts of their rifles. His last words before he fell unconscious were: "Enough, you have ruined our lives." Hana cried—not out of fear, for she had abandoned those feelings when she saw her brother's disfigured body in the hospital morgue—but out of remorse at the sight of her parents from the military jeep as it sped away, leaving Burqin behind. Her complaints that her handcuffs were cutting her wrists were futile at first, so she kicked the soldier in front of her so that he would not be able to ignore her pleas. Another soldier had the idea to loosen the plastic handcuffs with a lighter, burning her hands and dress. Hana's arms were too numb to feel the burning of her flesh, and she only discovered the wounds when the prison guards gave her a numbered placard and took her mugshots, from the front and from each side. She was prisoner number six thousand and something. She did not care to remember the exact digits that marked her captivity inside the Israeli prison service, the Shabas.

When they tossed her inside that dirty little room, she felt as if it were only a dream that she needed desperately to wake from. But she was too tired to think, so she used one of the two old blankets she found on the floor as a bed, and the other to cover herself as her body folded into a fetal position, and she slept. Only two hours later she was awakened by loud knocks on the door. She was bewildered and disoriented, and found herself wearing a brown prison outfit. They blindfolded her once again, and dragged her upstairs, downstairs and up again, into offices and rooms where the air was different from the air she breathed in Burqin, and where the language was unfamiliar and cold.

She found herself sitting in a chair like no other. Its front legs were shorter than its back legs, forcing her to sit in a contorted position and making her feel very uncomfortable. It was glued to the ground in a fixed position. They tied her legs and arms to the chair, and when they removed her blindfold, she was introduced to her new interrogator.

"I am Shamus. In Arabic you can call me Shams al-Din," said the man. He sat on a comfortable chair, behind a large desk, dotted with photos of happy children and playful animals. He was unhealthily skinny, and shaven bald all around except for a small patch of hair on the front of his head. "I know so much about Islam, and read the Quran," he resumed in strange Arabic, peppered with classical words of someone who studied a language at a university but never valued the spirit of those who spoke it. "I also studied psychology, so do not try to lie to me," he continued, this time grinning as if impressed by his own credentials.

He threatened to keep her in prison for ninety days if she did not cooperate. Disobediently, she offered to make it a rounded one hundred, so that the math would be easier for him to compute. He quickly understood that Hana was not the type to be intimidated easily. The tools he normally used to break the spirits of ill-fated, handcuffed prisoners would be of little value even with the help of the torturing chair. He asked many questions that went unanswered.

"Hana. Such a beautiful name. It means happiness, no?"

"Why do you want to commit suicide, Hana, aren't you happy?"

"Why do you want to kill Jews?

When she remained silent, he changed his tactics. Moving closer to where she was sitting, in that same contorted position, he whispered as if communicating a secret, "Do you know that Samir was a collaborator? He worked for us."

"If my brother was a collaborator, why did he try to kill an officer?" she replied.

"Do you miss your mother, Hana? This poor woman, what did she do to deserve all of this? Do you want us to drag her to prison to bring some sense back to you?"

"I do not miss her. I do not want to see her," she answered.

Out of nowhere, he struck her face with a piercing slap that made her dizzy, and left her with a loud buzzing noise that slowly rose from the back of her head to the front, as if it were a barrier against his obscenities and insults. Getting nowhere with her, he left the room. She stayed in that position for exactly seven hours while the large clock on the wall ticked sluggishly, every passing second feeling like an eternity. On his orders, she was to be taken to the "seven-star dungeon," a pit much deeper underground than the first one. It was the month of Ramadan, and she carried on fasting even after sunset because she did not trust their clocks and her faith was a compass. The second time they interrogated her, the same officer pulled her hair, then hung her from the ceiling for nine hours straight, the tips of her toes barely touching the ground. The third time, the guard who brought her to the interrogation room tried to touch her, and she struck him in the stomach with her left elbow. To make her pay for this, they exiled her to the upper part of the prison populated mostly with Jewish criminals. They fought among themselves in that hell hole, but were united in abusing her. Still, Hana would not eat, so it mattered little if the cook spat into her food, or if an inmate spilled a glass of water slowly into her hair while the others laughed cruelly. On the fourth day she drank some water as she stood before a judge, and she could see her family sitting on the other side of her cage. She was ordered to be interrogated for thirteen more days. On the seventh day, she heard the recording of a woman who sounded just like her mother being tortured, howling in pain. On the ninth day, they told her that a man called Mayhoub had informed on her and that all of his admissions would be used to indict her. Knowing their capacity for endless deceit, she laughed, and was sent to another cell even deeper underground.

"I am Mayhoub," a voice whispered to her from the other side of the wall. He knocked on the wall for hours, repeating the same phrase, "I am Mayhoub." She did not answer, or even move, but kept staring at one point in the darkness, protected by it, as if it were clay to shape whatever colorful world suited her. A few days later, they placed her in front of a man who claimed to be a lawyer hired by her family. He asked her to trust him and reveal everything, but she remained silent. No matter what they tried, what outrageous claims they made, or what torturous methods they used, she was not answering their questions, not even reacting with the slightest facial expression. One day, however, even she could not remain unshaken, for the sight before her was too vile to witness. Male officers were brought in and sat all around her watching pornographic films. She lowered her face to the ground and muttered verses from the Quran to block out the lewd voices and obscenities. It had seemed that there was no lower they could possibly go in their shameless pursuit, but she was wrong.

One time Shamus placed a gun and the keys to his car in front of her, and walked away. Her handcuffs were entirely removed, as if she were being tempted to escape. Hours later he returned, questioning her decision to stay on her chair. "I cannot drive," she answered with a smirk that ignited his wrath once more.

The voices from the cells around her were multiplying.

"I am your brother. Please confess so that they release me."

"I am your cousin ..."

> "I am a member of the Islamic Jihad; I am told it is okay if you wish to confess. All members of the cells have escaped by now."

None of this worked. They resorted again to streaming her mother's tortured voice into her ears. She tried to sleep, but the moment her eyes would shut the knocking would start and the voices would resume, pleading, threatening, screaming, sobbing, for hours, for days. They brought in an Israeli woman disguised as an Arab. Using a fake Jenin accent and a sympathetic manner, she tried to gain Hana's trust and get a confession, but Hana continued to resist, huddled in the corner of her cell and staring into the darkness, conjuring up images only she could see—familiar and comforting memories to keep her sane.

Then the court sentenced her to six months in administrative detention, and Hana was once more exiled to the criminals' ward. But after thirty-five days of abuse, she refused to eat, and was then taken to the lower floors of the HaSharon prison where twenty-seven Palestinian women prisoners were held, some for a few years, others for many more. That prison was once a fort where the British police too had kept their rebellious Palestinian prisoners, before Israel became a state with its own dungeons and scientifically devised torture methods. Hana was kept there for twenty-five months.

Hana would have preferred a life sentence to administrative detention, not because she favored prison over whatever relative freedom Burqin offered, but because this was a form of psychological torture she could not bear. She would count the days to her release, get her clothes in order, celebrate her last day in jail with the inmates, and then stand before military court only to be sent back to prison to serve another term of six months, where she would go through the same stages of emotional torment, hunger, and isolation. The Israelis understood this well, and chose to let her know of the verdict just minutes before her term was due to expire. But the more versed the Israelis became in the art of torture, the more hardened and resilient Hana grew. She began memorizing the Quran, taught to her by a Ukrainian woman who had converted to Islam when she met her Palestinian husband in Kiev years before. He was a student and she was serving pizza at a small restaurant when they fell in love and returned to live in Bethlehem. She had been accused of transporting Arab fighters inside Israel, and was sentenced to twenty years in prison. Arina Sarahna, who refused to go back to Ukraine without her children in exchange for her freedom, became Hana's companion. She taught her Russian, made Arabic sweets and coffee, and led the other female prisoners as they embroidered dresses, scarves, and flags.

After a long-anticipated and grueling wait, Hana was released on October 18, 2011, along with most of the twenty-seven women who were held in HaSharon, and nearly a thousand Palestinian men from prisons across Israel. Their release was the outcome of an agreement between Israel and the Hamas resistance movement in Gaza, after Hamas set free an Israeli soldier captured some years before. Just hours before Hana stepped outside her cell to assume a life of relative freedom, a group of Palestinian women were brought in, blindfolded, handcuffed, frightened, and bewildered, as if they had been plunged into a sea of infinite darkness. Hana felt their pain as she watched them enter. Also left behind were seven women, including Lina, who had asked Hana to breathe in extra Palestinian air on her behalf and to eat more of her favorite food, shawarma, for her sake. The goodbye was bittersweet for the two women after all they had shared.

* * *

The celebrations lasted for months. They started at the government headquarters in Ramallah where Mahmoud Abbas, who presided over the very Palestinian Authority which had arrested Hana a few years earlier, was the first to greet her with a smile and handshake. Cameramen stood in the corner filming his speech about freedom, justice and revolution before he retreated to his fancy mansion. From early morning to late at night a tour of accolades ensued. Hana was bussed to every city she was allowed to freely enter. Everywhere she went in the West Bank, she received certificates that authenticated her heroism. Sometimes she was allowed to leave the West Bank for days or weeks and travel outside Palestine where other Arabs also celebrated her as a hero, and awarded her plaques on which her name was inscribed in golden ink. And when the celebration of her freedom concluded, and all the papers that certified her heroic status were hung on the walls of the family home in Burqin, Hana was arrested once more.

On the day of her second arrest, on February 16, 2012, neither the Israelis nor Hana wanted to go through the same routine again, but Hana was prepared for the worst. She was asked a few questions, and offered no answers. Her captors were brutal and wasted no time, and she was exceptionally determined, having grown thicker skin and a steel will. The Israeli newspaper *Yediot Ahronot* claimed that Hana had been plotting to kidnap a soldier, but Hana had no patience to engage her interrogators in a useless discussion. Her only request was to be searched by a female soldier instead of a male. But the drunken men, with their guns and terrible breath, paid no mind to her humane request. They stripped her completely naked and physically assaulted her, punishing, slapping, and kicking every part of her unclothed body. She fought back, but the handcuffed woman was overwhelmed by the armed, inebriated men. A soldier threw her onto the ground and kicked her face with his boot, and it bled onto her raw, bare skin and dripped down the stairs as they dragged her down once more to her seven-star dungeon.

Hana refused to eat. At first her only demand was justice and a fair trial for the soldiers who abused her, but her appeal was ignored. Then she demanded that Khadir Adnan, who was leading his own hunger strike at the time, be set free. And then she demanded her own freedom. On the fourth day of her strike, she was sentenced to six months of administrative detention. On that day, she learned that Khadir Adnan had suspended his strike for having achieved all of his objectives, and she became more determined than ever to go through with her own. On the fifth day, she was no longer able to stand on her feet to pray and could only do so with the help of one of three women who still inhabited her old prison ward. They included Lina, who tried to persuade Hana to end her strike. But when Hana was placed in solitary confinement, the three women launched their own hunger strike in an act of sisterly solidarity. Their only demand was that Hana be released from her individual cell so that they could look after her. Instead, Hana was punished further, and she was placed with the Israeli criminals once more.

A few days later, she was brought back to join the Palestinian inmates again. She was more fatigued and even paler than before. Luckily, Lina remained as her companion and advocate before the harshness of the guards and the prison administrators who refused to provide Hana with more than one blanket and one dress. They even refused Hana access to clean water. Lina scuffled with them often, and offered Hana her clothes and her blanket. Ironically, the guards were keen for Hana's strike to end, not because of any concern for her or for human rights, but for fear that the streets of Burqin, and all of Palestine would explode in fury if she died. The guards were even offered a raise and a trip to Sharm al-Sheikh in Egypt if anyone could get her to eat somehow. They took turns tormenting her, but as days passed, and as Hana grew physically weaker, her resolve grew stronger. Her gums swelled by day twenty. Her hair fell out by day thirty-five. And only when blood began to pour from her nose was she taken to a Haifa hospital.

A tender breeze rustled through her window and gently caressed her face. Hana opened her eyes. "Where am I?" she asked the nurse. "You are in Haifa," she was told, and Hana smiled. It was the first time in many days, perhaps years, that she had felt joy. "This is the land from which my family came," she said softly as her smile grew wider. Her declaration was communicated to the guards and in turn to the prison authority, which immediately ordered her removal from Haifa. Before that Hana had visited Haifa only in her dreams, but for a fleeting, beautiful moment she believed that she might actually die there. Her request to do so was denied.

Her brain began to hemorrhage blood and it seeped out through her nose, a sign that her death was imminent. She was moved to yet another prison hospital, in Ramleh, and on the thirty-eighth day of her strike she was taken to Me'ir hospital in Kfar Saba, where four soldiers guarded her frail body, which was secured tightly to her hospital bed. On the forty-fourth day she was taken back to Ramleh, where she learned that Thaer Halahleh and Bilal Diab had for weeks been leading their own hunger strikes in solidarity with her, and that hundreds of other prisoners were joining the prison rebellion. Hana's strike got daily news coverage in the Palestinian media, and posters of her image covered the walls of Burqin and all of Palestine. Then one day a lawyer arrived who worked with the Palestinian Authority and that moment sealed her fate. He had her sign a paper stating that she agreed to be deported to Gaza for three years. Hana was disoriented, confusing reality and dreams in those foggy moments. The paper was never found, and when Hana opened her eyes, she found herself in exile, far away from her family, from Burqin, and its beautiful mountains.

* * *

In Hana's new dreams, Samir lived, and time stood still in the innocent days of when she was eight and he was ten. He held her hand and protected her from every harm. In her dreams, it was always spring and Marj Ibn Amer was an endless horizon of Hanoun flowers, where she and Samir would run but never tire; where he wore a white shirt without a single spot of blood, and red was the color only of the Hanoun-shielded meadows. In her dreams, she rode a horse that could never be tamed and she galloped towards a horizon, determined to return to the beginning of her story, to her last earth.

Hana al-Shalabi's confinement was physical. But Sara Saba's confinement was of a different type. A Palestinian Christian born and raised in self-imposed exile, she was taught that she was Palestinian before anything else. Her quest to redeem her identity is similar to that of many Palestinians who are born in the diaspora, or shatta. But hers went a few steps farther. Her strength prevailed, and unlike many other Palestinian refugees, she chose to embark on a journey back to Palestine to reclaim her sense of self and of homeland. Sara told me how she found God, Palestine, and ultimately herself.

5
Jesus of Beit Jala

It was no dream, and no one could tell Sara Saba otherwise. Until this day she can perfectly envision the beautiful Palestinian face that looked down at her from above. She felt his hand caress her long black hair. She remembers the loving and assuring eyes. There was no need for words. His presence silenced all her questions and all her doubts, and brought upon her troubled mind a sense of peace. Her vision, lasting just a second or two, had shaken her belief that he was long dead, or rather had to be dead, or rather still, that she had felt dead inside for as long as she could remember.

"Please God, please God, please God," she had chanted for hours on end after endless nights of broken sleep, while the demons from her past haunted her in the depths of the darkness. But eventually the chants grew tiresome as if she were only going through the motions, unconvinced that He cared or bothered to listen. She had already declared Him non-existent anyway, she told her friends that God was dead to her. Where had He been when she needed him most? How could He sit there above the clouds and watch her fall victim to the violent whims of her father for so long?

"Please God, please God, please God." She still needed Him. Everyone else had turned their back on her. Even her mother, a sweet woman without a grain of self-confidence or the strength to resist her fears, was oblivious to her daughter's pleas for help. She could not help Sara because she could barely help herself, and so Sara felt no anger but only compassion towards her mother. Only God could send Sara to sleep and end her suffering. And as much as she tried to forget about Him, it was impossible. Growing up with a mother who taught her to make the sign of the cross when she passed in front of a church ingrained a faith in her Christian soul no matter how hard she suppressed it.

It had been four nights of interrupted sleep, or no sleep at all. Though her mantra persisted, her faith had begun to fade months ago. And just when her murmurs grew muffled, he appeared. When she first felt His touch, she expected to see her mother, and she opened her heavy eyelids and turned towards the bedroom door. But her mother was not there. Her door was closed and her eyes were open, wide open. The gentle stroking of her hair began suddenly, but it did not startle her. She let it happen. When she turned around and looked at the wall beside her bed, she saw him. She blinked once, and he was still there. It was Jesus. She was sure of it. He was the same Palestinian Jesus of Beit Jala; that familiar, tortured, handsome face adorning all the ancient churches that she had visited back in her homeland. He must have traveled all of that distance, passed through the checkpoints, evaded the immigration officers, and arrived at her bedside to assure her not only of his existence, but of the preciousness of her life as well.

"Please God, show me your mercy, and let me fall asleep," were her last words before Jesus arrived in the suburbs of Melbourne, Australia, to answer her prayers and numb her pain. She could not recall another time when she had slept so deeply. And when she awoke, she was more convinced than ever that the night before was not just a hallucination or dream. He was there to reconcile the battles she was fighting alone, and to show her that her search for identity and meaning had bridged the distance between Beit Jala and Melbourne. He was there to show her that God is living, and He is loving.

* * *

It was not exactly an identity crisis that tore Sara apart. It was something far more complex. She was born in Melbourne, and could not have asked to have been raised in a more agreeable and exciting place. It is a city of unpredictable landscapes and erratic weather where one can never really be sure what to expect or what to wear. Here the concrete blocks and hipster laneways intersect in a seamless disarray and the four seasons can manifest themselves in a single afternoon. Sure, winters in Melbourne can be disappointing, for the frigid cold is never accompanied by even an inch of snow to make it look like a white wonderland. But the sun here is hotter than in most parts of Aussie land, bringing the kind of warmth that, coupled with the infinite meadows and rolling hills, is entrancing and liberating. Yet the contradictions between this place and Beit Jala are unavoidable. "What's the point of a tree so big if it doesn't even yield fruit?" her Uncle George once said, pointing out the difference between Beit Jala's relatively small trees with their generous yield of fruit, and Melbourne's eucalyptus trees which are massive and unproductive domineering works of nature, whose roots cause damage to the urban infrastructure.

Sara was not born in the city itself but in its quiet suburbs, on May 17, 1991. She was the first born of Linda and Iyad, and was followed by Charlie and Tina. Her family struggled from the first day they arrived in Australia, and their struggle never truly ceased. Whether it was language, cultural navigation, or feeling forever like one of them had a foot on the gas pedal and another on the brake, Sara was far from being an average Australian girl. None of her friends had as many responsibilities as she did. She was already bogged down by many problems of her own. But she was smart and eventually learned to manage her dual identity quite efficiently, despite the nagging feelings simmering deep down that this country was never really "home." Whatever the circumstance required, she could be Palestinian, Australian, or both. Did she really have to choose?

Unlike the suburbs of Melbourne, the homes of Beit Jala do not all look the same, and the history of that ancient Palestinian city is far more intriguing. Beit Jala's tumultuous history has been both a curse and a blessing. Many centuries ago, the town was known as Apezala, during the age of the Crusaders who invaded Palestine and eventually fled when Arab armies chased them back to Europe and wherever else they came from. As far back as recorded memory can trace, Beit Jala was largely Arab and Christian. And when the modern Palestinian identity began to evolve over the course of centuries, it was readily incorporated into the collective identity of the Bajajleh, as Sara likes to call the people of Beit Jala, who saw themselves as intrinsically linked to the Holy Land. No one could ever dare say otherwise.

And Beit Jala was indeed special, at least for Sara. That small town, tucked away only a few miles south of Jerusalem, has sat opposite Bethlehem for millennia and has never abandoned its innocence. It remained authentic in its heritage and traditions, like an open-air museum watched over by its caring residents. These disciples of Jesus wanted the simple things in life like the rest of God's children, so they married and had children. But for some, the challenge of leaving was simpler than the challenge of staying. Many sought asylum in Australia to escape the biting grip of poverty and war. Yet, despite the waves of outward emigration, and the eventual Israeli army takeover, a decisive majority of the town's small population remained Christian followers of the Orthodox Church. Though many Christians were forced out of Palestine, Christianity never abandoned Palestine, and it remained particularly rooted in

Beit Jala where Jesus once roamed speaking the word of God, teaching love and forgiveness, and comforting the outcasts.

The charm of Beit Jala derives from an inimitable simplicity. Sara was struck by its energy during her first visit to Palestine when she was a young child, when she met the people who shared her bloodline and her name. With all her family's kissing and cuddling, and proudly being shown off to all the neighbors, she was transformed from the awkward "foreign" kid who spoke no English on her first day of school, to a popular child who learned more about herself in this faraway place than she ever did in the land of her birth. Her many cousins in Beit Jala led her through the town's ancient roads in a seemingly endless procession where Palestinian sweets were offered at every turn, and where older kids took turns carrying her around despite her protests. Her Uncle George was right, El-Rass was the highest point of Beit Jala, and when she stood on the roof of the family's old house she could see as far as the Mediterranean Sea. Over the years, on her four visits to Beit Jala, Sara learned that air could be sweet and free of the suffocating fumes from cars and factories. For her, Beit Jala became a beautiful blend of scents from olive, apricot, and fig trees, while ancient scraggly sanasels and white-stoned, flat-roofed houses scattered in the hills opened her heart to the wisdom of this ancient land.

It was clear that the ancient Bajajleh did not build their city anticipating war nor seeking one. It was never a fortress and it could never be. Invaders came and went—the Crusaders, the Ottomans, the British, and the Israelis—yet Beit Jala remained committed to a peaceful existence. Its sloped land, carpeted with green grass, is divided into lots that are passed from one generation to the other, mostly Christian, but also Muslim peasants who had little interest in expansion or the accumulation of wealth. The city remained quiet even when the Israelis devised a concrete wall that was massive, oppressive, divisive, and ever-growing. It eventually found its way to the land of the Bajajleh, depriving them of their most prized farms and threatening their very existence. Many fought back, and the Bajajleh never thought of abandoning their old homes and their ancient churches. They knew from hard-earned experience that invaders, no matter how strong or how well-armed, no matter how brutal their tactics or how long their stay in Beit Jala, would eventually leave.

* * *

Sara's grandparents were committed to that place. They would never have thought to break ties with that ancient town no matter how difficult things might become. Jamil was born in 1910, in the final years of the Ottoman Empire when Palestine, along with all of Ottoman Syria, was divided into administrative divisions called Sanjaks. The Jerusalem Sanjak included Bethlehem, Beit Jala and Gaza. Along with Nablus and Akka Sanjaks, the three regions constituted modern Palestine. But Jamil was too young to remember the Ottomans and the colonial intrigues of that period. His childhood memories were of the British who had occupied Palestine and imposed themselves as caretakers when he was ten years old.

Back then most Palestinians were concerned with survival, and the young Jamil had no other choice but to leave school after second grade to work in construction. The war had left many scars on Palestinian towns and, as had been the practise in past wars, every invader arrived with ambitious plans to construct their own government buildings, police stations and prisons. But in reality they were masking the damage they had inflicted upon the inhabitants and their humble homes. Brick by brick, Jamil negotiated his existence from his days as a young boy to those of a young man ready to start his own family.

Then came Nabeeha. "She is as sweet as an angel," Jamil was told by the elder women of the family. And it was true. They were married and had seven children in the following order: Musa, Nabil, George, Maria, Linda, Issa, and Iyad. The last was Sara's father. Raising this number of children was incredibly difficult on the unreliable income of a cheap laborer. Nabeeha had no choice but to go to work in a biscuit factory outside town. When she came home after a long day's work, the children would be waiting anxiously for their happiest moment of the day. Surrounding her and tugging at her dress, they demanded their share of the damaged biscuits that she was allowed to take home at the end of her shift.

Jamil and Nabeeha could have continued like that for a long time, and in fact they had planned to educate some of their children. But the war of 1948 forcefully displaced hundreds and thousands of refugees throughout the region, and sent the Saba family back into survival mode. To their dismay, the children, some of them teenagers and others too young to work, had to leave school. They ended up in various odd jobs to make a living while death hovered over Palestine.

Eventually life took its toll and they both died in Beit Jala. Nabeeha died in 1973 at a young age from an unexplained illness, and in 1992 Jamil died an old man from Alzheimer's disease. In his final years, the Alzheimer's ravaged most of his memory and motor skills, but whenever he stood on the roof of his house and gazed at his surroundings, his own village, Bethlehem, Jerusalem and on a clear summer's day, the Mediterranean Sea itself, peace would be restored in his heart. Beit Jala had been his home and that of his ancestors ever since Jesus walked upon its grassy hills, two thousand years before the Israelis came and stole his land.

The last of Jamil and Nabeeha's children was Iyad. He was born in 1961 when the West Bank was still administrated by Jordan. Iyad's early memories were of the Israeli invasion of what remained of historic Palestine. In 1967, Beit Jala fell under Israeli occupation and was strangely united into one single entity containing Palestinians who were once divided between the three Ottoman Sanjaks, and later between Israel- and Arab-administrated regions. But they were still militarily occupied and collectively oppressed. It was around that time when the Sabas began leaving Palestine. First George left in 1973, and then Issa a few years later. Iyad followed suit in 1983. All of them arrived in Melbourne, the land of those tall eucalyptus trees that bore no fruit.

Sara's bond to her Uncle George was always strong. It was through him, not from Iyad and Linda, that she first learned about Palestine and the meaning of diaspora. George was born two years after the Nakba and the pain in his heart over the loss of his homeland had shattered his sense of belonging to anywhere else. Food was scarce when George was born, and although the family was spared the pain of exile, at least at that stage, they were badly affected by the consequences of war. The famine-like hunger, the lack of medical care, and the general insecurity were among the horrors that they faced. George was as thin as a stick and lived a childhood of poverty and sickness. When his mother, Nabeeha, suddenly died in 1973, it was devastating for the whole family. None of them would recover completely, especially the younger ones. The sweet angel of the biscuit factory was no longer there to assure her offspring that all the trials of life were a part of God's plan. No longer could she promise that things would ultimately work out, and that justice and peace would finally prevail. Only months after she passed away, George escaped Palestine with his young wife, Angel. Together they embarked on a new life in Australia and opened a small milk bar. Apart from the culture shock and trying to understand customers ordering in their Aussie slang, the tiny convenience store served as a base for many of the Sabas who came to Australia.

When Sara was born, both her parents worked long hours to make a living. There was little time for baby Sara from the tender age of six months. Until this day Sara does not understand exactly what they did at work. Their job titles were "machine operators," yet what machines they operated and for what purpose remains a mystery. Much of the first six years of her life were spent at the home of her Uncle George and Aunt Angel. They taught her how to speak Arabic with a Bajjali accent, told her hundreds of Palestinian fables that had been told by thousands of Palestinians before them, and took her on weekend trips around Victoria. Because of them, she could say that at least some of her childhood was happy. The relationship was a perfect match: George and Angel had no children of their own, and Sara hated her parents' home with all her heart.

Aside from sporadic happy moments, her parents seemed to live in perpetual misery. As the years passed, Iyad's temper turned violent and Linda was at the receiving end of it. With time she learned to remain quiet as Iyad raged, blaming her and everyone else for his suffering. Deep down Sara understood it was the mark of a man who could not love and accept himself and consequently, anyone else. What Sara couldn't understand was why her mother remained silent when her children were the subject of that abuse; or when little Sara's head was smashed against a concrete wall until it burst open, bleeding; or when her face was hit with determined blows; or when her body was bruised by the metal buckle of a leather belt. His violent words produced the deepest scars of all. Sara felt nothing but pity for him. Though she was still very young, she understood that his anger was a mask that hid the true face of a man who feared his past. Sara dreamed of a father who was loving, supportive, accepting and most of all, honest with himself and with his family.

"Why are Uncle George and my father so different from each other, when both were born in the same town and to the same parents?" Sara often asked herself. When Nabeeha died in 1973, Iyad was only twelve years old. As the youngest of all the children, he was spoiled according to Beit Jala's natural order of things. But everything changed when his mother suddenly passed away. The father's grief was so profound that he could not heal the wounds that afflicted his children, especially the youngest of them, and especially Iyad. With no school education and no skills other than basic carpentry, Iyad fled to Australia. When he arrived in 1983, he had no sense of purpose or direction. He was angry and confused by this new and different world. God spoke a different language there and the cold churches were largely empty. From being a coddled young boy, brimming with his family's attentions, he found himself lost on the other side of the world.

Returning home to Beit Jala was not an option. It offered little work and a violent military occupation. Yet Australia was an impossible, frightening, and alien place. This was felt not only by Iyad, but also by his brothers and their families. To cope with this sense of banishment, the family referred to everyone in Australia who was not Arab as an *ajnabi*—a foreigner. It was a strange conciliation, but it served the family well during those first years.

So Sara grew up hearing the word *ajnabi* very often and the ramifications were palpable. Before she started school, she believed the word referred to an entirely separate breed of humans. Later she realized that they were speaking of the Australians, and that it was her father's way of keeping her rooted in Palestinian tradition and identity in this strange new land. Whenever she asked why she was not allowed to join her friends camping, swimming, or on sleepovers, the answer was always "because they are *ajaneb*." She knew there was Palestinian Arab blood flowing through her veins, but Sara, frustrated, was also a young Australian girl. On her second trip to Palestine, she would discover that ironically Palestinian girls her age had more freedom than she did, and this made her love that country all the more.

Perhaps Iyad and Linda's attitude was the result of their own denial of the reality that they were no longer in Palestine, and that they were, in fact, now foreigners in a peculiar land. So Sara started school not speaking a word of English. It was not a deliberate attempt by her parents to deny her the language of their host country, but they themselves, even after years of living there, had not mastered it. In time, Sara found herself assuming the family responsibility as the unofficial interpreter, form-filler, telephone operator and problem-solver. More and more, her parents relied on her for every little English-related thing, and she resented them for it. It was not just about the daily burdens of a child having to bargain with a gas company over a high energy bill, or with the welfare office over a problem with family welfare payments. Sara resented the social disconnect that her parents, Iyad in particular, had imposed on themselves. It was as if they were caught between two different worlds, unable to claim that they belonged to either. They were displaced and painfully alienated, and Sara was suspended in mid-air trying to put her feet on the ground.

* * *

Two years before Sara was born, a group of Bajajleh in Melbourne formed an organization for people who had left the village; it was a way to ease the hardship of being so far from Palestine. They called it the Beit Jala Palestinian Association. Bajajleh's voyagers had set up associations worldwide from South America to various African countries, and of course, in the West and Asia. Exile from their homeland, from that village on the side of a green Palestinian hill because of military occupation and conflict, had embittered them, compounded their fears, and advanced their sense of loneliness. They needed a kind of virtual Palestine to alleviate their isolation; a place to get together and dance, to eat the delicacies of Beit Jala, to teach their kids *dabka* (an Arabic folk dance), and to talk about home and of course, politics. They also fundraised for various causes, particularly Beit Jala schools and charities, especially when they felt helpless, or perhaps guilty for not taking direct part in the collective burdens of their village and its people's constant struggle to maintain its Arab-Christian identity. The moments of happiness they shared were often interrupted by pangs of guilt for what they had left behind.

Sara remembers the association during its heyday, before the kids got tired of performing *dabka* and the members grew bored of their same old stories. The association, no matter how authentic, was not Beit Jala and a true sense of home could not be recreated. No matter how hard they tried, home was somewhere else—somewhere besieged, overwhelmed, but surviving.

But when times were good, Sara danced with the rest of the Bajajleh, she giggled and ran in circles and wore her special Beit Jala thoub embroidered with its unique designs and colors. Sure, she also rolled her eyes quite often: when the older Bajajleh would break suddenly into prolonged *mawaal* songs (originally an Egyptian form of vocal music), triggered by a little too much alcohol; or when the old people would jump on the podium, stand shoulder to shoulder and perform a less energetic form of *dabka*, one that was more intimate and draped with sorrow and nostalgia. In their songs, life was simple. Themes were centered on rich harvests and the love of shy women with long eyelashes. In their lyrics, there were no soldiers, Ottomans, British, or Israelis; and no walls had sneaked upon them like a snake poisoning their humble existence, stealing the joys of life and, sometimes life itself.

There was another reason why the association grew lackluster with time, hosted fewer parties, fundraisers and other social opportunities where the Beit Jala women could wear their traditional thoubs and men their finest outfits. It related to Sara's generation who were born in Melbourne, spoke with Australian accents and did not remember with fondness the "good old days." For them, the pain of exile was much less, if it was present at all. But it never escaped them that they were not fully fledged Australians, whatever that identity entailed, nor were they real Bajajleh either. Their funny Arabic accents were often ridiculed by their elders. They did not break into song when sorrow proved too overwhelming. Images of modestly clad, beautiful-eyed women with long eyelashes, fetching water from the village well, were not a part of this younger generation's identity or sense of belonging.

Sara's parents were determined that she would grow up to defy that norm by recognizing herself as a Palestinian Arab Christian from Beit Jala. But they could not protect her entirely. Sara's understanding of herself came into question one day when her second-grade teacher Mrs. Levy asked her pupils a simple question: "Where do your ancestors come from?"

The exercise was meant to highlight the wonderful fusion of cultures that Australia is supposed to represent. Mrs. Levy had planned to have the children color the flags of the countries that their families had come from, and then hang them around the classroom. It was a testament to inclusion and multiculturalism in which Mrs. Levy strongly believed. Yet all of that ended when Sara declared enthusiastically: "I am from Palestine."

Sara did not know that Mrs. Levy was Jewish. Even if she had known, she would not have cared or have even understood the layered meanings of that identity in relation to Sara's as a Palestinian Arab and Mrs. Levy, according to some, her political antithesis. Until that moment, Grade 2 had been quite uneventful. Sara had focused hard on school. She was always happy there, away from her stressful home life. Sara's English skills were constantly improving and aside from her father's violent temper, things were going quite well for her.

But when Mrs. Levy said that "there was no such thing as Palestine," and immediately moved on to another student, ignoring Sara's bewildered expression, something inside the little girl forever changed. It could not be that Iyad had been lying to her all of her life, and that her mother and even Uncle George were part of a conspiracy to convince her that she was something she was not. And for what purpose? So that she would be denied sleepovers and swimming pool parties with the "foreign" kids of Melbourne? Palestine was a fact. She relived the memories of her visit. She had been there. She had smelled the fruit trees and tasted the dried thyme and olive oil and had dipped her falafel into the home-made hummus. She had seen the villages and the welcoming children who spent their entire summer vacations plotting ways to acquire candy, and the kind village elders whose kisses left traces of a unique and ancient scent. Palestine had its own gods that all got along just fine; in Palestine mosques made calls to prayer and church bells rang loudly, summoning deep spiritual reflection among believers. Palestinian Jesus may have looked tortured and dazed as portrayed in Beit Jala's many churches, but he was kind and he said gentle things about the poor, and he called on those who went astray to return to God's Kingdom.

When Sara returned home, she threw her heavy backpack on the kitchen floor and told her parents that Mrs. Levy had denied the existence of Palestine. A crisis meeting was hurriedly assembled, bringing George and Angel and other Bajajleh into Iyad and Linda's small living room. The men spoke angrily and the women, folding their hands above their bellies, shook their heads in silent disapproval. The family council declared that Mrs. Levy must not be allowed to impose her bias against common sense, and that Sara should respond saying this and that and a thousand other things. Of course, no one spoke enough English to compose an articulate message to Mrs. Levy, leaving little Sara alone with the task of challenging the insufferable teacher with retorts such as "Jesus was Palestinian," and "Palestine was mentioned in the Bible," and that Palestine had a flag, and a map, and a people, and so on. Ultimately, it mattered little whether the flag of Palestine was to join the other crayon-colored flags in the classroom. For Sara Palestine had to exist, because without it Sara was lost, neither here nor there, trapped in the margins of many cultures and homelands, never home.

* * *

It would be no exaggeration to say that Mrs. Levy's denial of Sara's Palestine was the spark that inspired a seven-year-old girl's ceaseless search for identity, and in some way altered the course of her life. Sara Saba's search for "home" from that day forward took on many manifestations, not merely personal, political, or even nationalistic, but spiritual as well. If Palestine did not exist, did it mean that Jesus himself, a Palestinian, was a figment of the imagination of a group of Bajajleh in Melbourne who wasted a great deal of time fixating on a homeland that did not even deserve a crayon-colored flag of its own? Was it a collective denial of something deeper? Was there really a God?

When she got older and could intellectualize her crisis, Sara spent a year and a half of her university studies immersing herself in a more eloquent rendering of that very question she had pondered as a little girl. She wrote an 18,000-word honors thesis defining "home." The outcome was quite coherent, but largely removed from her reality, because her life was more complex than that of the rest of her Bajajleh–Aussie compatriots. For some of them, "home" was the antithesis of exile. To discover her own relationship with her homeland, she needed to first articulate what exile meant:

> "According to Alejandro Vallega the meaning of exile originates from the unchanging nature of roots, origins, the concept of the native homeland and the ideas and influences that arise from these notions. In this view what is fixed is not the actual experience of exile itself as this is subjective. It is the unchanging origins found in the native homeland that the exile wishes to remain in or to return to that is concrete. In the circumstance that a person is forcibly removed from their place of familiarity and exposed to a new environment, what occurs in most cases is the exclusion from inherent influences found in bloodlines, family, friends, language and religion."

Is that why the Bajajleh came together and sang about a place called Beit Jala, and of beautiful Palestinian maidens with long eyelashes fetching water from the village well? Is that why Iyad and Linda kept calling everyone who was outside the confines of their culture "foreigners"? Were they afraid that by embracing their exile, they would cease to belong to a collective idea called Palestine? If the key issue is exile, which cannot be resolved until the homeland is restored to the Bajajleh and reclaimed in its original form, how could Sara claim her own Palestine, and hang its flag proudly?

> "As Edward Said further argues; 'Exile has a special role to play in the tumultuous relationship the human has with his or her native homeland. It acts as a rift or a barricade, 'between the self and its true home', restraining the person from residing in a place of comfort."

Is this why Iyad lost his mind, and why Linda seemed so removed from Melbourne all those years, speaking little English and sending Sara to school with za'tar sandwiches for lunch? Was grasping onto the past and that which was familiar to them simply an exercise of self-preservation? When the kids asked Sara what was the olive-oil-dowsed green powder pita bread sandwich that she was eating, she had no answer—there was no real cultural equivalent in Australia, at least to her knowledge. Her mother, who with her inadequate vocabulary suggested "tell them it is grass," did not know that because of this response, Sara, the girl with unruly, curly hair and a funny accent, would be the object of ridicule for days. The Arab girl who ate grass was not exactly popular to begin with, especially since, as it turned out, her country of origin had an imaginary flag and never existed in the first place.

> "Home, according to Madan Sarup, is a place that provides unconditional love, security, comfort, identity, stability and warmth, a place that is familiar, where there is no need for roles to be assumed by anyone. For each individual, home is defined and identified with on different levels. What it constitutes of exactly and whether the image created is real or imagined is not so important."

But Sara had little of that in her life. Melbourne never felt like home, no matter how familiar the place was, how nice the houses were or how easy it was to walk around the flat land. Palestine, for many years, remained frozen as an image that was approximate, reduced through the drama of daily news to a prolonged conflict that often mirrored the conflict in Sara's own heart.

With time, Sara's Palestine became a mere construct of a homeland. It was draped in sadness, familial conflict, grass-like za'tar sandwiches, the gossip of the Bajajleh and their sweaty group dances, philosophical concepts conjured up by dead poets, an embroidered map in the corner of her family's living room, a framed flag that was recognized mostly by the Bajajleh themselves, and the tortured face of Jesus of Beit Jala whose agony was inherited by all the Bajajleh since the time he passed through on the slope of a hill, preaching about peace and his Father's Heavenly Kingdom.

* * *

Sara's first trip to Palestine was in April 1995. She was four, and her world was a more innocent place. She accompanied her mother and Auntie Angel who went to Beit Jala via the Allenby Bridge that separated Jordan from the Israeli-occupied West Bank. Her memories of that trip are hazy. The three of them waited at the Bridge for many hours, and when they finally got to Beit Jala their much-anticipated arrival was met by a barrage of wet kisses and tight, warm, bothersome hugs. She was kissed the most, first by her grandmother, then uncles and aunts and every member of the extended family and neighbors; then everyone else all over again. Once she became used to the invasion of personal space, Sara basked in the glory of being a returnee from Australia who wore the kind of fancy, unfamiliar outfits that only "foreigners" wore, and charmingly mixing her Bajajleh Arabic with a few English words and phrases she had picked up from watching television. As unfamiliar as the surroundings were, it soon felt more like home than anything she had felt before.

For Sara, this home was a place of endless, unmitigated fun, unmatched even by the largest, cordoned "play areas" that Melbourne's malls had to offer. She roamed the streets with her cousins and newfound friends feeling free and loved; spent countless hours making messes of her relatives' homes and throwing parties with other kids her age under an old, shady mulberry tree and basked in the flavors of Palestinian fare that tasted more real than the imports back home. Her first weekend in Beit Jala coincided with Easter. The festivities were not commercialized like the ones in Australia, and their spirituality was strong under the warm sun and blue skies; churches, cheerfully adorned with colors and lights, rang their bells playing songs that Sara had learned back in Melbourne; the faithful dressed in their finest attire and called to one another from verandas, church windows and on the street: *El Maseeh kam, hakan kam!*—Jesus Christ Has Risen! Truly, He Is Risen!

Home was warmth and friendly faces of people who would stop and hug one another at every corner and at every chance; where mosques kept track of time and their calls to prayer followed the movements of the sun; and where small churches, filled with harmonious hymns, huddled among the poor houses as they have for a thousand years. Sara was not a foreigner here, she was as Palestinian as everyone else and the feeling held fast. Yet as Sara fell in love with her new home, the reality of life called her back and she was once more uprooted to the other world that she had come from; where an angry dad barked orders; a submissive mom held her hands helplessly in front of her; and where "foreigners" walked the streets without even saying hello to the few Bajajleh of Melbourne who met every month to eat, dance, and retell the same old stories.

The hazy but happy memories of Sara's first visit to Beit Jala came back whenever life became hard in Melbourne and whenever she felt like she belonged nowhere. The source of her pain was not only the sense of alienation that by then had been deeply rooted in the Saba family psyche, but also from her parents' fighting, or more accurately, her father's verbal and physical abuse of her mother. The discord in the family was constant, but by spending time at her Uncle George's house, Sara was shielded from much of the conflict during her early years, and this was a Godsend. At least she had those joyous moments to teach her that not everything had to be suffering. Every child deserved that. And she was not to blame for the mess her dad had created.

When she grew older, however, she became more aware of the commotion and the horrifying insults, and she could remain silent no longer. When Sara finally collected her courage to stand up to her father in defense of her mother, she in turn became a party to the conflict and the dynamics within their family forever changed. Grabbing Sara's carefully braided hair, he tossed her across the room, slapped her and accused her of all sorts of unspeakable things. There was no rationalizing with him. One day Sara would learn to accept that and be at peace, but in the meantime, the courageous fourteen-year-old young girl, compelled by love for her mother to defend her, became the focus of her father's cruelty.

It became a life of horror, an almost daily show of mistreatment and abuse that even Uncle George could do little about and only God himself could stop. If only Sara could find the prayer that would end it all.

> "Not only so, but we also glory in our sufferings, because we know that suffering produces perseverance; perseverance, character; and character, hope. And hope does not put us to shame, because God's love has been poured out into our hearts through the Holy Spirit, who has been given to us."

Hope indeed arrived in the form of a second visit to Palestine. It was in December 2008, when Sara was sixteen years of age. She had just finished Year ten at school. The unkindness of her father was reaching a point where Sara was on the verge of declaring that God was dead, and where she was praying for her own demise. Instead, it was a winter that transformed her life into one where new possibilities existed. Unlike her first visit as a young child, in the memories of which home was a cluster of happy flashbacks, this time she was old enough to truly experience Beit Jala and the rest of Palestine on a whole new level. It was a gift to meet her family properly and understand their problems, their virtues, their struggles, and their pride. It was a time to converse with her elders to pray in the town's ancient churches and connect with the God she was beginning to doubt. Moreover, home took on yet another meaning. It was a temporary respite, although not a salvation from abuse. As soon as she arrived in Beit Jala, she jumped out of the car and ran into her uncle's place. Unlike her last visit, she was the one who initiated the hugging and kisses. She was home again and it felt so good.

She also fell in love—her first love. It was not his physical charm that appealed to her, rather the kind look in his eyes that made her feel safe. Serendipity cast its magic in Beit Jala when they met in this unexpected encounter. In the twinkling of an eye she knew without a doubt that she loved him, intensely, madly, uncontrollably. Her love was so deep that it shattered all the hate for her father that had crowded her heart and all the resentment of a world into which she was born but never belonged. A few weeks later, she left the boy with a simple goodbye, a nervous touch of hands and many lessons that would eventually help her to free herself from emotional insecurity. She had grown as a person and as a budding young woman growing closer to full self-possession and self-love. But there was no escaping the reality that her Palestinian dream-life had to come to an end. She packed her bags full of memories and heartfelt souvenirs and was uprooted once more, back to what was increasingly looking like a dismal life where neither love nor warmth existed, and where God was all but dead.

Sara never learned to tolerate abuse, nor internalize it as a normal part of life. Deep down she knew there were alternatives to the silent suffering. On her worst days, she thought about suicide, but did not muster the strength to act on her urges. Or maybe it was just the opposite; maybe it was precisely her strength that stopped her from making such a mistake. Her prayers grew less convincing as her faith weakened and withered. Following a particularly horrible night at home when her mother's hair was pulled in a most humiliating and painful way and her father beat her senseless, Sara finally declared that God no longer exists. In her mind, not only did God cease to live in Melbourne, but in Beit Jala as well. Despite this sense of loss, Beit Jala continued to offer a breathing space that made Sara long for any opportunity to return. Looking forward to that independence kept her going.

In December 2011, she traveled again to Beit Jala for the third time. This trip was filled with painful contradictions. As much as she longed to see her Beit Jala family once more and reunite with the young man she had loved and left there three years earlier, at her father's stubborn insistence he joined her this time, leaving Linda behind. Sara was devastated. Torn between two worlds, one welcoming and the other painful, home took on yet another new meaning as a place for tragic, helpless, doomed love. For forty-five days, Sara experienced those contradictions, and every day it made her cry. The physical abuse, and the mental torture followed her to Beit Jala, and it was relentless. It reached a point where suicide became a real possibility rather than a passing thought. But a glimpse of sweet, innocent love helped her survive the agony of abuse. This moment took place on December 30 when Sara experienced her first kiss. Sure, it did not wash away her misery, but for an eternal minute all her pain came to a sudden pause. It was a moment she would remember and cherish. Their love could not be sustained once she returned to the other side of the world, and they both knew that. So it ended just like that. But without love and God, there was nothing that was worth living or fighting for, not in Beit Jala and certainly not in Melbourne.

* * *

On her return to the Melbourne suburbs where all the houses looked the same and where the trees were large but bore no fruit, Sara finally hit rock bottom. She lay in the bathtub crying, with a determined plan to end it all right there and then. This time she meant it and she had all the tools she needed: a small towel to cover her mouth and mute her screams, a large bottle of disinfectant to poison her body, and a wooden cross to redeem her soul in the slight possibility of God's existence. Though she was tempted by the sweet release of death and the end of her misery, she was torn by guilt for the anguish that her mother, sister and brother would inherit for the rest of their lives. Unsure if she was about to commit the most selfish act of all, many thoughts and questions crossed her mind in a flash of images. What have they done to suffer so that her suffering may cease? Should she leave a note? What would she say?

"Dear Mother, Tina and Charlie ..."

She could not think of anything else to say. In fact, nothing could be said to justify what she was about to do.

"Why am I asking myself so many questions? Why is it always about others and not about myself?" she thought as her body stiffened, and she gave herself a final push to execute her plans. She reached for the bottle, unscrewed the cap and brought it to her lips.

"Is this how I want it to end?"

As the moment of delirium peaked, something stopped her and a wave of lucidity set in. She could not do it, like the time when she sat with a razor over her wrist but lost the courage to make the deadly cut; or when she held the open bottle of methylated spirits and failed to drink the poison. But this was it. She decided that this would be the last time that she would contemplate doing such harm to herself. On that same night she saw Jesus.

Sara knew he was the Jesus of Beit Jala because he looked exactly like his image adorning the ancient churches of the Palestinian town. He appeared for just a second or two, and a single loving stroke of his hand upon her hair gave Sara enough courage to make a stand the next morning, file a complaint with the police, march to court with her mother and demand freedom for herself and for Linda, Tina, and Charlie. The fears that had been crippling her were suddenly gone and her innate self-worth and dignity came back to her.

It had been a long and agonizing journey. Her father had tried to resolve his own life crises at the expense of his family. What had young Sara done to deserve all the torment? Surely Iyad was also tormented, but whether he had made his own choices or they were made for him, Sara was not to blame for his pain, his mother's early death, his exile, his split between Gods and places and languages and everything else. Why is it that people hurt the ones they love the most? And even when they know it is wrong, why do they continue? Sara would often ponder such questions, but was yet to find the answers.

God returned to Sara, but as quickly as he appeared, he was gone again. Day by day, Sara grew closer to Him and in July 2014, she decided to embark on her journey to find love and home and retrieve her God. There was no better place to seek that personal and spiritual salvation but in that Palestinian town on the side of a hill. This time, there was no turning back. Her beloved was waiting for her. She intended to hold his hand and kiss him a thousand times or more. God was also waiting, and His appearance this time was likely to last, beyond a second or two, for eternity.

Life was a beautiful routine in Palestine filled with effortless pleasures. She stayed with her mother's side of the family and spent precious mornings drinking hot mint tea with her grandmother. When no one was looking, she would sneak to the corner shop for her daily dosage of falafel, hummus, and pita bread. An incredible sense of self-reliance beamed through her as she walked everywhere by herself, took taxis back and forth to the town square, and went to Bethlehem and Jerusalem to see the Holy Land's treasures.

Though it was difficult to ignore, she did her best to overlook the ugly concrete walls that loomed over Palestinian existence like an ominous nightmare. She did not want to give the occupiers any satisfaction by getting upset, especially regarding the Jewish settlements that had been constructed on stolen land where the ruins of Palestinian olive trees languished under the earth. These lifeless structures looked like the Melbourne suburbs where all houses looked the same. Sara organized her reality and fashioned her "home" exactly the way she wanted. Home was the freedom to love and be loved. It was the ultimate redemption. But this tranquility came to an end when the most brutal of wars erupted that summer. The skies turned grey as Palestinians united and mourned for Gaza. Hundreds of people were slaughtered every day; entire families were blown up while protecting their babies; and the face of Jesus Christ of Beit Jala was more distraught than ever.

Hidad (mourning) was declared repeatedly, but the victims were too many and three days did not seem sufficient to cry for their stolen souls. And Gaza, that place that has stood as a testament to Palestine's pain for all of God's children since the days Jesus taught love and shared wine among his disciples, was hurting and bleeding. Sara could do nothing except pray, and she was grateful that she had found God again; at least she could talk to Him. The skies of Beit Jala in July and August were always brilliant blue and sunny, but not when Gaza was slowly dying. They were shrouded in dark clouds and the people wore black clothes and implored Jesus for mercy. Sara recalled her most trusted of prayers and repeated them nonstop. She prayed with all of her heart which pounded with anticipation at the sound of bells tolling and the calls of the mosques summoning the devoted to prayer. She knew that the God she had seen, who helped her redeem her soul, would have to stand up for Gaza; its pain, abuse, and loneliness mirrored all too well all that Sara had experienced.

> "And after you have suffered a little while, the God of all grace, who has called you to his eternal glory in Christ, will himself restore, confirm, strengthen, and establish you."

The news from Gaza was worsening by the day. Alongside the scathing broadcasts came thousands of harrowing images of dead children and of resolute men and women, Palestinians just like her, who stood and fought to the bitter end for a new beginning. Home had become a place where injustice was resisted, despite the pain. Sara knew that also.

When a truce was reached, and Gazans roamed the streets removing rubble and collecting their fallen martyrs, Sara was ready to go back to Melbourne, albeit a changed woman. On her last evening in Beit Jala, she stood on the flat roof of her grandmother's house, sipped strong Arabic coffee, and shared the moonlit evening with the man she loved, even as she knew there was no future for them together. She was at peace with herself. God had a plan for her as her grandmother, Nabeeha, used to teach her children. Though it would be marked with challenges, Sara was beginning to see a future ahead; a path where pain and love were destined to walk hand-in-hand along a Via Dolorosa of anguish and deliverance until the end. She learned how damaging and beautiful love could be; that whilst weeping for its victims, Palestine could also put her children to sleep in peace. Sara Saba had found home at last. Palestine was an embracing mother who dried up Sara's tears and promised to heal her wounds and it was that promise that kept Sara standing and fighting.

Home was also the place where Sara resurrected God, whose face carried the pain of a hundred generations, yet still embodied the hope born along with a newborn Gaza baby in the midst of war.

> "And after you have suffered a little while, the God of all grace, who has called you to his eternal glory in Christ, will himself restore, confirm, strengthen, and establish you."

* * *

Kifak inta?

My beloved,

I know I shouldn't be writing this letter to you. I know you said we need to move on. I promise I won't say anything to make you feel uncomfortable or sad. Although I know it probably won't make a difference to you. Because unlike me, you've moved on. You're happy now. So maybe this letter won't have an effect on you.

I have been hearing Fairouz's song, *Kifak inta* everywhere I go. And it represents so much of me right now. And that's what I want to know. How are you?

I also have a lot of thoughts that have been roaming around in my head. You were there for me in my hardest, cruelest times. Sometimes you stuck by me, sometimes you turned your back. But I know that you got me through hell, and for that, I will be forever grateful. I know you're thinking that I'm babbling on now, like I always have. I'm sorry, but keep reading. I need to get my thoughts down on paper.

Imagine if your life was recorded. Just for a moment, step back, sit down and take a deep breath. Imagine what it would feel like to rewind, pause, stop or fast forward certain moments in your life. Or better yet, to erase them. I ask myself this question often.

Would I be able to do this?

A couple of years ago, I had a dream. In it, my twenty-two-year-old self was walking with my twelve-year-old self. "I'm sorry Sara, I'm so sorry," my older alter ego cried to my younger self. "Please be brave, be strong, I wish I could do something to stop it." But just before I woke up, I uttered the last words that would later become my salvation. "I know you can pull through this, you will survive."

Spoiler alert. I did.

But you know that. I walked, ran, cried and fought through life. I sit here, in a beautiful, forgotten park, surrounded by the greenest grass and rolling hills that stretch into the distance, with the brilliant sun warming my back, and here comes the gentle breeze caressing my skin. Stillness envelopes me like a warm blanket on a cold day. This is peace. This is the beauty of God's creation. I've almost always believed that planet earth in all its majesty was too beautiful to be created from nothing. It is in these moments when I am most alive, in the company of my pen, my paper and God. I felt like this once before too; when I was with you.

I wish I could say that I am now happy. Or that I've found myself in some sort of magnificent discovery. Or that I'm on my way to love again. But what I've realized is that, before I love another human being again, I must first fall in love with myself.

I want to start writing you some regular letters. They will take me back in time, through my childhood memories, through my teenage years, up until where I am now today. When we used to sit together, you would always ask me to talk, to open up to you, to be honest. I never could, because sitting in front of you, I lost my train of thought, I lost my sanity ... But now, now that I know you have moved on, I can open up to you better, because I know it won't affect you in the same way it affects me. I hope that's OK with you.

Write soon.
Love, Sara
Melbourne, Australia

Like Sara was, Heba is lost. But Heba is lost in the true sense of the word, somewhere in Syria. Desperate to find his only daughter, Heba's father, Ali Abumghasib, has not stopped looking for her. A Bedouin refugee whose family was ethnically cleansed from Palestine in 1948, Ali's life is a journey to find the way back to his shattered tribe in Palestine. Ali was fatigued by the many wars he fought in and scarred by the torture he faced in various Arab prisons. Yet somehow his spirit remained as rebellious as ever. When Ali and I first spoke, it was so that I could help him spread the word about his family in Syria. To explain how his family went missing, he began his story at the very beginning, the Nakba of 1948. Ali's tale is told in a different style because he originally asked me to draft a letter on his behalf, addressed to his daughter for delivery via the Red Cross. But what was meant to be a short and pointed letter became a long, encompassing life story.

His family is still missing in Syria.

6
Letters to Heba

My dear,

It has been forever since I last saw you. Time ticks by so slowly now. You are the eternal compass guiding my thoughts. I pray to Allah that these letters reach you during my lifetime. But if I am destined never to see you and your brothers again, I will depart this earth knowing in my heart that your names were the final words my lips would ever speak. I hope Allah will forgive me for my bad deeds. Only He can understand why I felt compelled to make the choices I made in my life, for the sake of my family and my homeland. If this letter reaches you after my body returns to dust, please read it with an open heart and mind. Here there is only my truth. Pass it on to your siblings, and if you have children of your own, which I pray you do, please tell them about me. Tell them that Ali Abumghasib was a good man. Tell them I was born in a world that had no place for poor people or wanderers like me. But tell them also that I fought back the demons of this earth with all my strength until the last day of my life.

Heba, I tried my hardest to shield you from all harm. You saw me in my heyday, as a fighter in my military fatigues, but also as a broken man who worked under the burning sun as a manual laborer. My pocket hid the secret of a fake name on a forged identity card. All the while, I was fighting for you. And I really thought we could win, I long fantasized about our final trip to Palestine once it would be liberated. I imagined you wearing the thoub I bought you from Burj Al-Barajneh, embroidered with the colors of the flag. I imagined Ahmad as a fighter too, wearing a khaki outfit, adorned with a black and white kufiyah. In that fantasy, I was always old, but strong enough to remember everything clearly. I would guide you through our village in Wadi Al-Shalalah in Bir Al-Saba. "This is where your grandfather, Ayish, fell in love with your grandmother, Hamda," I would say, and you would smile and insist I tell you the story all over again. And you needed to know every detail from the color of the sky to the flowers that bloomed. He was a poor man too, a Bedouin like me. And like me, he was short, dark and wrinkled. But unlike me, he had little patience. His life was always hard and when he was forced out of his village, that small piece of land we called Al-Tour al-Abbiad, he lost his mind. He lost everything.

I wish I could tell you more about him, Heba. But I left him and my mother when I was only fifteen. Our lives after the Nakba was worse than those of the poorest of refugees. My father, the proud Bedouin of Bir Al-Saba, became a shepherd tending the sheep of a feudalist by the name of Mohammed al-Bashaireh. His family alone owned more land in southern Palestine than all of us refugees combined. Two hundred thousand refugees fled to Gaza in '48, and overnight they became homeless and penniless. Their fight was for freedom, dignity and the never-ending quest for their right to return. I remember seeing him with a long stick herding the animals, this way and that way over the fertile grounds. His mind always seemed to be elsewhere. He never sang to the sheep as shepherds often do. Never smiled. Not once. Can you believe that? It was as if he was playing the role of a guard dog that felt no devotion to his master. I was born in 1951, and I ran away from our single-room mud-house up north into the orchards when I was a teenager. Before that I never saw my father smile once. I heard him cry often, but not ever in front of us. I could hear him whimper after the *Fajr* prayer at dawn when he thought he was alone. His forehead would touch down on the prayer rug, and he would break down in tears and not be able to finish his *sujud*. I watched his silhouette trembling at that moment every day and I could do nothing for him. I could not dare injure his pride by letting him know that I saw him at his weakest, asking Allah to end his misery and deliver him from humiliation. Maybe this is one of the reasons I left. It was too hard to witness. I wanted to fight for him and for all of my people.

Your grandmother, Hamda, was more composed. She never raised her voice no matter what your Uncle Mohammed did and no matter how difficult I was. She was kind and content with life and had a simple philosophy: "Whatever God gives is always sweet," which she often muttered during the hardest of times. I remember her clearly on the night I ran away from home, just months after the Israelis occupied Gaza in 1967. It was summer, and she was wearing a long traditional *fustan* made of Egyptian cotton. She was building a fire in front of our home to boil water so that my father could soak his feet and feel some relief from the back-breaking day. Your grandfather was not home yet, and it was dark. I ran away without saying goodbye to anyone. This I regret. But there is no going back now. Don't have any regrets, my dear Heba. Sometimes we only get one chance.

By that time your Uncle Mohammed had fled Gaza as well. He was only a month old when the Bedouins were forced out of Bir Al-Saba in '48. He was a fighter in Ahmad al-Shukeiri's army and was one of the very few who remained alive in his unit. Their Palestine Liberation Army was made of ragtag soldiers—poor *fellahin* compelled by their passion to defend whatever remained of their homeland. Of course, they never had a chance at winning a war. When the Egyptians were routed, our defeat was complete. Your uncle ran away into the Sinai desert. A whole army fled without air cover, and he too never said his goodbyes. It pains me that I have never seen my parents after that day which is etched in my memory. They died refugees. My father remained the shepherd he never wanted to be, and my mother boiled water for his aching feet until they both died in that same mud room. I was told that he passed while kneeling down for prayer, and that his last wish was to see my brother and me. He never did. Am I paying a price for the pain I caused them? Will this be my fate too? Will Allah forgive me? Have they forgiven me?

I have to see you, Heba, even for one last time. You are the light of the stars that keeps me going through this difficult journey called life. My vision is fading, and my battle scars from the bullets still throb. Sometimes it feels like my left leg is about to come off, like it's attached to me by just skin. The doctor visited me in my trailer, and when he saw how I live he refused to accept any money. I had none to give him anyway. He told me that my years in jail and the torture I suffered in Arab prisons have taken a toll on my body. He gave me medicine, and when he heard my story, he offered me money. I refused. My dignity, my sweet child, is all that remains, that and the hope that I will see you one day, and hold your hand for a moment before my eyes close for the last time.

I must be honest with you so I can cleanse my soul, at least before you who are of my flesh and blood. I am ashamed to tell you that I often prayed for death. But I assure you it was not cowardice that compelled me. My pain was so excruciating and death seemed like the ultimate relief. They did awful things to me. The Jordanians poked me with hot rods in my back and they hammered sharp objects into my head. That is how my seizures began before I was assigned to four years in a mental hospital. The time I spent there is suspended somewhere I cannot find, and to be honest, I do not want to find it. No Heba, your dad was not *majnoun* [mad] even if the children at school teased you about your crazy father. It was those damn seizures that made me that way. There are scars all over my body, reminding me of those agonizing years. Kids in the neighborhood often ask me to show them my scars, and I do. "It is the price you pay for revolution, for freedom," I tell them. And I mean it.

* * *

Dear Heba,

Today I registered at the Red Cross and I filled in the "Missing Family" form. I gave them all the names and our address in the Deraa Refugee Camp in Syria. They told me that thousands of families are missing, and it could take a long time before they locate you. This gives me some hope at least. A young man gave me his old mobile phone so that I could receive news about you. He also opened what he called an e-mail account for me, but I told him I could not check it since I have never used computers. He promised to do that for me and I ask him every day if there is any news. If they had these machines when I was young, I would have sent a letter to my father and told him how sorry I was for leaving him, mom, and my sister Aziza. I would have told him that by my leaving, Aziza had a better chance at surviving since she could eat my share of whatever little food he managed to find for us at the end of the day. I would have told him how sorry I was about his pain, but I would never have told him that I heard him weep at the dawn of each new day. When we are young, we think we know everything. Not saying goodbye was a foolish mistake, but I do not remember what I was thinking at the time. Maybe I was just not thinking at all. I certainly was not listening to my heart.

Did I ever tell you that when I ran away from home, I walked for three days across the orchards and valleys before I reached Al-Khalil? I simply followed the path of the Gaza Valley which led me to the southern Naqab, and finally to the mountains of Al-Khalil where I hid in a cave. I was found asleep by a Bedouin girl. Unafraid, she went home and came back with her father, a kindly sheikh who fed me and hosted me in his tent for three days. Then his tribe left the West Bank for Jordan across the Bridge. They hid me at the bottom of one of their trucks buried underneath mattresses and piles of clothes. The Israeli soldiers drew so near that I could hear the panting of their dogs close to my face. But with the blessings of Allah our caravan crossed over. We arrived at the Ma'an region in Jordan. It was an empty, flat, arid land that the tribe decided to call home. I learned a lot from them and am grateful. Kindness is something very few have shown me. I stayed with them for over a year and then I moved to Amman, a totally different kind of life.

Sure, the Israelis used to frighten me. They still do. But courage is not a choice that we make in an easy situation. Courage is doing what is hard and frightening because you know deep inside you that it is the only way out. And whatever the consequences might be, you must face them for your ultimate freedom. I wanted to fight the Israelis, to kick them out of Bir Al-Saba and restore my parents to their village, to give them back their honor and everything that was rightfully theirs. As for how I joined the Resistance, well, it happened very quickly as if it were destiny.

In Amman I saw a handsome man wearing a military uniform. His jacket had a Palestinian flag insignia on its left pocket. I asked him if he was a Palestinian fighter, and he directed me to a building where I enlisted to join the fedayeen. I registered at the Fatah office in the Wihdat Refugee Camp. That moment changed the course of my life. I was seventeen years old and it was my time to finally start doing what I was meant to do. There I met a man by the name of Walid Nimr, with the *nom de guerre* of Abu Ali Iyad. He was in charge of the camp. Everyone who joined Fatah had an assumed name, including the women. Mine was not assigned to me until I went on my first mission inside Israel. After that, they called me Shadad. I was tough back then, and I promise you that if I had the chance to fight for Palestine once more, even at this age, I would.

After a brief drill on marching, saluting, and other basic training in Wihdat, inside Amman, they took us to the Karameh military training camp that was closer to the border of Palestine. Our trainers were Palestinians and Iraqis. In the division I joined they taught me to assemble and disassemble many types of weapons, mostly Russian-made. I became an expert on the Simonov and Kalashnikov. The sergeant responsible for our division thought I was a natural sniper. So they sent me to Egypt in 1969 to train for three months in Al-Tal Al-Kibir military school. We had to carry heavy weights and walk very long distances to build our strength and endurance. My trainers were mostly Palestinians but also Egyptians. My superior, Mohammed Baroud, was young and different from the others. He loved politics and Russian literature and anything else that could reveal truth. His skills were unmatched by anyone else in the school. He was a refugee with shrapnel scars from the previous war, and he proudly showed them when making his opinions known.

When I returned to Jordan, I discovered that your older Uncle Mohammed was a fighter in an elite force called 201 that was a part of the PLO. He was married and lived in the Jarash Refugee Camp. When we met, we embraced strongly and cried. I cried the hardest. It felt like after many years of being lost with no sense of direction and no blood relative in sight, I had finally been found. My brother's face was almost a copy of my father's before it collapsed into wrinkles and infinite sadness. Unlike me, Mohammed's actions did not seem to be driven by fear. He too was angry, but he was more composed and determined, like my mother was. I was proud when I told my unit that my brother was a fighter with 201, and that his face was as handsome as a movie star's. I was happy to be chosen to join forty other fighters from several factions for my first mission inside Israel, which for me of course will always be Palestine. Your uncle told me that I was not ready for those kinds of risky missions yet, and he volunteered to go instead of me. But I refused. He had children, but I did not have you yet. If I died, I thought, I would die inside my homeland. If I lived, I would redeem my father's broken spirit.

* * *

Darling Heba,

The news today reported that Deraa came under heavy shelling and many people died. What are the chances you are no longer there and are instead safe elsewhere? No longer in Syria or any other war-torn place? Maybe you got a chance to escape? My God, I hope you did not have to meet unscrupulous traffickers, or cross cold and unforgiving waters. With all of my heart, I hope you are free from harm. A voice inside me tells me you are safe. And if that is the case, why have you not contacted me yet? The young man who checks my e-mail told me that no letters from you have arrived. My mobile phone did not ring once. I have not seen or talked to anyone for days, except the shopkeeper where I buy my cigarettes and bread. He is always busy, and I don't want to bore him with details of my life. I hate it when his customers look at me with pity in their eyes. If they knew how strong and brave I used to be, they would keep their pity to themselves; the story of my first mission to Israel would make them tremble.

I was the youngest of the forty fighters and one of the ten selected by Fatah to join the mission. The others were from the Popular Front for the Liberation of Palestine, the Democratic Front and Al-Sa'iqa forces who were trained in Syria. We were sent there with clear instructions and told not to smoke at all, as the light of a cigarette could be spotted miles away even inside canyons and especially at night. Smoking is not good for you, dear, so please make sure that none of your children pick up that bad habit. We all smoked, all forty of us, all the time. We followed the path of the River Jordan into Palestine and headed south to Eilat. The code name of our mission was the Green Belt. Our ultimate aim was to capture Israeli soldiers and exchange them later for Palestinian prisoners. We also wanted to blow up the Eilat port before heading back to Jordan through the Aqaba Desert. But things did not work out as planned. There were many Israeli military camps along the way of which we were not informed. We had to constantly improvise our plans. We struck them hard and killed many. We lost ten of our men, from all of the factions, and we hurriedly buried them in the desert before returning to camp. We could not reach Eilat, but we captured two Israeli soldiers. They were white and skinny and frightened. One was tall and had orange hair. The other was so afraid, he wet his pants. I felt sorry for the guy, but I kept that to myself. I am not sure what happened to them once we arrived in Jordan.

Our revolution was building momentum and we were finally regaining initiative after the Arabs' astounding defeat in '67. When Fatah came on the scene in '65, things began to change for us. No longer were Arab regimes speaking on our behalf, and we were no longer waiting for the Israelis to attack us as we scrambled for cover. We went after them in the heart of their cities. The terror that they had inflicted against our people in the refugee camps was coming back to haunt them. They attacked us in the Karameh Refugee Camp in '68, hoping to destroy our bases and push us away from the border, but they failed. Sure, they killed more of us than we killed of them, but we stayed strong and fought like lions. The PLO factions and the Jordanian Army fought hand-in-hand.

The Israelis destroyed most of our camps, but we drove them out. Karameh had freed us from the demons of defeat less than a year after the Arab states were beaten on all fronts.

After the Karameh Battle, we evacuated our bases that were too close to the River and re-established ourselves deeper in the country. Although we grew stronger, some of the factions lacked discipline and caused political chaos. The Hashemite King felt his sovereignty threatened, and we believed the King was conspiring with the West and Israel to push us out of Jordan. A conflict with King Hussein followed, so our mutual victory in '68 became our collective shame two years later in a quasi-civil war. We fought against the King, who showed no mercy as he unleashed his wrath, killing thousands of innocent people in refugee camps who had taken no part in the war. There was one massacre after another, and no Arab country moved to prevent it despite our desperate pleas for help. The Syrians hesitated for too long to intervene, and Egyptian President Gamal Abdul Nasser, who sympathized with us, died in that same Black September in 1970. Our people were slaughtered in droves, with over five thousand killed in ten days.

It felt like our revolution had collapsed after the massacres, that we would not be able to redeem ourselves ever again. Fatah members who rejected the agreement between Yasser Arafat and the King of Jordan formed a group called Black September, and tried to exact revenge on the King and his followers. I was caught placing dynamite in the Emir Mohammed Airport, a military airport that largely served the monarchs. I was busy connecting wires and whatnot when the soldiers arrived, and it was too late for me to escape. They beat me up badly, and threw me in a large cave between Jarash and Irbid. Many men were there, handcuffed, bleeding or dead. I was then taken to the mukhabarat unit in Abdali where they would coerce me to confess. I told them: "I am a Bedouin shepherd." They took a large knife and began slowly slicing the back of my neck. I felt the blood pouring onto my back and shoulders. I screamed: "I am a Bedouin shepherd and never held a gun." Then they hammered sharp metal rods into my head. I could not hold back the vomit. The blood gushed from inside of my mouth. I cried: "I am a Bedouin shepherd and was looking for my tribe." They sent me to court and handed me three death sentences: for resisting the army, attempting to blow up a military airport, and for entering Jordan without papers. I retorted that they could only kill me once. I was incarcerated in Mahata Prison for fifteen days, then moved to Al-Jafr Prison in the vast desert between Jordan and Saudi Arabia where only a few lived to tell of its horrors. I awaited my execution order, then decided to make a break for it. Death was coming to get me anyway, so I had nothing to lose.

Heba, one reason that I am happy I lived is that I later married your mother and she gave birth to you. But sadly, I do not have you beside me in my old age. I don't know if you are alive, or God forbid … I cannot even bring myself to say the words.

* * *

Dear Heba,

Red Cross workers came to my trailer today and asked me for more information about you. They said "describe your eldest daughter" and I told them that "her face was like the moon, and when she smiles, it is as if the sun has risen." They laughed and told me that such a description did not help them. But it helps me. On the day you were born, it was the first time in my entire life that I felt truly happy. It was an overwhelming sense of joy that I did not anticipate. Silent tears of joy streamed down my face when I first held you in my arms. I said, I will call her "Heba" because she is a gift from God, a gift that a nomad like me does not deserve. I promised Him that I would never harm you, or allow anyone to hurt you, ever. But I lost you. I pray to God every waking hour to find you. I beseech Him for mercy, for a second chance. And once I find you, I will never lose you again.

When people ask you, Heba, do you tell them that you are Bedouin? I always say: "I am a Palestinian Bedouin." I am only a nomad because I am trying to go back to my country. I did not seek this lifestyle even though the Bedouin will always be a part of me. I still look at the stars when I want to orient myself or try to find home. That is one skill that my father passed on to me before I left my parents. That gift alone saved my life. I wish I could teach you, Heba. It could be our tradition and you could pass it on to your children.

When I left Al-Jafr, I walked through the deserts of Jordan to Syria, guided by the stars. I walked at night and dug holes in the ground to hide from border guards and the blazing sun during the day. I knew that the tail of the Milky Way led to Damascus, so I followed it. And as Bedouins do in times of starvation, I held a pebble under my tongue for hours on end to keep my mouth salivating. You can be proud, Heba, that we know how to survive. At the border, I was caught by guards who handed me over to Syrian intelligence. Experience has taught me that all Arab mukhabarats are the same—brutal, demeaning, and heartless. But lucky for me, my cousin was a member of Fatah in Syria, so I was handed over to him.

It was then that my seizures began. I would lose consciousness in an instant. My body would convulse and I would fall to the ground. It is frightening to lose complete control of your body. They thought the Jordanian torture I endured had made me crazy, so they put me in the mental ward in the Ibn Sina Hospital where I stayed for four years and was often tied to a bed for hours on end. There is very little I remember about those years. I recall how once in a while I would be brought back to the hospital, naked. They told me I'd taken off my clothes and walked into the street. These episodes subsided, and the Military Administration of Fatah eventually managed to get me out of that place. I was very grateful for Ali Hajjaj and Hajj Mutlik, two fine Fatah officers, for standing by me during those years. If not for them, I would have perished in that place as a crazy man in a foreign land.

It was towards the end of 1974 when I joined the Resistance in Lebanon. I was twenty-three years old. The guys thought I should not have been sent on any more missions inside Israel because of my condition. Instead, they had me work in the Wounded Affairs unit in Burj Al-Barajneh Refugee Camp in Beirut. It was part of Yasser Arafat's office at the time, but later was renamed Force 17. I slept in the office since I had no home and nowhere to go after work. Soon after I arrived, the Lebanon civil war began, and I found myself fighting in that war too.

I am not sure how I became entangled in that war. I didn't view the Lebanese as the enemy, nor did I perceive Lebanon as my home. When the PLO left Jordan and arrived in Lebanon, they upset the delicate demographics of that country. You see, the Lebanese have always been in conflict. Many sects and religions and groups all fought to survive or dominate one another. There were many Palestinians in Lebanon, first as refugees who arrived after the Nakba in '48. When armed Palestinians began organizing in Lebanon, the refugees felt a kind of freedom they had never before experienced in that country. Soon the PLO formed an alliance attacking Israeli settlements, causing internal tensions in Lebanon.

While I regret that the war occurred, I do not regret taking part in it. What else could have I done, when Palestinian refugee children were massacred in Ein Al-Rumaneh? They were innocent children, for God's sake, wearing black and white scarves and singing national songs in a bus on their way home to the Tal Al-Zatar refugee camp when Phalange militias ambushed them. They killed most of them when they opened fire from three different positions, and then began stabbing the wounded with their bayonets. What kind of monsters can murder harmless children? Are there no rules at all? Those savages have never hesitated to work with the Zionists against their own people and against the Palestinians, and for what? So that they remain the rulers of Lebanon?

I thank God that I had no family at that time in my life. If you knew what the Phalange and their Syrian allies did to Tal Al-Zatar in '76, the second year of the war, you would be appalled. They besieged the camp for many days until people began to starve. Then they massacred thousands of them and destroyed the camp completely. People were killed if their ID cards showed that they belonged to the wrong sect. I was still at the Force 17 office, sleeping, cleaning, and processing papers for the many wounded. I happened to hear a conversation between fighters about a large pickup truck with a machine gun mounted on its back, which the Christian Phalange used to terrorize Lebanese Muslims and Palestinian refugees. Without hesitation I knew what I had to do. I said to them: "I will take it down." They were surprised as I was an office worker who had laid down my weapons years ago. They had not seen me in action. I took an RPG from one of the fighters, and climbed a wall near a graveyard that opened onto a church located on Old Saida Street. I waited there for the pickup truck to show, and it did, driving slowly like a predator on the hunt. I blew it up with a single shot. Then out of nowhere, I felt as if I were standing in a puddle of warm water, and I fell. Blood was everywhere.

One of their snipers had seen me from the other side of the street and fired an explosive bullet into my arm. It shattered the bones into many pieces. I don't know how the doctors managed to put it back together. I was taken to the Gaza Hospital inside the Sabra Refugee Camp, and then to a makeshift hospital that was once the Arab League building in Fakahani. It was a struggle getting me there, as the whole of Beirut was divided between us and our allies, and them and their allies. Fatah, other PLO factions and their Lebanese allies controlled West Beirut, and the Phalange were in the East. In the southeast were the Druze, and many more factions occupied small pockets all over the city, taking over streets, schools and offices. Snipers were all around. Many people were shot after taking a wrong turn, or crossing the wrong street.

I woke up in Fakahani wearing a large cast. I was livid. I left the hospital immediately and borrowed a Simonov. I bought a small monocular, taped it on top of the rifle and walked to As'ad al-As'ad Street where I hid inside an abandoned building that was pitted with hundreds of bullet holes. I mounted the rifle to the side of a window that opened onto the heart of the Ein Al-Rumaneh where the Christian Phalange roamed unhindered. I remember a large tree in the middle of the road that was abloom with red flowers. On the other side, there was the main street where Phalange militias were crossing back and forth. I learned how to be a good sniper in Tal Al-Kibir in Egypt. I thought I would be using my skill to fight Israelis, not Lebanese. But life is never what you expect, dear Heba. Why did they have to butcher those kids? Why did they butcher the whole of Tal Al-Zatar? I took my revenge, and five Phalange soldiers lay on top of one another in the street.

My arm healed after two weeks and I joined a small unit that included Hasan Abu Ali, Bassam and Muntaqim. We guarded Jamal Abdul Nasser Street in Burj Al-Barajneh, and we opened fire at the Phalange militants whenever they drew close. We were fed by the house of Khadir al-Annan, a Lebanese Muslim family who were oppressed like us and were fighting for a greater share of their country. There was widespread discrimination against Muslims, all Muslims, both Sunni and Shia.

That was when I met your mother. She was an Egyptian maid. She was dark-skinned and very sweet. She was kind to me and asked me if I needed food. My brother Mohammed, who was fighting in Lebanon as well, was pressuring me to think of marriage. I hadn't seriously imagined that someone could love me, or that I could love someone else. My mind was always occupied with other problems. I realized that I did not want to lose the opportunity, so I asked her mother, who was also a maid in Lebanon, for her hand. Karima was precious and so good to me from the day I first saw her until the day I lost her many years later. How I miss your mother. I know she misses me too. She never knew that I was in prison all of those years. She must have been angry at me for not coming back to rescue her. I will explain everything to her, Heba. I will make things right. I will do my best to bring my family back together. Everything will be OK when I find you, Heba.

* * *

Sweetie,

I have no photos of you. If I did, I would put them by my bedside so your image would be the first thing I see when I wake up, and the last before I fall asleep. But it's OK, you are stamped in my memory. I remember you exactly as you were. The day you were born was the day my life mattered most to me. I am not a materialistic person, but when you arrived, I wanted to make more money so I could take better care of you. When the civil war subsided in '76, I spent a week working in Arafat's office. I saw him once and ambushed him. "I need more money, Old Man," I told him. He laughed and hugged me. He took his three-color pen and wrote a note to the Fatah finance office. I asked him to make sure he signed it using the color green because for whatever reason, that was the only color that the finance people would accept on a signature. At the time I was getting paid 211 lira per month. Arafat ordered I receive a 500 lira bonus. I was grateful to him. I took your mom for dinner that day. I bought her a dress and a silver necklace, and still had enough for cigarettes and two pairs of trousers and I gave her the rest. She was so happy. It felt good to do that for her. I wish for the chance to do that again.

Arafat was always in high spirits, even in the most difficult of times. He managed to keep us together. Fatah had other great leaders, but no one even comes close to him. I do not think I would have stayed a fighter with Fatah if it were not for Arafat. He was like a father to me, to all of us. I do not care what other people say. They do not understand. I was there.

After the war, I became a trainer in Madrasat Al-Qittal, in Lebanon. In the years I spent at the military academy, I met many interesting people. Some of those I trained grew to become great leaders and many of them were martyred in missions inside Israel, or fighting the Israelis in Lebanon, in Syria, and in Palestine. There were many volunteers who poured in from Algeria and Pakistan, as well as many indigenous Americans who didn't mind that we called them Red Indians. Some became my friends. They are down-to-earth people who understand what it means to be a people fighting for their land and identity. In the years that followed, some of them died fighting against the Israeli invasion of Lebanon. We celebrated them as martyrs and buried them amid chants and recitations from the Quran. I sometimes wonder how their people are faring in America.

When I trained Imad Mughniyeh, I felt that he would become a great leader, but I did not expect that he would hold such an important position in Hezbollah many years later. Hezbollah emerged from a small group called Harakat al-Mahromin that was a strong ally of the PLO. I trained many of them myself.

Imad is originally Palestinian. His family lived in Rouis, between Hadas and Burj Al-Barajneh. We became good friends although he was younger than me. He was a tough kid and was hand-picked by the head of the military academy to accompany Arafat. Imad was polite and incredibly brave. If his mission was to jump into a blazing fire, he would do it as long as fighting Israel was at the core of his mission. He did not see the Phalange as his enemy, although he hated them for their treason. The Mahromin were indeed oppressed. If it were not for Hezbollah, the Shia would have been oppressed in Lebanon forever. Later their movement splintered between Amal and Hezbollah, which turned its focus to fighting in Syria instead of securing Lebanon's border against Israel.

Do you think I have abandoned you Heba? Do you hate me? If you did, it would break my heart, but I would not blame you. As far as you are concerned, I left and never returned. But it wasn't like that. I had planned to spend my life with you and my family until the end of my days. I wanted to raise a strong girl, who would carry on my fight for Palestine. I had wanted to call you Dalal after Dalal Mughrabi, who was killed only months before you were born. When she arrived with her fiancé at the academy, she was eighteen. I trained them both to use various types of rifles, and to disguise themselves in diverse environments. A year later, they landed on the coast of Tel Aviv, and killed many Israelis before she and her fiancé were killed. Her mission was aimed at capturing Israelis and exchanging them for Palestinians, but things did not go as they had planned. After that many girls came to volunteer with the Resistance at the academy. Dalal had lived in Fakahani where we eventually moved. You were born there. But I decided to call you Heba because your birth was a miracle.

You were born amid a new, awful war when Israel invaded South Lebanon. They intervened at the invitation of Lahd Hadad and the Phalange, but we fought them back in

Nabatiyeh, in Burj Al-Shamali, in Rashidiyeh, in Al-Bas, and Ein El-Hilweh. Our weapons came from Russia and Cuba, and even though the Israelis occupied large areas in the south, we mounted our resistance from Marj Al-Zohour, Shiba, and the Occupied Golan.

There is so much that I miss about Lebanon. Despite everything, it was still a beautiful place.

* * *

Salaam my dear,

Today I was thinking about your mother. Karima lived up to her name. She was indeed generous. She used to mix salt, dried green pepper and the smashed pits of apricots. We used to dip our bread in the mix after adding some olive oil. It was a humble meal, but this is how we survived.

My pay of 211 lira a month was not enough for me to take care of you and your mom. You needed clothes and visits to the doctor and toys. So, I also worked in construction for the PLO. They had large contracting companies in Lebanon. I got paid 25 lira a day and it made a big difference. Your brother Mohammed was born a day after your birthday. Karima was worried about having to feed another mouth. She did not want to put even more stress on me. Oh, what a gift you are, Heba. I told her that children would keep our revolution alive.

Whenever I felt like a failure for not being able to provide a good life for my family, your mother, although an Egyptian, always told me: "It is okay; it is all for Palestine and for Heba." But things got harder, and she had to work again as a maid though I did not want this. A bus picked up you and your baby brother to take you to daycare. It was not too bad there. All the kids were refugees, mostly coming from Burj Al-Barajneh.

When Israel invaded Lebanon in '82, I no longer felt it was safe for you and your brother. But it was too late to sneak you out of the country and into Syria. I moved the three of you further into West Beirut where there were civilian shelters. The military academy became a fighting unit of its own, commanded by a man named Jabbar. The Israelis tried to deceive us by landing in the airport wearing Lebanese army clothes, but we repelled them. The PLO was tough in those days. We would liberate an area and then hand it over to the Syrians. But then they would lose it to the Israelis, and then once again we would return to the battle and push the Israelis back. It was like a game of chess and we knew the moves well.

We could not move freely in East Beirut because the Phalange traitors collaborated with the Israelis. Some Christians were on our side, and Palestinian Christians fought alongside us because we are all brothers. Whenever we needed to operate in East Beirut, we had to go through the sewers. I did that more than once when my unit mounted attacks against Israelis stationed in the Al-Mathaf area.

It was hard to trust anyone in Lebanon in those days. Several assassination attempts against Arafat failed, and some of those who had helped the Israelis locate him were working for him. Can you believe that? Some of the collaborators were shot on the spot. One of the executions happened in front of me. They caught the guy contacting the Israelis after a building was blown up in which Arafat was having a secret meeting. He survived by a miracle. And when Arafat was rushed to his car, the car blew up only a few meters from him. Be careful who you trust, Heba, sometimes even angels' eyes disguise the devil.

As the war continued, I moved you from one place to another. But nowhere was safe: massacres were everywhere and the shelters were attacked, incinerating people alive inside places where they should have been protected from harm. When we received orders to leave Lebanon, we knew it was all over. You were with your mother and brother in a shelter in the Sarayah area in West Beirut. Later I found out that your mother took you back to Burj Al-Barajneh.

I had to leave you behind, as only PLO fighters were allowed to board the ships. We were not told our destination and we were accompanied by Italian and French navy ships until we reached the Red Sea. When the Italians left our ship alone, we were nearing the Saudi coast and ran out of water. The captain phoned in the Saudi coastguards and sought permission to anchor near the shore and stock up on water and other supplies. They told him if he dared reach the Saudi waters, they would blast him and his ship. So he continued south.

I was worried sick about you, and I had no idea where our ship was meant to stop. The only thing that gave me some comfort was knowing that my Lebanese friend Abu Ali Jafar was going to look after you. He smuggled weapons and cigarettes for a living, and he treated me like his son. I trusted him completely.

The ship was filled with fighters, men and women who fought to return to Palestine. Suddenly they were floating on the high seas with no sense of direction. Some of the fighters thought that we would ultimately be sent to Tunisia. Others thought our destination was Algeria, but we landed in Sanaa, Yemen, where thousands of people came to greet us. They thought we had come from Palestine, not Lebanon. Yemeni jets circled the sky to celebrate our arrival. Drummers marched all the way to the ship and children threw flowers at us. Their President, Ali Abdullah Saleh, came to the ship and hugged us. We told them we were thirsty and hungry, so they brought water and *khat*. We thought the *khat* leaves were like some type of *mulokhiya* (jute leaves, eaten as food). I did not know it was a kind of drug. I stuck a whole bunch in my mouth and chewed on it. Then I felt like I was floating upside down in the air.

Within a few days, morale was high again. We set up a military camp that hosted nearly 2,000 fighters and resumed our training. Our superiors told us that our exile was temporary, but when we learned that the Israelis and Phalange forces had attacked Sabra and Shatila, killing thousands of refugees, we felt sick to our stomachs. We urged our camp commanders to go back to Lebanon and help our people. We had left the country on the understanding that international forces would protect the refugees. If the Italians had been stationed there, those refugees would not have been butchered.

We were angry and felt betrayed by our foolish leadership. Fatah sent some of its leaders to talk us out of leaving Sanaa, but we fought with them and beat them. Even Abbas Zaki who was then the PLO ambassador to Yemen was physically beaten. We shouted at him: "Our children are being slaughtered, our women gang-raped and mutilated, and you ask us to be patient." They were all scum. When I think of that day, my blood boils. The war started with the murder of our children in Tal Al-Zatar, and ended with the slaughter of our families in Sabra and Shatila.

They finally gave us a thousand dollars each, bought us tickets and sent us to Syria. Over one hundred of us had opted to leave Yemen. When we arrived in Damascus, Syrian security held us at the airport. It was a Tuesday and they said: "You will be sent back to Yemen on Wednesday." They put us in the airport jail. I had a small TV and I sold it to someone in the detention room. I told the guard I needed to buy cigarettes. He let me out. The moment he got distracted, I fled. There were hundreds of people in the airport so he had no chance of catching me. I wanted to go back to Lebanon and find you. The risk was worth it. I took a taxi to the center of Damascus, then another to Zarzar Lake, not far away from the Lebanon border. Then I crossed the border to Haloua where Palestinian fighters remained and had a checkpoint on the Lebanese side. They gave me a ride into western Biqa Valley.

In those days it was hard to navigate Lebanon. There were too many sects and too many fights. No wonder Israel managed to exploit our differences. Al-Biqa was divided between Shia and Sunnis. I went to the Sunni area, but could not go further because the Israelis were too close. I met a Bedouin from Arab Al-Faor who was selling oranges. I gave him money and he gave me his word that he would go to Burj Al-Barajneh and find you. I was overcome with relief when he came back and told me that you were all still alive. I waited for days in a motel but your mother did not show up. By then I had spent 600 dollars and had only 400 left.

While I was lying in my bed, I heard her voice in the parking lot. I ran out in the street and only when I was outside did I realize that I was wearing only my undershorts. You were five and Mohammed was two-and-a-half years old. I hugged you with all the strength I had, and we all cried. What else can you ask God for but to have your family with you? And the woman who completes you.

Your mother was very clever. She sold our small house in the camp along with the few pieces of furniture we owned. It totaled 14,000 lira, which she sewed into the inside of your jacket in case the Phalange thugs searched her clothes. The few pieces of gold she had were hidden inside Mohammed's diapers. Your uncle in Tripoli helped me obtain papers certifying that your mother and I were freedom fighters and that we were on holiday. He drove us back to Al-Biqa and from there we went to Syria through Haloua. It pained me to leave him in Lebanon, but I had to ensure your security outside that hell. I thought Syria would be safe. It seemed like there was some stability there as long as one did not create problems or talk badly about the regime. I had no idea there would be a war there one day even worse than Lebanon's.

Where should I have taken you, Heba? Forgive me for not seeing that nightmare coming.

Once we reached Syria, I instructed the driver to take us to Deraa where your uncle's wife and children were living. His son, Abdel Aziz, was the first to greet us. We stayed with your uncle's wife for one night. The next day we bought blankets and pillows, and a few items for the kitchen, and rented a room in the camp. It was nice to be like a real family. I stayed with you for two months, then I had to return to Yemen. First, I reported to the Fatah Military Administration in Damascus and they assigned me to serve in Aden, not Sanaa. It was 1983, and I had to say goodbye once more. For a year and a half I lived in a tent. My responsibilities included taking care of supplies in the camp where over 1,500 fighters trained and lived under the leadership of Abu Al-Abed Khatab. He was a good man.

* * *

Dear Heba,

I know this is a lot for you to take in. I'm afraid that I will have little to leave you when I die. I have no money and the few items in my trailer were donated by an Islamic charity, I'm sure when I am gone, they will probably donate them to someone else. But I am leaving you with my stories. I am not trying to paint myself as a hero, only to provide you with the true account of what happened to me. I want you to know that I am a good man, and I want you to tell your children, "Grandpa Ali fought for Palestine." I do not mind if you tell them I died poor. Money has no soul, and it never mattered to me. If it had, my life may have been different. It is important that they do not think of me as one who lived as a coward. I am not. I know I ran away from my family when I was a teenager because I was scared, but I wanted to fight the Israelis and my father was too poor to take care of me. I never ran away from you. My damn luck and circumstances were out of my control and forced me into places I never wanted to go. In fact, these circumstances almost forced me to fight my brother after the Fatah split. I refused. I told them: "I left Palestine to fight Israel, and I found myself fighting Arabs. But I will not spill my brother's blood." Always protect your family, Heba. And make sure your children understand this too.

You see, the split between brothers began when Colonel Abu Musa led a mutiny against Arafat in '83. He was helped by a few others like Musa Al-Imleh, who we called Abu Khaled, and Nimr Saleh. The latter was in Damascus, as the Syrians were also involved. Arafat suspected that the Libyans were supporting the mutineers. Abu Musa and other officers were fed up with Arafat's corruption, at least that is what they claimed. They said that he had contact with the Americans, and had open channels with Israel through Israeli Jews who presented themselves as peacemakers. It is true, many in Fatah were not happy with the circumstances after '82. The Fatah leadership agreed to disperse its fighters across the world, so there was no one left to defend the refugees in Lebanon. Only corrupt commanders were left in charge in Al-Biqa Valley. I disliked Colonel Hajj Ismail because I couldn't understand why someone who fled his post as the commander in South Lebanon during the Israeli invasion would be reassigned as a senior commander in Al-Biqa and the South.

We thought, well, Arafat must have a reason. He always did. He kept his enemies closer than his friends. But Abu Musa did not agree. He was a tough fighter, that Abu Musa. Arafat summoned the mutineers to be investigated and duly punished, but they did not hand themselves over and a war followed. In Lebanon, this was the last nail in the PLO coffin. The fighting spread from Tripoli to Al-Biqa. The Syrians were involved too and it ended with a catastrophe. I met Abu

Musa in Jordan. He loved Arafat until he lost faith in him. Abu Musa was originally from Al-Khalil. Khalilis are known to be hardheaded, like Gazans and Bedouins. When the war started I was in Syria on a short vacation from my post in Yemen, and I was deployed to Al-Biqa to fight when I discovered that my brother, Mohammed, was with the mutineers. There was little fighting among the Palestinians, though we fought the Syrians. I told them: "My brother is with Abu Musa, please spare me that fight." Then I was deployed to Tripoli. Fatah lost and Abu Musa remained in Tripoli and later started an offshoot branch, calling it Fatah Al-Intifada. We were shipped away from Lebanon once more.

My ship went to Cyprus. From there we were sent to the airport right away and were flown to Baghdad in Iraqi planes. I was assigned to my base in the "Revolutionary Council" camp, under the command of Sabri Al-Banna. In '85, I was overwhelmed by restlessness. I thought, the Iraqis were good to us, but I was neither fighting for Palestine nor close to my children. So I took a taxi to an area in Baghdad called Allawi, then a bus to the Syrian border. I had 500 American dollars and 200 Iraqi dinars. I reached a sand barrier and walked to Bokamal. I exchanged some money and took a bus to Damascus, and a few hours later I was home. You were sixteen then. You had so much you wanted to tell me and there was so much I wanted to say. I said to you: "I will get some rest and in the morning I will take you to the market and get you new clothes." But the mukhabarat came at night. I was trapped. The house was surrounded by men in those suits they wear. You can spot them a mile away. There were over forty of them and several military vehicles. They said: "Are you Shadad, Abu Mohammed?" I said, "Yes." They handcuffed me and took me to the Palestine Branch prison in Mezzeh where the mukhabarat headquarters was based. It was as if all the poor people of the world were stuffed into row after row of underground cells. There was little food, no cigarettes, and zero hope for any acts of compassion.

They stripped me naked and had me stand facing a wall for hours. They demanded that I confess to being an Iraqi spy. I denied being in Iraq, they would have killed me right away. I said: "I am a freedom fighter and I do not care for your fight with the Iraqis," that it was not my fight. They told me I was reactionary, and burnt my back with their cigarettes. The scars still dot my body. Then they put electric wires on my skin, sending shocks through me. They tortured me for days and then threw me in a cell, three meters by three meters, with seventy-five other people. I know it sounds impossible, but it is the truth. We took shifts sleeping. Some would stand against the wall and in the corners, and some would sleep pressed up against one another on their sides, hugging each other's feet to gain space. That alone was torture enough to make anyone mad. Eating was tricky too. We only ate bulgur and lentils mixed with rocks, dirt and insects. After surviving so many near-death calls, I didn't want to die choking. I was there for two years.

I was not aware until a year later that your brother, Ahmad, was born in '86. I was in my cell and your mother had received no information about me. I wanted to pray in the correct way, but the Syrians would not let us. They did not want anyone to practice religious rituals. I made a good friend there in Dr. Abdullah, an anesthesiologist who prayed a lot. The mukhabarat accused him of being an extremist. He was a kind man and cared for all of us. He had no medicine to help prisoners when they became ill, so only the strong survived. Many people died there, but mostly it was under torture. He was tortured but he withstood it. Two of his friends died. I left in '87 and he was still there. I wonder if he made it out alive.

I wonder how many of those incarcerated were fumblers who ended up in the wrong place at the wrong time.

Eventually I was released, handed over to the Immigration and Passports Unit and deported to Lebanon in a police car. I was dropped at the border. I walked back to Syria through Haloua and the mountains, and then I took a taxi to Damascus. There I purchased a fake ID, and named myself Atieh Abdallah al-Zoubi. It was the only way I could see you, and I visited only late at night. I continued like that from '87 to '92, seeing you and your brothers occasionally and in secret. You were asleep most times. I would kiss your forehead, and sometimes you would wake up and we would have a snack together and talk. How I miss that. Then Mahmoud was born. I could not say openly to anyone that I had had another baby boy out of fear that I would get caught. I bought him presents and clothes and toys and gave to your mother all the money I had saved working as a laborer in construction, and then I fled again. Somehow the mukhabarat got the news that I was secretly living in Syria and they raided the house again. It was almost impossible to see you during those days, or to find work. I was like a prisoner without a prison. I hid in friends' homes and lived with a fake identity in the hope that I could see you and your brothers for even a few minutes every now and then. It was obvious to me that you were not happy with that situation. It broke my heart, but I could not do anything about it. Life in Lebanon would have been hell for you, as it was for all of the refugees. And if I had left for Lebanon by myself, I would have not been able to see you. Please try to understand, my child, I know that it was not the ideal life for a family. I called you Heba because you are my gift from heaven, and I needed to be close to take care of my little princess. I am sorry for the pain that I have caused you all.

* * *

Dear Heba,

A group of young Palestinian men put my information and photo on that Facebook thing. They told me that they would do their best to help me. They placed a video appeal from me, asking anyone with information about my family to come forward. It is hope that keeps me alive. I hope to hear from you soon. When I think that I have not seen you all of these years, my heart breaks into a thousand pieces. That was never the plan. Allah gave me a gift and I squandered it. But when I was forced into hiding and was left with no money for my family, I had to take drastic measures. I thought, if I go back to my camp in Iraq, I should be able to cash in all of my back pay. I snuck out of Syria through Bokamal and went back to my old base. Abdullah Abdullah was in charge. He told me: "We don't owe you anything." He said a Palestinian Authority was now in charge and the PLO has no money. But he gave me a month's salary and a travel document that said "Palestinian Authority" on it. I had no use for it really. I just needed money for my kids and to resume my fight for Palestine.

Then I thought, my health is failing me and I do not want to die before fulfilling my duty of pilgrimage to Mecca. I snuck into Saudi Arabia, but was caught by the police after walking for two kilometers. I begged them: "Please, let me do pilgrimage," but they refused. They told me: "Let Saddam Hussein help you." They gave me 150 riyals and sent me to Bokamal. I crossed another sand barrier and found my way back to Deraa. I again assumed my fake identity, working in construction for three years for a man from the al-Hariri family, not the Lebanese family, but the Syrian one. They had so much money, but all I wanted was enough to send to your mother in order to buy you decent food and respectable clothes.

Then the mukhabarat caught me again. I knew it was coming. I was lucky to have stayed free until 2004. "Why did you come back after we sent you to Lebanon?" they asked me. "I came back for my children," I answered. They sent me to court and charged me with attempting to sneak into Israel. They kept me in a small underground room for eight long years. It was room number nine. I was there with eighty people. Your mother never knew that. I never saw her or you again after that.

We soon learned that a war started in Syria. I prayed to Allah that the war would reach our prison, so that we could be set free and I could rescue you and take you to a safe place. People were starving in prison, and the number of prisoners kept growing. Many were also dying under torture. No one would believe the things that happened within those walls.

I thought about you for eight years. In the beginning, I tried to hide my tears. Then I realized all the men were crying, so I cried openly with them. It was freeing to let out that pain. I hope you have someone you can cry with, Heba. In 2012, I was released from jail looking like a skeleton. The Syrians dumped me in Lebanon once more. A Lebanese officer kindly assigned me twenty-five thousand lira and took me to Shatila. It was late at night and I was so cold. I slept in a vegetable cart in the old market. In the morning, I looked for my old friends, but could not find them. I went to the Mar Ilias Fatah office and found Abu Sameer Afash. He told me "your friends were killed in the war or left Lebanon." The Palestinian Embassy gave me 300 American dollars which I sent to you through a bus driver. Did you receive them? I hope he was an honest man.

Abu Sameer told me my brother was killed in a car bombing in an area called Dhahr Al-Bydar, which was under Abu Musa's control. It was in the Al-Biqa area. Three of his children, Abdel Aziz, Itaf, and Fakhir, died with him in the car. Atef and Talat were still alive, but I'm not sure if they made it through the war. I really hope the 300 dollars reached you, Heba. It was all I had. Please remember to always put some money aside. Money is nothing, but you never know when you'll need it.

I stayed in Lebanon for two years, until 2014. They paid me 100 dollars per month. I know it was charity, but at least they respected me enough to give me a uniform and assign me to guard duties in the Fatah offices in Ein Al-Hilweh. Then the Lebanese police arrested me while walking in Al-Hamra in Beirut. I told them that I had papers and I worked for Fatah, but they deported me to Egypt anyway. The Egyptians detained me at the airport, and deported me and others to Gaza in three buses. There were 150 of us, each with a story more complicated than the next. It reminded me of the time I snuck out of Syria to Iraq with a group of volunteer fighters in 2003. We were about the same number of people, but we drove there in four buses. We went to fight the Americans who along with Israel are the source of our suffering—they were then and they still are today. An American plane blew up one of the buses and all of the young men died. They were Syrians and Palestinians. We arrived in Umm Qasr and fought the Americans for a few months. Most of our group were eventually killed: Mohammed Sobhi, and Ziad, and the young man from the Masalmeh family, and the one from the Aba Zaid tribe, and the Saffouri ... The Iraqi resistance told me, "You can go back to your family." So I did.

I do not regret that. When I go into battle, I am ready to die for those I swore to protect, but that trip to Gaza through the Sinai Desert was different. It was full of shame for me. I felt it was my final defeat. I was not going to war; I was going to die. The Egyptians were rude to us, and swore at the women and the men alike. When I crossed the border into Gaza, I fell on my knees and wept. I asked God for forgiveness. I went looking for my family, but no one was alive. There were only distant relatives who did not know who I was. I told them: "I am a freedom fighter." They respected me when I said that, but they could not relate to the stories I told them. An Islamic charity gave me an old trailer where I still live now, waiting to hear your news. If you ever make it here, I will find a job and rent you a big house. I will make up for lost time. I have learned that time is not always on our side, dear Heba. Please use it well.

* * *

Dear Heba,

I went to the Red Cross offices today to ask if they had heard anything about you and your brothers. They seemed impatient with me, but then they brought me tea and cookies and asked me to wait. After two hours, a young secretary told me they had no new information, but took new photos of me to update my profile. My looks today may surprise you, Heba. My hair is white, most of my teeth are missing and my beard is long and uncombed. If you see my photo, please do not be sad or shocked. As soon as I hear from you, and know you are safe, I will get a haircut and trim my beard. I will buy new clothes if I can afford it. You will be proud to walk next to me. Make sure no one disrespects you, dear Heba. You deserve someone who treats you kindly.

Heba sweetheart, I pray all the time now. In the summer, I sat outside my trailer on a plastic chair waiting for you. It is winter now. My small heater is broken and the trailer roof has holes that leak water onto the floor. A young man told me that he would come and fix them, but he never showed up. I am sure he is busy. Maybe there are more important things for him to repair. I collect rain water in a pot, and when I run out of water I use the rain to wash myself for prayer. I pray that you are safe. I pray that if I never hear from you or see you again, you will lead a happy life far away from war; that you may never be hurt and that you will always have a home. If you cannot come back to Palestine, may Palestine always be in your heart, as it is in mine.

Heba, I miss you. I am alone and afraid. Please tell me you are okay. Just a letter, a line, even a word, so I may close my eyes and rest.

Your Loving Father,
Gaza, Palestine

Ali was driven back to Gaza when the world rejected him. Joe Catron went to Gaza by choice. He was not a refugee, but what is a refugee anyway? It is true, he fled towards war, and not from it. But he too was pushed forward by his fears, guilt, and a sense of purpose. Maybe a sense of not fitting into the world one is born into, or liking the game one is forced to play, made him a refugee to a certain degree, and perhaps he still is one. Maybe exile can be a self-imposed act of volition. Maybe Joe's last earth is never meant to be found.

7
Alive in Gaza

"Gaza has a way of making you grow up in a hurry."

His eyes were agape as he scrutinized his surroundings from wall to wall. Rest is not a luxury one can indulge during times of war. You have to face the danger and welcome moments of calm when they come. This takes its toll no matter how strong or resilient one is, but the Gazans certainly know how to put on a strong face, especially for an outsider. Dignity is everything. And even when you can take a break, the mind takes you on journeys that nothing could have prepared you for, no matter what you packed in your suitcase or what you might have read on a blog; or what books you might have devoured from the icons of Palestinian history. Nothing can substitute for actually living in Gaza. It is true, no one who goes is completely selfless and everyone has different reasons to be there, whether they talk about them or not, or whether they even know it themselves. Maybe one feels more alive there than in some New York coffee shop.

For Joe, Gaza was real and he was as present there as he could possibly be, doing what he believed was right. Whenever he attempted to close his eyes to regain some energy in something resembling sleep, not a moment later they would be wide open. Even though he had not slept for days, his worry was too intense to brush aside and his fears were multiplying by the minute. This place had changed him more than he had anticipated, and his perception of death had also changed: a fear that he had inherited from some distant past was forever cured. But this place, this miserable, poor, alien, inspiring, besieged, disfigured, magnificent place, where columns of smoke rose from every square mile of landscape, had only swapped his fear of death with the guilt of surviving when so many he cared for were dying or being maimed all around him.

What kind of life was that anyway? And what if they all did die, every single one of them; the Swedes, the Venezuelans, the Americans, the Italians, the Palestinian doctors and nurses, and all the patients? What anguish would it be if they all died and yet he remained alive and all alone? How could he justify this scenario to anyone, but more importantly to himself? If they could not be saved, the volunteer human shield should die too. He should be the first to fall, in the line of duty; at least that is the logic he could accept and live with.

He closed his eyes once more, but again he was forced to open them. It was not the sounds of explosions that demanded his attention, but his thoughts laced with compounded fears and apprehension. He tried to distract himself and keep busy, and resist his solitude by calling friends in faraway places. An exhausted Gaza was falling all around while the world's so-called peacemakers spewed their usual spiel of diplomatic chatter. The sounds of the city that he eventually grew familiar with—market vendors hawking their wares to customers; bargain hunters demanding higher discounts; cab drivers announcing destinations to random passersby; the laughter of schoolchildren and the routine calls for prayer—were replaced by the deafening noises of bombs dropping, whistles from missiles being launched from the sea, screams of pain from bodies trapped in coffins of rubble, whimpers of the dying on the verge of taking their last breaths, and shouts from hospital staff when ambulances would arrive as they carried limbless and stunned civilians.

"Wake up, Joe. Just wake up." A voice bellowed through his head and startled him into an all-systems-go position. He hoped that none of it was real, but it was as real as the heart pumping rapidly in his chest. He had lived through this nightmare before, during the war of 2012, but back then he did not yet possess the awareness of its implications. As soon as the Israeli army named the offensive Operation Pillar of Defense, scores of people began falling in a calamitous war that once again did not distinguish between military targets and civilians. An entire family was claimed when a bomb blew out their whole building without the slightest warning. By the time the flames were extinguished in that cruel November, hundreds had perished in the war on Gaza with its beguiling name that echoed in mainstream media propaganda. While Gaza's graveyards expanded in various directions as people scrambled to bury their dead, to Joe's astonishment Gazans were still grateful that the number of casualties was not as high as that of the previous war. They all kneeled down and prayed for their martyrs before burying them and hanging up photos of men and women across Gaza's streets. It was a bid to keep their smiling faces alive just a little bit longer, before the elements beckoned the evanescent visual poems back to ashes. And the faces of inculpable dead children were immortalized in graffiti tributes atop somber gray walls throughout the refugee camps, reminding all who saw them how life can betray you. The following morning, they began crushing the destroyed concrete remnants of collapsed buildings, turning the gravel and grit into bricks, trying to rebuild the homes, schools and clinics that were demolished. The task was great if not impossible because Gaza was still recuperating and under reconstruction after thousands of homes were destroyed in the earlier war a few years earlier, deemed Operation Cast Lead by the Israelis. The destruction was happening at a much faster rate than the reconstruction; yet somehow Gazans ignored this and kept on fighting—weary and angry, but steadfast as ever.

Gazans are a unique people, unmatched in their kindness and spirit of rebellion—at least that is how they struck Joe Catron when he first arrived in the Strip in the early months of 2011. He came to stay for a couple of days that somehow turned into a few years. Gazans were full of contradictions. They wept for their dead for hours, but carried on with life full of faith that things would without a doubt someday get better. They spent much time in their mosques, praying more than the compulsory five times a day, seeking God's forgiveness from sins they had never even committed. And they hardly ceased moving despite the confines that obliged them such limited access to the outside world, rightly earning Gaza the designation of being "the world's largest open-air prison." Two million people in perpetual motion, in a place measuring less than 365 square kilometers. Gazans were loud, often enraged by the slightest irritant; they were also quick to forgive and did not stew in jaded resentment. They kissed and hugged and smoked, and made children, and then went to sleep with a last prayer in case they never woke up.

Joe survived the war of 2012 and recorded some stories of those who had survived that onslaught and previous wars as well. But he never fully embraced war as a fact of life until July 2014, when its most unconstrained manifestations became real for him. From his arrival to Gaza in 2011, after crossing through the Rafah–Egypt border, until the start of the 2014 war, day by day he slowly began to understand a new set of unwritten rules. Learning through observation, and with his own origins in conservative America, he was able to navigate the cultural differences easily by comparison to some fellow activists, and was sometimes even mistaken for a Palestinian himself. Adopting both good and bad habits and characteristic rituals, he walked everywhere and greeted everyone he encountered; smoked incessantly; spoke about everything from politics to Jinn, from poetry and love to the contradictions of the sea (offering a possibility of escape while simultaneously being part of their prison), to the meaning of life and death.

Maybe all this was the perfect training ground for the ultimate test of July 2014. The Israelis called their new war Operation Protective Edge, but it was Gaza that needed protection and Joe felt compelled to do something, anything. Gaza had been under a strict siege for years. As a consequence, in order to push back the invaders, local fighters collected their own weapons as well as improvised bombs and rockets. They dug tunnels because the earth below offered the only protection, though there was also within them the risk of suffocation or flooding; through them food, flour, toys, and cement, as well as rudimentary rocket launchers, were channeled across deserts and borders. And when tunnels crumbled and the bodies of those who had dug them could not be retrieved, Gazans would carry out symbolic funerals, chant for the martyrs who remained underground, vow to fight, and then dig more tunnels. There was no alternative for Gazans, it was either that or bow down to the occupier. Joe of course did not have to be a part of all this, he had a choice. When the air strikes began in early July, he could have run away and no one would have ever chastised him for it. In fact, others did leave. Many internationals rushed to the Rafah border and beseeched unsympathetic Egyptian guards to let them into Sinai so that they could go home from there. But Joe begged no one, remaining in Gaza not to dig tunnels, but to explain to the world why Palestinians had to build them.

Gaza was very different than Hopewell, Virginia. The latter was an industrial town, bereft of the lights and noise of big cities, but it was good enough for Joe. His house comprised one floor with three bedrooms, and it was nestled near the converging point of two railroad lines that served the chemical factories of the town. Childhood for him was a long, uninterrupted bike ride upon a dirt road. The path was an unfinished project left to the whims of young kids who reveled in its simplicity, free from the confines of middle-class play dates in safe environments that offered little risk of scabbed knees. The city planners ran out of money, or for whatever reason lost interest in the road. This was good news for Joe and the other neighborhood kids as the dirt road was connected to a seemingly infinite grassy field. Both the road and the meadow were a child's heaven. One day, though, he left it all behind. Compelled by a curiosity stronger than himself, he chose Gaza. It was not the last earth to which Joe would travel, but it was the most vivid physical and emotional contrast that could be imagined for a child from Hopewell.

Joe could have rushed back to Hopewell, Virginia, as soon as the children stopped screaming and the evening news repeated the final death toll and announced that the war was over. He could have packed his bags and left his little flat near the Gaza port, and gone home to the mother he had not seen in years. Barbara would surely have taken a day off from driving her cab across Virginia, come and greeted him at the airport, bringing him a gift or at least wearing a proud smile. She would have certainly honored him for following his heart, and like any loving mother maybe would have admonished him for not visiting sooner. And he would have reminded her that it was because of her guidance that he learned to think for himself, to take risks and understand the world as it really was: unforgiving at times, but grand. He had never really had plans to leave Gaza in the first place, even after the bombs stopped falling, and the well over a thousand dead were counted and buried. He simply could not leave. Not yet. If he left, his guilt would have been a burden to carry for the rest of his life, and anyway he still did not understand why he had left Hopewell in the first place.

In one final attempt to fall asleep, Joe closed his eyes, but rest was out of reach. A bomb had shattered much of the building's fourth floor, and it was Joe's turn to speak to the reporters huddling in the basement of El-Wafa Hospital. They kept asking him: "Why is the army bombing a hospital?" And to that obvious question, he kept telling them again and again that he just did not know the answer.

* * *

It was Joe's maternal grandparents, Homer and Barbara, who first got him thinking about the world outside Virginia. He had never seen his Dad, or perhaps he did once, but he was too young to remember. Joe's father died many years ago, after he had abandoned the boy and his mother, leaving Joe with no memories that would give him a reason to love his father, or perhaps hate him. It was Homer instead who took the role of father figure in Joe's life. Homer and Barbara were the products of the profound historical circumstances that had shaped them and by extension their whole family. They survived the Great Depression and were both swept up by the promise of "relief, recovery and reforms" as enunciated in President Roosevelt's New Deal in the mid-1930s. Both of Joe's grandparents had come from the Scotch-Irish highlands of Virginia's Appalachia. There in the mountains poverty was extremely dire and the painful memories were often repeated to young Joe as a reminder that his generation was a lucky one. In their final years, Homer and Barbara managed to realize their own modest version of the American Dream—having a home of their own, two cars and some money in the bank. Yet they fought many battles to get there: a figurative war against poverty and want, and actual wars against whomever the United States deemed the enemy at the time.

Homer was a tank gunner on the front lines of what was referred to as the "European theater"; a war that saw the destruction and rebirth of Western civilizations. Then, sometime in 1940, he joined the Army Air Corps only months before it was rebranded to become the US Army Air Forces (until 1945). Joe never had a clear understanding of his grandfather's politics early on, but many signs indicated that Homer had fought enough to eventually loathe war completely. When teenaged Joe began expressing his desire to join the army, deterring him seemed to become Homer's main mission in life. Homer eventually prevailed, changing the course of Joe's life forever. Homer had always regretted his own lack of education. During his youth, education was considered less significant while surviving poverty and war were the nation's top priorities. He struggled to read newspapers, while Barbara read novels; and when he opened the papers every morning, the disquiet caused by his handicap was visible on his face. By the end of his life, Homer had declared himself a socialist, implanting a thrilling idea in Joe's head: that when socialism would one day prevail, as it had to, all of the world's political systems would be transformed from those that ensured the dominion of the rich over the poor, to those in which infinite possibilities of social justice and equality were more than just the wishful thinking of an aging ex-soldier.

It was Joe's mother, Barbara, named after her own mother, who helped Joe translate his new desire for change in the world into intelligently articulated language. She loved books and subscribed to several magazines, those offering political commentary, but especially fine photography. She encouraged Joe to read and engaged him in endless discussions about right and wrong, morality and ideology, and how to live a meaningful life. Born in 1954 during the baby boom years, old enough to understand that American wars were taking on a more covert and sinister character, Barbara was at the forefront of societal dissent. A degree in mathematical science, rooted in structure and rules, did not make her a conformist in the least. She hated compliance, particularly the kind that was typical of the dreary, uneventful existence of the class known as white collars. Instead, she finished university and after trying various career paths, she found driving a cab most to her liking. Barbara's personal history taught her to be strong. She lost her only brother to a car accident when he was in his early twenties, and one of her three sisters drowned. Left with Marie and Ava, who also faced their own struggles, she carried on with a smile on her face.

Conflicts in the Middle East were staples of the news consumed in many American households. These viewers were informed, one generation after the next, of Israel's righteous battle against hordes of encroaching Arabs. The Catron family did not fall prey to this propaganda. They knew how to read between the lines, having been influenced by a self-declared socialist grandpa, and a younger generation that grew to distrust the official version of everything. They knew the truth was quite different than what was presented on the evening news. Ava had joined her husband while he worked for Aramco in Saudi Arabia, where they lived in an expat compound. Whenever she came home to visit, her sympathies for the Palestinians and the reasons for them were eagerly communicated to the family. After she separated from her husband, Clint, and finally moved back to Virginia, much time was spent conversing with Barbara and a very curious Joe.

Then there was Keith, who along with Joe was a fixture at Hopewell's local library. Through their long conversations, Joe's politics took yet another leap far away from the mainstream thinking of what was acceptable in his town, indeed his entire country. Keith, in his thirties, bespectacled with short curly hair and a handsome face, was an advocate of a curious blend of Marxism-Leninism and Black Nationalism. It was only later in life that Joe questioned whether Keith's variations of the two revolutionary brands were compatible, but without a doubt Keith's enthusiasm galvanized Joe and their days became a prolonged, unsolvable argument. Between his work as a union activist and postal worker, Keith read voraciously on a wide range of topics while Joe was still a student trying to form his own unique political identity, with no practical experience to help him differentiate between achievable goals and wishful thinking. Eventually Joe decided to delve further into the world of fiction when he designed his own major at The College of William & Mary, studying Folklore and Mythology. Joe's interest in the supernatural was not new. He had spent much of his young life seeking solace in fantasy novels and as a young teenager tried to write his own. Sure, they were mostly a child's adaptations of widely available fantasy books, the *Lord of the Rings* trilogy in particular, but he did labor to breathe his own identity into them; his character, hopes, dreams, and fears as well.

During this exploratory time, Joe remained concerned with the real world around him. What troubled him most during those years was how to achieve actual, definite, and tangible change in society. He joined every group that purported to offer progressive politics, looking for an answer. The anti-globalization movement was particularly attractive, for it claimed to offer a global context to everything that had gone wrong in the world. From a distance, it seemed to be the ideological extension of all the anti-war movements that had thrived during America's dirty wars in Vietnam and the rest of Indochina. As Joe drew closer to the global justice movement, however, it became less appealing because of what he saw as the lack of an effective plan of action or even a serious attempt at building one.

He still marched in every rally he could, and took every opportunity to exhibit his placards chastising one American foreign policy or another. But the causes the movement backed seemed too numerous, the costumes too frivolous, and the signs ill-considered. It was more like an activist circus than an actual platform through which a coveted paradigm shift could be achieved. It was a strange mix of people supporting causes that seemed rarely to overlap. Back then Joe argued that those who did not take themselves seriously were unlikely to convince anyone else of the seriousness of their cause, but he had no other option but to keep on marching, rallying, chanting, and demanding one form of justice or another. Deep down the urgency to do something more tangible grew.

It was not until Israeli tanks rolled once more into Gaza in 2008, declaring war against the besieged inhabitants of the Strip, that Joe found his calling. That was still a few years before he actually crossed the Atlantic and then the Mediterranean to finally cross the Sinai Desert into Gaza, and found himself a de facto spokesperson for El-Wafa Hospital days before it was leveled to the ground. He was angry at the plight of all of those dead children and furious at his own government for defending and arming their murderers. So, one morning Joe folded his most trusty placard, put on his favorite kufiyah, and took the subway to Manhattan to join an anti-war protest called by the Palestinian community in New York. As he reached his destination, he found himself in a whole different world of activism. It was an entire community wearing kufiyahs and flooding the streets of New York City in a sea of emotions, an abundance of tears, and a single chant that was so focused and penetrating that it left the young Hopewell activist in reverence. "Free Free Palestine," "Free Free Palestine," they all cried, delineating over and over again this overriding priority of a mobilized community. It was invigorating. Joe was not asked to conform to any particular ideology, or expected to declare allegiance to a precise line of politics. All that was required was a kufiyah, which he was already wearing upon his shoulders, in order for him to merge seamlessly into the burgeoning mass of scarves and flags, whether in Brooklyn, Bay Ridge, or Manhattan. It was a massive community where neither color, nor gender, nor class mattered; the important thing was being unified around one cause with distinct demands for freedom, justice, and an end to a war that had already taken the lives of hundreds. "Free Free Palestine," he shouted along, his voice unique, but also a mere echo within the thousands of other voices. This time the words had an authentic taste and he grew even more determined to bring about this change himself.

* * *

He carried on chanting even louder, but soon he was actually in Gaza. When he arrived, his first self-assigned chore was to hold a placard that he had designed himself and squat alongside a group of mothers demanding freedom for their sons and daughters in Israeli jails. It became a custom Joe looked forward to every week as part of his humble Gazan life. Most Mondays for years, in front of the Red Cross building in the heart of the Remal neighborhood in Gaza City, Joe would be there to support their cause. The mothers had been gathering in that same spot for years before Joe had joined them, but once he did, he became a permanent companion of the grief-stricken women, and later of other supporters and family members who were also separated from spouses and children without any news for years at a time. The Red Cross building would also be the backdrop for the twelve-day hunger strike in which Joe later partook along with two other international activists, in solidarity with the mass hunger strike of Palestinians in Israeli jails protesting against their inhuman conditions.

It was the happiest day of his life when 477 prisoners were freed in a prisoner-exchange deal that saw the largest and most clamorous celebrations that Joe had ever seen. Not only did he experience total exhilaration, but he felt like he had contributed to something much bigger than himself.

More tasks were added to Joe's schedule, which grew busier by the day. He tried to teach himself Arabic, and whatever he could not communicate using his limited vocabulary, he attempted to convey using facial expressions, mostly those of sympathy and solidarity, but also of amusement and felicity. The rest of his days were spent meeting people and walking around refugee camps where he was repeatedly mistaken for a refugee himself. His fairly dark skin and unassuming demeanor obscured his ethnic roots and evinced an air of familiarity, so he was often approached by people who would speak to him in a rough Gazan accent, and he would smile. "Ana Ajnabi," he would say. Some would question if he was indeed a foreigner, for he dressed in familiar humble attire and did not walk around brandishing cameras or electronics as other foreigners typically did. He did not drive around the scruffy streets of the refugee camps with a new car dotted with foreign lettering, and did not have a "fixer." Instead he had friends who were mostly refugees, and who eventually began to see him as one of them. Joe tried to integrate as best he could and find his place in Gaza as if he were a Palestinian, not an outsider with one agenda or another. In time, Gaza had become his new Hopewell and he was just fine with that. Of course, this new Hopewell was very different—it was welcoming and beaming with life, yet it was also teeming with great danger.

Joe was not in Gaza as a thrillseeker looking for his next fix, and hated it when the international press wanted to make the story about him rather than focusing on the Palestinians. This predicament presented itself often to him and other activists who felt a moral obligation to be in Palestine. But what was he to do? Risk not telling the story, or not have the story told at all? How could this norm be dismantled? This paradox had to be ignored to a certain extent, as the dynamics of racism and colonialism regarding media coverage was too big of a beast for him to decipher. So, he put his efforts into his daily tasks. He accompanied refugee protesters to the northern Gaza borders where the towns of Beit Hanoun and Beit Lahia were separated from southern Israeli towns by an army that opened fire whenever a kid raised a flag or a farmer ventured on to his own land. It was through these northern towns that Palestinian refugees crossed into Gaza in 1948, barefoot and bewildered. Many of the youth that Joe accompanied to the heavily militarized zone came from a village or a town that either still existed under a new designation, often a Hebrew name, or had been entirely erased from the map. Their fathers and forefathers had made Gaza their temporary home and were told that returning to Palestine was only a matter of time. They all fought hard to speed up that return, but to no avail. So, their children kept on returning to that very border, gathering at the fences of what was once their country, chanting, "Free Free Palestine," and Joe would chant along.

Gaza had changed since 1948. Nearly 200,000 refugees fled for their lives at that time, escaping massacres and systematic destruction of dozens of towns and hundreds of villages. After that, the Strip was ruled by Egypt, and following the latter's defeat in 1967, it was overrun by the Israeli military and armed Jewish settlers who claimed their own beaches and used much of the water for their massive fortified settlements, industrial lakes, mango farms and swimming pools. As the colonies expanded, the refugee camps diminished in size. Even after the Israeli army evacuated its colonies, deployed its forces to border areas, and besieged the Gaza Sea in 2005, Gaza still continued to shrink. For one, its population had grown to nearly two million, but also its most arable lands that adjoined the Israeli border were declared military zones. Not far away from what became a death zone, snipers took their positions above reinforced watchtowers. Even the sea was beleaguered by the Israeli navy, which instructed Gaza's fishermen to venture no further than six nautical miles from shore, which was then reduced to three, compounding the issue further as fish would be difficult to find in the shallower waters. And whenever it suited their twisted whims, they blew the small Gaza dinghies out of the water and watched the survivors swim back to shore. Joe had even accompanied some of these fishermen and no matter how much he screamed at the military boats that he was an American and they should leave the poor fishermen alone, they seemed to care little for him or the international laws they were breaking. Their faces were stiff, their guns mounted and ready to fire, and not even Joe Catron of Hopewell, Virginia, was capable of changing the dynamics of that disproportionate war.

Joe's stay in Gaza was initially meant to last only a few days. But something impelled him to remain. The internationals in Gaza were not many. Some were affiliated with NGOs that had managed to carry on with their operations despite the siege imposed on the Strip by Israel and the Egyptians as early as 2006. Others were activists like Joe, although each had different reasons to be there. There was the rich English kid who walked around Gaza as if he were a savior of the miserable multitudes; and there was also the older small-town American woman who chastised Gazans for fighting back, preaching to them the nonviolent teachings of Mahatma Gandhi and Martin Luther King. And, of course, there were the many journalists who would stay in Gaza for a few days or weeks only to return to their countries to write thorough investigations or even books about everything the world needed to know about Gaza's militants, underground tunnels, and history of political movements. But there were also the unpretentious ones who knew that by the end of their journeys they would have learned more about themselves than they could ever possibly have taught Gazans about life, survival, and resistance. Joe was one, but there was also Vittorio Arrigoni, the man who had proudly tattooed on his right arm the word "Al-Muqawama"—Arabic for "Resistance."

Vittorio was murdered soon after Joe had met him. He had anticipated becoming friends with the Italian, who at times seemed to physically resemble Che Guevara. But Vittorio was kidnapped by a Jordanian and some Gazans and later found dead in circumstances many regarded as mysterious. Palestinians wept for Vittorio as if he were one of their own, just as they had wept for Rachel Corrie before him when she was repeatedly run over by an Israeli army bulldozer, and Tom Hurndall, who was shot in the head by the occupying army. The Palestinians called them martyrs and inscribed their names and pictures all across the refugee camps. Vittorio, unlike Rachel and Tom, was killed by Gazans with whom he had come to declare solidarity. He arrived in Gaza in 2008 atop a small boat that carried a group of activists challenging the Israeli siege, and acted as a human shield during Operation Cast Lead. Vittorio befriended hundreds of people and with time became a popular fixture in most of Gaza's activities, conferences, protests, and many celebrations. In addition to his solidarity work on the ground, he also wrote books, articles, and entries on his blog *Guerrilla Radio* when he was not protecting farmers and fisherman. Joe and Vittorio spent little time together before his tragic end. They first met at a café in the university district in Gaza, but the last time Joe saw Vittorio alive was at a party on the roof of Joe's apartment building in Gaza City. That night Vittorio was quiet and reflective, with little to say, perhaps lost in his own thoughts.

It was not the impression that Vittorio had left on Joe that lingered the most. It was the shock and pain of his death that lived on. Gaza's small community of activists from around the world sought comfort in each other's company. So, when a friend, who had risked his own life for Gaza, was killed in peculiar circumstances, the pain was mixed with confusion, as Vittorio's motto "Stay Human" reverberated across the world.

Joe and Vittorio's time in Gaza overlapped by only a month. Joe had been with the International Solidarity Movement for about a week when this baptism by fire took place. The ISM was a group of internationals who stayed in Palestine for various lengths of time, each with his own spin on solidarity and direct action. Before Joe arrived, death was hovering over Gaza and his coming changed little in the course of bloody events. Operation Returning Echo in March 2012 was a crash course in the punishment Gaza had been subjected to for all of those years. "Only" scores were killed then, but it was a taste of what Joe and all of Gaza would experience in November of the same year, when hundreds perished under the rubble of their homes as they took shelter in schools, or even in their hospital beds when seeking medical care.

In November 2012, Joe's trial of guilt began. He had not felt useful during that war. Mere words of solidarity seemed frivolous when graveyards were swelled with corpses of whole families. That war left Joe with a dilemma that persisted for months. He could either dwell on his fear of death or do what had to be done—more importantly, what was expected of him and what he expected of himself. He chose the latter course, and then the 2014 war began.

* * *

The relatively large El-Wafa Medical Rehabilitation Hospital was bombarded for days on end. It was mostly empty. The majority of its patients had already been evacuated, but fourteen remained because their conditions were too critical. Attached to machines keeping them alive, any attempt at relocating them was likely to endanger their already vulnerable lives. The logic was perplexing. Basman Alashi, the executive director of the Al-Wafa Charitable Society responsible for running the hospital, had appealed to Joe and a few other internationals to come and to invite international media to see for themselves that the hospital stored no arms and that no rocket launchers were mounted anywhere within its facilities. Joe obliged, not only for the obvious humanitarian and ethical reasons, but also because of his profound respect for Basman Alashi. Joe and the other activists were certain that the Israelis knew without a doubt that El-Wafa was not a base for Hamas or any other local resistance group. And he was going to prove this, showing to the world and himself that the time had finally come when he would overcome all of his fears.

El-Wafa was located at the eastern end of Gaza's main commercial street, Omar al-Mukhtar, in the Shujaya neighborhood. The location was convenient when patients needed to be transported from nearby clinics and hospitals for urgent care, but when Israel launched Operation Protective Edge in July 2014, El-Wafa's strategic address proved to be a curse. Only meters away from its main gate stood a large separation barrier that divided Gaza from a military zone at Israel's southern borders, making the hospital a position that could potentially benefit their long-term strategy. From an Israeli military viewpoint, it needed to be conquered, no matter the price. For Joe, this was a critical moment. Refusing to be stationed in a hospital-turned-military-target was to betray the very essence of his journey to make the world a better place whatever the risk. He answered the call, serving shifts of twelve hours at a time, along with other activists like the

Swede Charlie Andreasson, who also was trying to resolve his own moral dilemmas.

Journalists had gathered together so that Joe and Charlie could inform them of their decision to serve as human shields to safeguard the critically ill patients and the hospital staff. But the presence of international activists barely changed the scene in any way. The day before Joe arrived, four small Israeli "warning rockets" slammed into the hospital's roof and walls. In the afternoon of Joe's first day on the job, a large missile struck the fourth floor, leaving a gaping hole, shattering many windows and unhinging many doors. A massive Israeli strike seemed imminent, regardless of the fact that patients could not be evacuated nor could the staff leave them there alone.

Elsewhere in the Strip the casualties were mounting. The horrors of the war were unprecedented even by Gaza's grim norms. Over fifty entire families perished in a matter of weeks, in every part of the Gaza Strip, especially in the northern neighborhoods where Israeli tanks attempted to advance but failed due to stiff local resistance. Hundreds of fighters were trapped in the tunnels which they used to combat the advancing soldiers. Airstrikes never ceased; thousands of flights were conducted in the sky above that tiny patch of earth that was Gaza. It seemed that everyone was on the target list: schools were demolished; over 20,000 homes were destroyed; seventeen hospitals were damaged or fully razed; and half a million Gazans were on the run with nowhere to go because no place was safe or sacred. Even UN facilities, where nearly 300,000 refugees sought shelter, were targeted, sending the refugees on the run yet again. Even in this inferno, many opted to stay home without running water or electricity, and very little food. Prayer was abundant, because only God could help them.

Joe stayed too. He sincerely wanted to. He knew that Alashi had summoned him—not to die, but because as far as the Israelis were concerned, Palestinian blood was cheap. Though it was a long shot, the hope was that the presence of an American and a Swede might make the Israeli government pause and consider the consequences of its actions. The unity of the activists intensified along with Israeli threats against the hospital. The number of internationals there grew. Joe and Charlie were joined by an Australian, a Brit, a French national, a New Zealander, a Spaniard, and a Venezuelan. Days passed and missiles whistled by. The activists were prepared to die so that others would have a chance to live. And in that very moment, Joe Catron had stepped over the boundary that separated his old self, an activist with many questions and few answers, to his new self, a man, still with very few answers, but with a clear sense of a calling and a purpose.

Unlike the prolonged conversations between Joe and Keith back at the Hopewell Public Library, Joe's conversations with the other internationals who gathered as human shields at El-Wafa Hospital were more lucid and far simpler. They bothered little with grand plans aimed at changing the world. There was no time or even desire to figure out whether national liberation movements could be streamlined into Marxist–Leninist theories within an anti-globalization platform that could effect a paradigm shift the world over. Their reflective and almost spiritual conversations at El-Wafa were focused largely on their determination to save lives, sacrificing their own if necessary. Eventually El-Wafa was entirely destroyed. A barrage of missiles struck on July 17, prompting a chaotic evacuation of all those inside. Other hospitals were also destroyed in the following days, and not even the presence of two Swedes at the Beit Hanoun Hospital spared its total ruin on July 25. Aware that their Western passports mattered little to the advancing army, Joe and his international companions still moved to serve as human shields elsewhere, this time at the largest Gaza hospital, Al-Shifa. There was no turning back once they had made their choices, notwithstanding what little affect their actions had. There still would have been the guilt of "What if?" haunting them had they not stuck to their ideals.

* * *

It was in late August that news of a looming ceasefire began to surface, though the sounds of the blasts which shattered many windows were telling another story as Joe filled his Twitter feed with the latest casuality figures. His stint as a human shield at the Al-Shifa Hospital was less frightening than his days at El-Wafa. The explosions grew closer after midnight for some reason while he sat in the hospital's library, not far away from the overflowing morgue. Yet the sounds of bombs never grew familiar to Joe's ears. Each and every boom was accompanied by the same adrenaline rush and fear for his life. But he wanted to save others more than he wanted to save himself. Those who live through wars develop a range of psychological methods to pacify themselves, to survive the violence while maintaining their sanity. "Once you hear or feel a blast, you have already survived it," is what Joe used to say to console himself and others when the bombs came closer.

Al-Shifa Hospital staff had already informed him and the others that even Gaza's largest medical facility, far away from the combat zones, was no longer safe. In fact, when heavy explosives were unremittingly lobbed from the ground, sea, and air, all of Gaza became a combat zone from which there was no escape. Joe's typical response to all of this was eventually reduced to "*mashi*," accompanied with a nervous smile and a fading hope that the war would soon come to an end. The reality was totally opposite. There was nothing "fine" about it. And although the war carried on for much longer than anyone anticipated, fifty-one days, Joe never grew numb to the sight of bodies of mutilated children and women, or to the decomposed, agonized corpses coming to Al-Shifa morgue. He was so far from Hopewell and his days reading about astronomy and mythology. The two worlds were so different, and he struggled to make sense of it all.

In Gaza he learned to bridge cultural gaps because the presence of death teaches people to care more for one another than for themselves. When the survival of a whole group is at stake, the individual, although he still matters, becomes a secondary aspect of one's unyielding fight for existence. The point is to save a collective being. Joe Catron not only reached that realization in the last days of the war, he internalized it as well. He never really abandoned his fears completely, but fear over his personal safety shifted to fear for that of others, changing Joe's relationship with himself and the world. He could finally understand why war made a "socialist" out of Homer. The old man could hardly decipher the language of a newspaper, but it turned out that solidarity was not really conveyed through a written word, but through action.

Indeed, one aspect of Gaza's culture that struck Joe as odd when he first arrived—to stay for a few days that turned into years—was how young people, the *shabab*, would often run towards explosions, not away from them. They did that to save those trapped under the rubble of some building or pull out the bodies of those whose flesh and bones were melted together in the burning metal of blown-up cars. Towards the end of his stay he was doing the same thing, exactly what he once perceived as peculiar. Unlike many other, more sensible, foreigners, his instincts made him rush to rescue someone he had never met before or even knew existed, rather than run away to save himself. Whenever a ceasefire was declared, he found himself along with other internationals rummaging through the wreckage of destroyed neighborhoods, looking for trapped bodies. This led him back to Shujaya neighborhood when it was almost entirely destroyed, and hundreds of its residents were killed or trapped under the concrete of their homes. The Red Cross had by then suspended its operations in that area since the invading soldiers neither respected humanitarian ceasefires nor had any particular regard for ambulances with large red crosses on them.

It was then that Joe met Salem Shamaly, the archetypal Gazan teenage boy with short hair buzzed on both sides, skinny jeans and not fully developed facial hair. Salem was the only son in a family of seven sisters. He was somehow separated from his parents and siblings during the chaos. When a temporary truce was declared, he returned to a devastated Shujaya, walking hazily amid the rubble, yelling the names of his loved ones, unable to recognize his home or even his neighborhood. When he met Joe and his friends as they too looked for survivors, they tried to dissuade him from going any further, knowing that Israeli snipers were positioned atop the tall adjoining buildings of the neighborhood. He was desperate to find his family, and they agreed to join him in his search.

There were eight of them in total, seven internationals and Salem. Joe captured much of the undertaking with a camera, and the captured images would gnaw at him for probably the rest of his life. They decided to walk in two groups, crossing streets as quickly as they could so the snipers would have little time to shoot at them with their explosive bullets or reload their guns for another go. Salem either didn't understand the plan or was eager to cross the once familiar roads once again. He crossed alone, just after Joe and three others ran to the opposite side of a dirt road, and just before they gestured for the others to follow their lead. It was a matter of seconds that determined it all. A single bullet struck Salem in his lower body. The young man, wearing a green t-shirt and carrying a cheap Nokia phone, remained conscious and expressed his pain through agonizing shrieks that echoed across the streets of the now destroyed Shujaya. He raised one arm to the snipers so that they would stop firing, but they did not heed this call for mercy. They fired a second bullet, and a third, and a fourth, and with each shot his voice faded, his body stiffened and eventually he ceased to move altogether. Joe and the others stood frozen by the horror of the moment. Nothing could have prepared them for this. When Salem's body gave in and shells began to fall all around them, there was no other choice but to run back to relative safety, leaving Salem behind in that spot where he stayed motionless for several days until it was safer to retrieve his body.

Salem's death, so quick and ferocious, the sight of him grasping his outdated Nokia and the sound of his voice crying the names of his seven sisters and parents, had an impact on Joe like no other experience he had had before in Gaza. The team of witnesses shared the videotape of the incident, recorded by Mohammed Abedullah, on every social media platform they knew of, aiming to compel the Israeli army to allow the evacuation of the teenager's decomposing corpse. Salem's family never dreamt that one day they would watch footage of their own flesh and blood leaving this earth in such a brutal way. It was one of his seven sisters who recognized him while viewing a YouTube video of what she expected to be some unnamed dying Gaza kid. Hearing his cries for her just made the experience all the more scathing. Salem did not deserve such a cruel final walk on his last earth. By the time she saw the video, before the final carnage, Salem's sister had managed to escape from Shujaya along with the others and was deep in the heart of Gaza City.

"Gaza has a way of making you grow up in a hurry," Joe wrote to a friend soon after he left Gaza. He quoted a poem of Mahmoud Darwish which he had read every single day during the 2014 onslaught.

> Time there does not take children from childhood to old age, but rather makes them men in their first confrontation with the enemy.
>
> Time in Gaza is not relaxation, but storming the burning noon.
>
> Because in Gaza values are different, different, different ...

Was Joe referring to Salem? To all the children who grew up underneath the ground, digging their own tunnels to freedom, only to end up fighting an impossible war and being buried under sand and water? Was he referring to himself, to that child from Hopewell, Virginia, who grew up without a dad and escaped his demons on a rickety bike over a dirt road that led to an infinite meadow? Some months after the war, he wrote with the cynicism and stubbornness of a true Gazan:

> I've emerged more energized and determined to support Palestinian liberation than ever. This doubtlessly has something to do with basic human impulses: engaging with people and sharing their lives has a way of making you understand their motivations and goals more intuitively than you might otherwise.

Joe returned to New York a few months after the war ended. Upon his return, he rarely engaged in conversations about grand theories of social change. His experience in Gaza made him all the more engaged and focused, but at times also very cynical, the same syndrome that afflicts many Palestinians once they leave their homeland. This was especially true for Gazans, who fear being far away from home when the next onslaught comes. Joe's worry for his friends in Gaza, who initially mistook him for a refugee, overwhelmed his thoughts. That small strip of land, a microcosm for all the conflicts burdening our imperfect planet, would stay with him forever. His relationship to it was now that of true devotion to a brother, or a family. In fact, Joe's feelings were not all that different from Salem's when he called the names of his seven sisters just before he was shot down, nor from the hope that he would remain alive long enough to find them.

Between the Last Earth and the Last Sky, all stories converge into one somewhere in the Mediterranean, as Palestinian refugees from Lebanon, Syria, Iraq, Gaza, and elsewhere find themselves on an island that no one wanted to be on. A navigational error led their small boats to a place with no land access to continental Europe, trapping them on that useless ground. Greece may as well have been millions of miles away. Their predicament seemed to reflect that of all Palestinian refugees.

The island remains nameless here upon the request of Leila (a pseudonym), to protect her identity while she continues her work with NGOs that help Palestinian and Syrian refugees.

8
The Last Sky

Her teenage depression was long gone, and the battle to find her identity was not over, so she took solace in the poetry of Darwish.

> The Earth is closing on us
> Pushing us through the last passage
> And we tear off our limbs to pass through.

Her earth was supposed to be different from theirs, and on the surface, it looked that way: how she walked and talked, the clothes she wore, the opportunities she had, the things she owned, the places she went, the homes she lived in and the foods she ate. She was worlds apart from the rest of them; she was sure of it. For one, she was not a refugee, or rather she had opted out voluntarily from that whole wretched enterprise. Did it really matter that there were similarities between her family's past and those of other refugees?

The Nakba, the genesis of all the pain that has been endured by every Palestinian over the last four generations, persists. It screams for attention: "I am the origin of all the sins of man, even those that are yet to be committed." She could not escape this truth, for her Nakba was their Nakba as well. But so what? She was a Jordanian–Palestinian, or, when circumstances called for it, simply a Jordanian. The allegiance to being Palestinian, wholly, utterly, and painfully Palestinian, did not surface until it was forced down her throat by the very people she was trying to help. Since she had arrived at that forsaken place on a miserable island, in a barren building they called a refugee center that was twenty-five kilometers away from civilization, destitute refugees kept pushing her out of her comfort zone, beckoning her to leave her lifelong bubble.

"You are not a Jordanian," shrieked the angry man from Shatila as soon as Leila introduced herself. His razor-sharp perceptiveness cut at her, so she omitted her clan's name from any introductions; problem solved. "My name is Leila Khalil," she would say, and leave it at that. But what she was omitting was as obvious to the refugees as the hunger eating away at their stability, or the frustration pushing them to their limits. While she was working to heal their pain, she wished not to participate in a shared celebration of an agonizing past. As far as she was concerned, she was a well-dressed volunteer who had flown three hours from London to help desperate refugees who were fellow humans in need.

"I'm not sure why they're so angry," she complained to a friend over the phone when she arrived at her hotel, after her first day of work. "Why are they angry with me?" The Palestinian refugees from Lebanon were the angriest of all, and were also the most frightened. Who would not be afraid given the stark reality that no country would accept them? How does one make sense of the fact that there is no safe earth to return to? Keeping their sanity intact was the notion of their homeland, an anchor to some solid ground that existed somewhere below in that sea of uncertainty, keeping them from drifting into an abyss from where they would never again return to find their last earth.

They carried that land with them in the symbols they brought into this hell-hole: it was a place tattooed on their bodies, a worn-out scarf that hugged their necks, or it was a poem etched out on pieces of crinkled paper. The elders among them spoke of a Palestine where simple villages and olive trees dotted the landscape, and jubilance was abundant. Their happiness came to an abrupt end the day that Palestine was overrun by gangs of terrorists from the north, and since then Palestine had to be felt through an outline on a map, a key, a color, or something to be worn and talked about, but never touched directly. How else does one survive after being told that one does not exist?

For the hundreds of refugees trapped on this island, this useless island where there are no jobs and no stable economy or useful currency, it was all one big horrible mistake that they had ended up there. The boats were heading to Greece, and, if all had gone as planned, just a few more months of difficult travel would have led the refugees to Germany. Nothing would have stopped them: no border guards beating them with clubs, no cold nights sleeping on frozen ground, no tear gas burning their eyes or choking their breath, no starvation or dehydration, no illness, no swimming through rivers of shit, no sexual predators, no violent thieves, no humiliation, and no theft of one's life savings would have kept them from freedom below the beautiful blue sky north of the Mediterranean. Had the world forgotten that refugees ended up here only because of the wars waged by the West? But they ran out of luck and were lost at sea, picked up by a boat flying the wrong flag. This error put in jeopardy everything they had risked dying for. But hadn't their whole lives till now been determined by a series of other people's mistakes?

The Earth is squeezing us.
I wish we were its wheat
So we could die and live again.

Leila had nothing to do with any of this. Her life was the epitome of diligence and success. But, on some level, did she carry the burden of trauma passed down to her from her parents and grandparents? Was it present in her DNA, whether she liked it or not? Will it live on in the collective psyche of all Palestinians until there is a resolution to the ongoing catastrophe? If anything, she thought, these refugees should be proud of her—a Palestinian who had made it despite the many odds.

Her grandparents fled Yafa in Palestine in 1948, and two years later her father was born in a Lebanese refugee camp. Leila was born in Saudi Arabia, and as for each successive generation life was in a state of constant improvement. Her family became a success story of Palestinian refugees. There did not seem to be a need to mention their refugee status, or include Palestine into everyday discussions. The family made Jordan their home, had a thriving business, helped out those in need, and lived the good life, yet joy and pride were tainted with a nagging sadness and an unconsciousness promise never to forget their people's continuing suffering. Until all Palestinians are free, true peace of mind would elude them, and guilt would remain.

The Nakba was rarely invoked at the dinner table or at family gatherings. Leila had little recollection of Palestine, at least in its tragic sense. When distressing past episodes were evoked, they were raised ever so cautiously and with one objective: to make the point that things had changed, that the past had been forever redeemed.

Her maternal grandparents had fled Tulkarm for Jordan. Her grandmother was pregnant then with Salam, and along with her husband and two other children, Hasan and Rula, they shared a room in a refugee camp before moving to the big city. Hasan drove everyone crazy, she was told, perhaps because he had to sleep in a suitcase for a month before they were able to rent a house in Amman. Little Hasan got his revenge though. Such a menace was Hasan that stories of his rabble-rousing and foolhardiness brought much laughter for many years.

The family moved on rather quickly, in more ways than one—and that was what they wanted. Back in Palestine before their exodus, they had hidden all the family photos in the attic. The albums were left behind and eventually lost, and with them apparently all their memories of Palestine. The elders said little about their past, and the young grew up not to question the elders' wisdom. It was just the way it was, or maybe the way it had to be. Many years later, when Leila wrote her Master's thesis on the experiences of people forced out of Palestine during the Nakba, she realized for the first time that memories presumably lost with the family memorabilia were still raw and not fully purged. Her grandmother, Hanan, who reluctantly agreed to be part of the study, broke down as soon as she began talking. "The wound is still so deep," she kept mumbling as she wept. "The wound is still so deep."

I wish the Earth was our mother
So she'd be kind to us.

To Leila's surprise and dismay, her family, whose story embodied the story of all Palestinians, no longer agreed to take part in her research. This ended her quest to go to the source of her family's pain.

But living in the Middle East, one cannot be fully sheltered from the tragedies afflicting this hotbed of conflict. Neither their money, acquired from successful businesses and hard work, nor the quality education attained by the children, spared them from the difficulties of life in that unstable part of the world. They moved from place to place, sometimes staying in place for a year, and sometimes for much longer. One side of the family escaped Lebanon's communal clashes in the 1960s, as they had escaped Palestine two decades earlier. The other side of the family escaped Jordan more than once, first during the civil war, and then again during the Gulf War.

One thing is for sure—having money allowed them to move about freely and privileged them in ways that most refugees or Palestinians could not even have imagined. They did not have to seek shelter in refugee camps, nor were they compelled to hang on to rickety dinghies running out of petrol in the middle of angry seas. They moved around within the region, buying what they needed and getting any necessary documents. No one wants a poor refugee, but when you are a rich one, money buys freedom.

And when the entire region was on fire, the family moved to the United States or to Europe, this time carrying all of their family albums.

I wish we were pictures on the rocks
For our dreams to carry as mirrors.

The photo albums were not the only thing they were careful not to leave behind. There was also a key; the same decomposing piece of rusty metal that had hung on the wall in every home they had claimed as their own. It was the only remaining family heirloom from their home in Palestine. Placed center-stage in every living room, in every house, in every city where the family had moved to, or fled to, the key seemed to contradict the way Leila's family had chosen to live their lives. Never openly acknowledged, it affected their thoughts, body language, and interactions. For Leila, Palestine was hardly present, but always there, hardly discussed, but felt with every beat of her heart. She was a Jordanian, but inside, always Palestinian.

Her father received a fine education in business management in the United States that allowed him to successfully run the family business along with his brother. Together they doubled the family's wealth and generously helped many Palestinians to pursue higher learning. Unlike other young women her age,

Leila chose education over marriage and received a doctorate in psychology. Her culture was important to her, but she believed that education was crucial for women from conservative societies. It was a means to protect themselves against abuse, and a weapon by which to achieve equality. This was a point of contention between Leila and her mother, who had traditional views regarding the priorities of young women. Proud of her achievements, Leila wanted to help people as she had been helped. At least that is what she kept telling her mother, who insisted that "one must help herself first, before rescuing others." To Leila's mom, "helping herself" referred to the institution of marriage. Fortunately, Leila's father was on her side. He took pride in his daughter as she took on outdated traditions, reshaped them to her own liking and won small cultural battles that contributed to her personal growth.

But it was not tradition that stunted the family's emotional wellbeing and drove them to deny their own past. Working towards a new life centered around a materialistic definition of "success," they did what they sincerely believed to be best for themselves and their loved ones. On the happy day when Leila finally became a doctor, she had acquired the knowledge to offer a diagnosis of the family's collective sense of unease. Sharing it with no one, she wrote in her diary a taboo conclusion:

> It is hardly a surprise how the traumas of our own parents and grandparents are passed on to us. Growing up in Jordan, I didn't understand why speaking of Palestine scared them. They were protecting us. I didn't understand or comprehend that they grew up in an uncertain life, the kind of crippling uncertainty that they did not wish to pass on to their children. They had inherited much anxiety about circumstances that were out of their control, but provoked

them to act, so that they can never experience it again or allow their children to relive their past fears.

After years of study, reflection and self-torment, Leila felt that she had cracked the mystery of her upbringing, and the seemingly paradoxical attitude of her elders. But did it really matter? And why should it have? She had a normal upbringing in Jordan with every comfort possible. Yet she felt that she could not liberate herself from a trap she had been in for so long. To her there was more to life than what was visible.

As a teenager, she had suffered from scarring depression. Succumbing to her own fears and anxieties, she left school and forsook social life for the safety of her home. The family hired the best tutors available to complete her high school years at home in Amman. She barely managed to graduate. Plagued by chronic restlessness, she wondered why such angst reigned over her apparently perfect life.

Her calling came in 2015 while she was watching the news on television. Boats filled with refugees from Syria had crowded the Mediterranean in desperate attempts at salvation from a war that worsened with every day. Many drowned in the frigid waters that sucked them down as they reached for their loved ones, while others appeared on screen as images of cold naked bodies washed ashore on a foreign land. Some were never found or identified, and their choking screams haunted those who watched them swallowed up.

The lucky ones who made it to safety embarked on new interminable journeys. Leila intensely wanted to help them pass through this trial; a new beginning worth the fees and humiliations demanded by cruel smugglers. Isn't security a basic human right? Wasn't the world failing these people again and again? This was Leila's chance to face her fears, break out of her cocoon, and find her place as a healer. Within weeks, she was on her way to the island as a volunteer in a refugee center that offered shelter to 400 refugees. Leila alone was responsible for helping the dejected refugees negotiate their pain and cope with their traumas.

"Leila, these are not Syrians. They are all Palestinian refugees," she was told as soon as she arrived with her brand-new volunteer garb. There was no escape now. Refugees stood before her in all of their anger, fears, needs, and plainness, imploring her help. They looked like the members of her family. No course at her prestigious university had prepared her for the emotions that hit her like a tidal wave. Over and over again they told her how they must leave this unbearable island, where the authorities refused to grant them refugee status. These human beings had no home to go back to, they had landed on the island by mistake. The sea had deceived them, no earth would accept them, and they had no last sky to which they could fly. Coming from refugee camps in Lebanon, Syria, and Gaza, these strangers were united by broken hope; by memories of dead ancestors who lovingly spoke about Palestine and simple villages scattered across hills embraced by the sun.

> We saw the faces of those who will throw
> Our children out of the window of this last space.
> Our star will hang up mirrors.

Leila was not much different from them, if the truth be told. Her family had labored to overcome, according to their conception, a mere historical handicap, but she too was a refugee. And like her, many of these refugees were educated. They had imagined that education would lead to a better life. Doctors among them had studied a lifetime and professed an oath to heal their brothers; teachers had taught the difference between right and wrong; poets had written songs of artistic resistance; laborers had raised buildings from an architect's dream; and mothers had made warm homes for their babies. Whether they were unruly children, handsome faces, or thugs with a record, she could not deny that to her each represented a curious manifestation of her family and of herself. She was them and they were her.

The refugee center had no staff except for a few volunteers from a local organization, and Leila was the first Arabic-speaker to arrive. "We are not here to beg, we just need help to get to Germany and to be able to stand on our feet again," said Khalid, who was elected as the representative of the group. The rest of them stared at Leila quietly and intently as if she had the power to alter the past and redraw the boundaries of earth, sea, and sky.

Khalid's beaming smile expressed his hope that rescue was only a matter of time. He simply needed a dictionary to learn the language to negotiate on the refugees' behalf, and to resume their journey away from this unbearable island. Khalid was familiar with suffering. He hailed from Shatila, the Palestinian refugee camp in Lebanon where thousands had perished in notorious massacres, and where children grew up plotting their escape from that squalid world where the mass graves of their fathers and mothers were used as a dumping ground by nearby Lebanese cities.

With his tattoos, Khalid's body language made a strong first impression. A map of Palestine occupied most of his right arm, and his left arm was largely reserved for the letter H, the first letter of his fiancée's name. His beloved had made it to Sweden after her boat reached Greece, and, like thousands before her, she walked to Macedonia, on to Serbia and then wandered towards northern Europe until the Swedes offered her shelter.

Where should we go after the last frontiers?

Unlike Khalid, Jamal was angry and had no concrete plan. When Leila's eyes met his, he exploded into a ten-minute outburst. "Why won't you help me?" he kept repeating. Though his large body and violent temper intimidated Leila at first, she saw his anguish as clearly as she saw the fresh wound on his neck. The bullet intended to end his life instead invigorated his anger, propelling him to leave the perpetual trap of internecine conflict. The gun may have been fired in clashes between Sunnis and Shias in Lebanon, or between Lebanese and Palestinians, or among Palestinians. Like all fathers, Jamal had wanted an education for his son. However, the mundane act of walking him to school became deadly when they were caught in a crossfire of senseless conflict. Without hesitation he acted as a human shield to protect his small child, and in a split second made the decision to escape that place.

"I want to protect my family, damn it!" Jamal cried, his aggression masking the fears of a loving father. Leila tried to help him process his experiences, but he provoked her by asking about her origins. "Why can't you say 'I am a Palestinian?'." But how could she say that? Was she really a Palestinian? Jamal's meaning of Palestinian was alien to her. But with each refugee encounter her perspective gradually changed. It took three months for Jamal to apologize for his outbursts, but less than that for Leila to reclaim herself.

* * *

Among the refugees was gentle Abu Ahmad, a middle-aged man who had been residing in the center with his son for months. A kind man with soft eyes, he was separated from his wife when a large group fled Lebanon on their way to Turkey. She remained in Turkey, but he was washed ashore with his son to this island limbo. Unlike the fretful, tense, and younger refugees in the center, Abu Ahmad's eyes were capable of seeing the world as it was. He accepted his fate. "I want to live in a place where my son is treated as an equal."

Where should the birds fly after the last sky?

Salman was thirty, strong in spirit, but with a visibly exhausted body. "Words cannot describe the life we had to endure until this very moment," he told Leila. "My children don't deserve to live the life I did." But did he deserve it? He spoke about the massacres of the past and the present: Sabra and Shatila, Yarmouk, Deir Yassin, Gaza, and Jenin. No, Palestinians are not unified by their massacres or their common pain, but by their pride and their endless hope, he insisted. "I shall raise my kids to be proud Palestinians as my father raised me," he declared. Then he sank into his chair, fatigued by his own memories.

Where should the plants sleep after the last breath of air?

Zahra was a thirty-three-year-old woman with big brown eyes, a beautiful face and many stories to share of a life uncommon among women her age. Circumstances had made her tough, but a childlike innocence emanated from within her. "Look, I decorated my home with teddy bears," she said as she showed Leila a photo of her "new home" in Lebanon, which she was forced to abandon before floating across the sea. "I grew up in the streets because my family abandoned me. My mother died and my father didn't want me. I grew up alone and married in Shatila. But I left him. No one tells me what to do!"

Feeling that she could trust only herself and the roots that grounded her sense of self, Zahra left many things behind: her abusive husband, Lebanon, and the war, and flashbacks of suffering that no longer served her. "We Palestinians have strong spirits. Take what's good from the foreigner but don't forget your roots. We Palestinians are too strong for life to tear us down," she told Leila while sipping mint tea.

We will write our names with scarlet steam.

There was also Mohammad, a ten-year-old boy from Ein El-Hilweh whose large green eyes sparkled with giddiness and a yearning for the life ahead of him. He wanted to be a footballer, and asked Leila if European teams would allow him, a Palestinian refugee, to join. He wondered if people in Europe were nice and whether or not he could attend a school, make new friends, play games, and be like other young boys. Assuring him that goodness existed everywhere, his mother stood behind him as she stroked his hair while flashing a look of doubt at Leila.

There was Basel, Khadija, Mahmoud, Safa, and hundreds more, waiting and waiting, each carrying a small bag stuffed with whatever they could salvage from their homes. There was also Laith, the adopted son of Salma and Mazen, the poet from Yarmouk who had published three poetry books in Syria. He had written a new poem on the boat. "I am not a refugee," said Mazen. "Refugee" was not his identity, but his destiny, he told Leila. He was hard at work on his fourth collection, in the tiny room where his family lived in the refugee center. To the middle-aged man with the rebellious old soul, poetry was a means of survival. "I didn't study psychology but I am a psychologist," he claimed. He and Leila had a common understanding of life, but he complained that his son did not like his poems. "Someday he will understand," he said with a smile, nodding.

We will cut off the hand of the song to be finished by our flesh.

Leila had the luxury of leaving and returning to the refugee center as she pleased, but the moment she stepped into that large edifice of concrete and barbed wire, where refugees arrived with utopian dreams on their sleeves, she became one of them. "A refugee lives abroad on average for seventeen years before going back home," her professor once said in a lecture. For these refugees, however, exile did not have a time limit. Their status was tattooed on their souls and in their exhausted, weary bodies which nevertheless contained within them enough hope and courage to keep them moving forward.

A long time ago, Leila's grandparents had built a house in Syria. It resembled their earlier home as closely as possible. Perhaps this replica of their place in Palestine was meant to heal old hidden wounds. Their little heaven, sprinkled with happy memories under the orange trees, and a fountain of stone and marble in the center of their small orchard, allowed them to travel in dreams to the home they longed for. During the war, they had to abandon this new house too and escape to Jordan where they became refugees once more. Where will they return when the war is over? To Syria? To Lebanon? Or will they stay in Jordan? But why not to Palestine? Why never Palestine? Though Leila had never been there, the rusty key in their family home was clearly marked: "The Key to Our Home in Palestine."

We will die here, here in the last passage.
Here and here our blood will plant its olive tree.

9
Dawn

Bureaucracy triumphed, and both East and West rejected them a thousand times over during the interminable months at the refugee center. Taking action into her own hands when humanitarians had failed her yet again, a fed-up mother woke her son at dawn. After performing morning prayers, they ate a simple meal and she packed their lives into bags ready for the journey ahead. It mattered little to her that they were on an island and there was no escape route but the merciless sea and the horizon which threatened death as one way to liberation. The boy wanted to be a footballer, and his mother was determined to find a place for him where people would be kind: "Mama, where are we going," he asked.

Engrossed in her thoughts, she said nothing.

They quietly snuck outside and crossed over the barbed wire fence. There was no other choice. It was of no significance that the mother's ankles bled, her blood was a small price to pay for what her chosen path might bring. What mattered was the safety of the boy on her back and that they were together. If they had to die, at least they would die as one. Step by step, they walked towards a vast green meadow, through a dark orchard, and reached a familiar shore where ragged dinghies were randomly scattered. Overtaken by a sudden feeling of optimism, they thrust forward with a rush of determination to make a new life in a new world where dreams were reborn, or broken, by breaking free from the indignity of the refugee camp.

The Earth is squeezing us.
I wish we were its wheat
So we could die and live again.

"Mama, where are we going …?"
"Home."

Postscript: Echoes of History

The present-day path charted by Khaled Abdul Ghani al-Lubani aka "Marco"—escaping the Yarmouk Refugee Camp during the Syrian civil war is the tragic after-image of an old dirt road walked upon by a young communist rebel. Decades earlier, Ahmad al-Haaj fled his village of Al-Sawafir in 1948 during a period that the Palestinians refer to as their "Nakba", or "Catastrophe."

Similarly, the echoes of a conversation between two women prisoners in an Israeli jail are a reverberation of an earlier conversation held between two refugee women from Gaza as they huddled together in an ancient orchard, escaping, however fleetingly, the misery of life beyond. The two pairs of women were separated by many miles and many years, but their shared fears, sorrows and hopes made their stories, inevitably, alike.

This book is an attempt at unearthing the common ground of the Palestinian narrative, often separated by political divisions, geographical barriers, and walls, factionalism, military occupation, and grinding years in exile.

The Last Earth is a unique document, in narrative form, of people's history that challenges both earlier academic and popular takes on the collective Palestinian story, regardless of who has told it and why.

The book's characters are complex in their own right. The circumstances in which they found themselves and the fact that each one of them was an active participant in shaping their own reality—as insurmountable as their obstacles may have seemed—gives each story a unique sense of urgency and depth. But only when these stories converge and overlap, the shared

Palestinian (in fact, human) struggle becomes a resounding echo of their deeply profound collective experience.

Each chapter, read individually, is like an icon for the experience of an entire generation. When read as a whole, the book tells the story of a people whose history cannot be reduced to a timeline of conflict, but rather is embroidered and torn with complex human emotions, hopes, dreams, struggles, and priorities that seem to pay no heed to politics, the military balance, or ideological rivalries.

While it sheds light on the past, *The Last Earth* is not meant to be entirely the story of the past but also an endeavor at presenting ordinary people as active agents in shaping the present and the future. Moreover, the book aims at more than just filling the gaps in disconnected historical narratives. Rather, it seeks to provide a unified perspective on Palestinian identity in modern times.

If memory is the active process in the creation of meaning, then *The Last Earth* interprets and distils memory as part of that process. But it is also a retort to the reductionism that has afflicted the Palestinian discourse.

Indeed, the main objective behind this book is to present a Palestinian "history from below" which directly defies two dominant narratives concerning this subject: the first is the elitist rationalization of Palestinian political reality (which sees history as an outcome of the workings of an individual or a faction/group); the second is the reductionist approach to any subject concerning Palestinians, a discourse that teeters between the extremist view, which denies their very existence or presents their struggle and national aspirations as a "problem" to be quickly—if not haphazardly—remedied.

The accounts in this book, then, are largely positioned within that alternative history. The stories of the individuals presented confront what some perceive to be the many misconceptions in official and academic discourse concerning Palestinian history.

Specifically, to provide a more vivid rendition of emotive personal histories, I have intentionally taken on the personality of each individual storyteller, internalized (as much as it was possible) and re-told their stories in a way that aims to respect the dignity of each narrative, while bearing in mind the receptivity of the reader and their ability to engage with the text. The final product is closer to the stories of Rosemary Sayigh and Salam Tamari's documenting of people's history than to that of typical, detached academic studies. At times, the narration style may seem somewhat similar to the work of Ghassan Kanafani, Ibrahim Nasrallah, Abdul Rahman Munif, or even Gabriel García Márquez, where reality and fiction merge to form a whole new category of literature.

However, these stories, with all of their characters and details, are true. What may, at times, read as a form of magic realism (for example, "Spirits of the Orchard") is, in fact, a reflection of the strong belief held by some of the characters, who truly believed—or needed to trust in—the supernatural and the miraculous.

I have written several books on Palestine, most of them dedicated to investigating an alternative approach to communicating the Palestinian story. *The Last Earth* is the culmination of all of these previous efforts, building on my Ph.D. research on People's History with Professor Ilan Pappe at the European Centre for Palestine Studies at the University of Exeter. In all of these, I was compelled by the imperative to relocate the centrality of the Palestinian narrative from an Israeli perspective to a Palestinian one, especially one that overlooks the typical elitist narrative and focuses instead on re-telling the story from the viewpoint of ordinary, poor, underclass, and working-class Palestinians.

As such, *The Last Earth* confronts both academic and popular takes on the tragic and criminal events that comprise Palestinian history. It weaves the dimensions of intergenerational time, as it stretches from before the Nakba—marking the brutal birth of the Israeli State—to the destruction of the Palestinian refugee camp in Yarmouk, Syria, to the flight from devastated Yarmouk to Europe.

This work is not mine alone. On the one hand, capable Palestinian historians have relentlessly pushed to liberate the Palestinian story from the deception of history and dishonesty of historians. On the other, this book is the outcome of a group effort involving mostly Palestinian writers, bloggers, and historians in Palestine, Lebanon, Syria, and across the world.

This decision—of involving mostly Palestinians in the composing, interpretation, and conveying of these stories—was hardly the outcome of any veiled ethnocentricity. Rather, it adheres to the wisdom of late Professor Edward Said:

> ... facts get their importance from what is made of them in interpretation ... for interpretations depend very much on who the interpreter is, who he or she is addressing, what his or her purpose is, at what historical moment the interpretation takes place.*

The Last Earth is a sorely needed reinterpretation of Palestinian history, internalized and communicated by Palestinian voices, so that the rest of the world can, for once, appreciate the story as told by its tenacious victims, not barefaced aggressors.

It must be restated—as it has already been by the brave characters of this this book—that *The Last Earth* was never intended to generate pity. Far from that, it aims at documenting the lives of a people, who, despite the untold harshness of life, stand tall and fight back.

* Said, Edward W., *Covering Islam*, New York: Pantheon Books, 1981, p. 154.

Methodology

A few months after I concluded my Ph.D. research in the summer of 2015, I contacted several Palestinian researchers and journalists to collaborate on a project where Palestinian history is re-told through the perspective of ordinary people. We agreed to challenge chronological narration of Palestinian history, since people who are living the everyday tragedy, whether of occupation or *shatat*—exile—don't compartmentalize their personal history based on time periods—for example, pre-Nakba, post-Nakba, First Intifada, Second Intifada, and so on. These classifications may be useful in traditional history, or in the field of journalism, but of little use to people whose lives, tragedies, hopes, defeats, and triumphs are far more compounded and interwoven.

Our first step was issuing a call for Palestinians everywhere to share their stories, while attempting to relate them to the collective Palestinian narrative. A statement, written in Arabic, English, Spanish, and French was made available via print and online publication and throughout social media. To reach Palestinians in refugee camps in Gaza, the West Bank, Lebanon, Jordan, and Syria, several young Palestinian journalists became actively involved in the process of collecting stories. Notable amongst these individuals is Yousef Aljamal—a dedicated Gaza-based writer and Ph.D. (candidate) history student—and Salwa Amor—an award-winning documentary filmmaker who spent years documenting refugee stories, mainly in Syria and Lebanon, but also of those who had escaped the Syria war for Turkey, Greece, and the rest of Europe.

Along with the very diligent and skilled American-Italian editor and journalist Daniela Loffreda, I sorted through hundreds of profiles; some submitted their initial stories directly, others were made available through our researchers. Nearly fifty profiles were selected for interviews—a process that lasted for several sessions, each session consisting of two to four hours. Most of the interviews were conducted via Skype, in the presence of one researcher, and with myself asking questions and recording answers on the other side of the screen. The selection of these stories was made to reflect a fair division between female and male correspondents, a rational distribution of the geographic location of the interviewees (that reflect, to some degree, the current distribution of Palestinian communities worldwide) and how representative is each story in terms of the collective story of the Palestinian people.

Although the book narrates the stories of eight individuals, it is indeed the outcome of this whole process. For example, "Shit River" focuses on the story of Marco, but the general information in that chapter was vetted through a series of interviews with several Yarmouk survivors, in Yarmouk itself, and others who fled to Gaza, Turkey, and Europe. Marco was chosen to be the protagonist in the chapter because his storyline appeared to be most compelling and his ability to narrate his own story in striking detail was most convincing.

Like Marco, Ahmad al-Haaj—"Abu Sandal"—provided the most vivid account of life in Palestine before the Nakba. Most astounding was his ability to render complex political ideas, specifics pertaining to the war, the tragic defeat, and the harrowing escape to Gaza, while cleverly dotting his narrative with personal stories about his family during these hard times. He is a fascinating human being; a brilliant storyteller, who can convey tragedy and humor without making his listeners lose respect for the profound and principled life he has led. I conducted the interviews with him over the course of several weeks. Although he was eighty-three at the time, his memory was very sharp and his resolve to return to his Palestinian village seemed as strong as it was in 1948.

Thus, the stories were selected on this basis. The narratives needed to be rich, complex, diverse, and representative to give me the needed space to mold them into complete stories, while keeping in mind that they must remain an honest reflection of the stories conveyed to me. Unsurprisingly, the narratives overlapped on many occasions. Even if the storytellers have never met, they were essentially describing the same events, from a different perspective, location, or timeframe. I tried to remain true to the spirit of that realization as well.

Although the stories are all true, some of the names have been changed, based on the request of some of the people I interviewed or by my own choice to respect the privacy of the people whose names were mentioned. For example, the names of three characters in Marco's story—a mother and her children—were altered to protect their privacy; this was also the case in Hana Shalabi's chapter. The only main character whose name was changed is "Leila Khalil", in the chapter "The Last Sky." She requested her name to be changed to "Leila" due to her involvement in the field of human rights, working directly with war refugees through an internationally recognized NGO.

A few other changes were made to the stories to ensure the continuity and cohesion of the narrative. For example, Hana Shalabi's dream of her brother has been relocated from an earlier part of the story to the final section so that it doesn't interrupt the flow of the narrative. The unnamed mother and her son, in the final short chapter, "Dawn," failed to reach mainland Europe and eventually returned to Lebanon. I made that discovery after the manuscript was completed. I gave myself the license not to alter the original story, where the book ends with them seeking an escape from the island. I wanted to convey the truth that the story of any refugee can never truly conclude until the journey of all refugees come to a just end as well.

As long as Palestinian refugees are stranded in refugee camps, aboard rickety boats, at border crossings, or on dusty roads seeking shelter from war-torn countries, as long as the mother and the son are going to seek some other destination, a safe place, a last earth, which, ultimately can only be their Palestinian homeland.

Ramzy Baroud

Index